FOREIGN POLICY ADAPTATION

To my mother and father

Foreign Policy Adaptation

STEVEN M. SMITH
University of East Anglia

Gower
Publishing Company
Limited

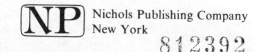

Nichols Publishing Company
New York

812392

Published by
Gower Publishing Company Limited
Gower House
Croft Road
Aldershot
Hants GU11 3HR

Distributed in the United States in 1981 by
Nichols Publishing Company
Post Office Box 96
New York N.Y. 10024

 British Library Cataloguing in Publication Data

Smith, Steven M.
  Foreign policy adaptation.
  1. Political psychology
  2. Adaptability (Psychology)
  I. Title
  327.1'01'9   JA74.5

UK   ISBN   0-566-00370-8
US   ISBN   0-89397-106-5

PRINTED IN GREAT BRITAIN

Contents

Figures

Preface

I have incurred many debts in the undertaking of this study; it is a pleasure to be able formally to record them.   This study was originally carried out for a doctoral thesis at the University of Southampton. In connection with this, I would like to express my thanks to my supervisor, Professor Joseph Frankel, and to my examiners, Professor James Barber and Dr. John Simpson, for their helpful comments regarding the original manuscript.   I would also like to acknowledge the financial support of the Social Science Research Council for the period of the original research.   I owe an enormous debt to Joseph Frankel and John Simpson for their advice, help, criticism and, above all, for their encouragement during my six years at Southampton.

I would also like to thank Dr. Brendan Evans of Huddersfield Polytechnic for his comments on an earlier draft of this study; I must also express my sincere thanks for all his advice, encouragement and help during the two and a half years that we worked together.

The final version of the study has benefited considerably from my being able to discuss it with the author of the approach that it tests - Jim Rosenau.   Although this study is somewhat critical of his adaptive behaviour approach, I would like to thank him for his comments and advice; above all, I would like to thank him for the open way in which he received my criticisms.   There was never any attempt on his part to explain away or to discount any problems that I argued were present in his work; indeed, he welcomed criticism, believing that that was the way for the subject to develop.   It is in that spirit that this study has been written.   I would like to thank the University of East Anglia Overseas Study and Research funds for providing the finance to enable me to visit him.

I would also like to offer my thanks to Mary Gurteen, who typed the manuscript.   I don't know quite how she coped with my writing and other quirks, but cope she did.

Despite all this help, there may be deficiencies in this study; the least I can do is to accept full responsibility for them.

Finally, I would like to thank Mary Smith, who has helped me more than anyone else.   She may not know that, but I do, and it is a pleasure to acknowledge it.

12 March 1981

University of East Anglia
Norwich

1 Introduction

This study arose out of a twofold desire: on the one hand, it arose out of a concern with explaining the foreign policies of two states - Britain and the Netherlands. On the other hand, it developed from a desire to subject to empirical investigation one theory of foreign policy behaviour - Rosenau's adaptive behaviour theory. This concern with the empirical material therefore determined the case study for the theory.

The approach to be tested - Rosenau's adaptive behaviour theory - was chosen for three main reasons. First, it represented the culmination of Jim Rosenau's lengthy, and important, attempts to develop a theory of foreign policy behaviour. As such, it was based on much of his earlier work in this area, notably his celebrated pretheory article (1). A second reason was that, in looking around for some explicit theoretical analysis of foreign policy with which to explain or examine the foreign policies of the two states, the adaptive behaviour approach was the one that had, at that time, been subjected to least examination. As will be shown in chapter two, the other major theories of foreign policy behaviour were clearly deficient. The third reason was that, just as this study was being undertaken, the author of the adaptive behaviour approach came out with a number of claims regarding the development of the subject area of foreign policy analysis. These claims made an examination of that author's most recent, and most elegant, attempt at theorising foreign policy behaviour seem of interest in answering these claims. For these three reasons, it was decided to undertake a series of case studies on the foreign policies of the two nation states in order to test the utility of the adaptive behaviour theory.

Therefore, the subject of this study is an examination of the utility of Rosenau's adaptive behaviour theory for the explanation of British and Dutch foreign policies from 1945-1963. It must be stated categorically at the outset that this study is not concerned with researching into Dutch or British foreign policy per se. The aim of the study is to utilise the two foreign policies to obtain statements about the foreign policy stances adopted in three issue areas and then compare these stances with those predicted by the adaptive behaviour approach. Given this aim, this study, although drawing extensively on empirical data concerning the two countries' foreign policies, does not claim to be concerned primarily with the unearthing of previously unknown details about these policies. Whilst it is contended that this study does provide a much more extensive discussion of Dutch foreign policy, in the areas dealt with, than has appeared in one source before, it is felt that such factors are clearly secondary to the main aim of the work: that is to test for the first time the adaptive behaviour theory.

As has already been noted, the idea of testing this approach was given a boost by the very strong claims by Rosenau about the development of the subject area of foreign policy analysis. In his conclusion to a series of articles reviewing the state of international relations theory, he claims that

> 'all the evidence points to the conclusion that the comparative
> study of foreign policy has emerged as a <u>normal</u> science . . .
> our differences now are about small points - the adequacy of an
> events data scheme or the scope of a governmental variable - and
> the great "debates" over the role of case studies and the appropri-
> ateness of scientific methods have faded into an obscure past. Now
> we can work at peace, without diverting energy to justifying our
> existence and beating back challenges from unsympathetic col-
> leagues.' (2)

Although he makes it clear that foreign policy analysis has not yet
'tied up all the loose ends', he states that the paradigm for the
study of the phenomena is in existence. Similarly, in a 1975 revised
version of an article that was originally published in 1968 (3),
Rosenau claims that the

> 'developments in the comparative study of foreign policy over the
> last seven years amply justify the conclusion that those engaged
> in the enterprise have nurtured a field into existence.' (4)

Indeed in his revised article, the original title 'Comparative foreign
policy: fad, fantasy, or field?' becomes 'Comparative foreign policy:
one-time fad, realized fantasy, and normal field'.

   Although, more recently, Rosenau has expressed doubts as to the cumula-
tiveness of foreign policy analysis (5), the strength of these claims
is clear. By the mid 1970s, Rosenau saw foreign policy analysis as
a normal science: indeed, in both the articles referred to above, he
discusses the use of the term in Thomas Kuhn's analysis of natural
science (6). Whilst it is never explicitly referred to, it is clear
that Rosenau sees the paradigm necessary for normal science as being
his work on pretheory and, based on this, his theory of adaptation (7).

   Obviously, any attempt to examine the nature of that claim would involve the analysis of not only the various theoretical approaches in
the field of foreign policy analysis, but also would require considerable examination of the relationship between empirical studies and
theoretical underpinnings. Furthermore, it would require detailed
analysis of Kuhn's work on normal science and paradigm formation (8),
especially as this has been subjected to a large amount of criticism
(9). Such an analysis will not be undertaken here (10); this study
will be limited to examining the utility of the adaptive behaviour
approach. Nevertheless, this examination will be put into perspective
by the importance attached to the approach by Rosenau in his claims
about the development of the subject area of foreign policy analysis.

   Even without these claims, the adaptive behaviour approach is an
excellent theory to subject to empirical examination. In a discipline
not noted for the generation of explicit theories, the work by Rosenau
on adaptive behaviour offers a rare example of a theory that not only
claims to explain empirical data, but also lends itself to the generation of falsifiable hypotheses. Accepting Kenneth Waltz's view of
the nature and role of a theory (11), the overriding criterion for
assessing the utility of a theory lies in the extent to which it ex-
plains the relationship between observed phenomena. As such, it must

be capable of leading to the generation of hypotheses. Although an approach may have tremendous heuristic qualities, it is the explanatory power of a theory that determines its utility. Hence, it was seen as a clear advantage of Rosenau's adaptive behaviour approach that it was open to such testing and examination. Indeed, the very fact that Rosenau's work was open to such examination made it appear to be the most promising direction in the quest for general theories of comparative foreign policy analysis.

Given, then, that the adaptive behaviour approach was chosen for testing, the question of how was it to be tested arose. As will be seen from the discussion in chapter three, considerable attention was paid to the methods by which the approach should be tested. The procedure eventually chosen was to utilise the adaptive behaviour approach to derive predictions as to the foreign policy behaviour of Britain and the Netherlands in the post war period. These predictions would then be compared to the findings of three case studies of the two states' foreign policies. This comparison would form the basis for an evaluation of the utility of the approach. The need for case studies is obvious: without undertaking detailed case studies the only way to develop statements about the foreign policies of the two states in the language of the approach would be to assess the 'general character' of the foreign policies. Such an assessment would obviously be extremely subjective. With this problem in mind, the case studies were chosen on the basis of providing as wide a coverage as possible of the two states' foreign policies. Thus, it was decided to take one case study of an issue area in which the two states followed very similar foreign policies (West European security 1945-1963); one case study of an issue area in which the two states followed fundamentally divergent foreign policies (European integration 1945-1963); finally, it was necessary to choose an instance of considerable interaction between the two states (the Netherlands East Indies 1945-50). By so doing, it was felt that the two foreign policies would be given the widest coverage concomitant with the detail of analysis required. It is fully recognised that the three case studies represent very broad categories and that they only represent a small proportion of the issue areas that could have been chosen. It must be stressed again that this study does not seek, nor does it claim, to offer either detailed case studies of specific issues or an overview of the foreign policies of the two states; rather, the choice of the case studies was determined by the requirements of testing the adaptive behaviour approach.

This study will proceed by examining, in chapter two, the theoretical approaches that dominated the foreign policy analysis literature in the 1960s and early 1970s. A series of major approaches will be outlined and criticised, both for their theoretical deficiencies and in terms of their unsuitability for this examination. In chapter three, Rosenau's adaptive behaviour theory will be outlined and it will be used to generate hypotheses as to the foreign policy strategies of Britain and the Netherlands from 1945-1963. In chapters four, five, and six, the case studies of differences, parallels, and interaction will be summarised. In chapter seven, the empirically derived strategies will be compared with the predictions obtained in chapter three. Chapter eight will offer a lengthy review of the approach in terms of the findings of this study and also in terms of the internal consistency of the approach and the problems found in operationalising and testing it.

3

This review will be undertaken in the light of the claims made by
Rosenau concerning the development of the subject in the 1970s.

Leaving aside the question of whether or not the adaptive behaviour
theory was the paradigmatic basis for comparative foreign policy analysis (especially in the light of Rosenau's own later statements on the
extent to which this paradigm has decayed (12)), Rosenau has published
a considerable amount on this theory. Most of the pieces were published in the early 1970s, although even in the late 1970s he was still
developing it. Indeed, the year 1981 will see the publication of a
collection of the key articles and papers on the theory (13). What
this collection reveals is that, for Rosenau, the adaptive behaviour
theory is a central component of the explanation of the foreign policies
of states. Whilst Rosenau argues that global interdependence has
altered the nature of international relations, he is clear in his
reliance on the adaptive behaviour theory for the examination of foreign
policy (14). As such, this examination of the utility of the approach
in the explanation of the foreign policies of two states is all the
more relevant to Rosenau's current position regarding the most appropriate methods of explaining foreign policy behaviour. In other words, in
terms of Rosenau's work, this examination of the adaptive behaviour
theory is revealing in that he has made a series of claims regarding
the paradigmatic development of the subject area based on his view of
the strength of this theory, and that, even if he is now concerned that
this paradigm has decayed, he still sees the theory as being central to
explaining foreign policy behaviour in the contemporary international
system. Obviously, the conclusions arrived at in this study are the
result of only one empirical examination of the theory, but, not only
is this the first published empirical examination of it, it is also the
primary means by which such theories are to be evaluated. Therefore,
whilst this study can neither evaluate fully the accuracy of Rosenau's
claims concerning the development of paradigms in comparative foreign
policy analysis, nor assess totally the likely utility of building ex-
planations of foreign policy behaviour on the foundations of the theory,
it can inform both enquiries.

NOTES

(1) J. N. Rosenau, 'Pretheories and Theories of Foreign Policy', in
R. B. Farrell (ed), Approaches to Comparative and International
Politics, Northwestern University Press, Evanston, Ill. 1966, pp.27-92.
(2) J. N. Rosenau, 'Restlessness, Change, and Foreign Policy Analysis',
in J. N. Rosenau (ed), In Search of Global Patterns, Free Press, New
York 1976, p.369.
(3) The original version was published as J. N. Rosenau, 'Comparative
foreign policy: fad, fantasy, or field?', International Studies
Quarterly, Vol. 12, (September 1968), pp.296-329.
(4) J. N. Rosenau, 'Comparative Foreign Policy: One-Time Fad, Realized
Fantasy, and Normal Field', in C. W. Kegley, G. A. Raymond, R. M. Rood
and R. A. Skinner (eds), International Events and the Comparative Analysis of Foreign Policy, University of South Carolina Press, Columbia
S.C. 1975, p.35.
(5) See J. N. Rosenau, 'Puzzlement in foreign policy', Jerusalem
Journal of International Relations, Vol. 1 (4), 1976, pp.1-10, and
J. N. Rosenau, 'International studies in a transnational world',

Millennium, Vol. 5 (1), 1976, pp.1-20.

(6) See J. N. Rosenau, 'Restlessness, Change, and Foreign Policy Analysis', op.cit., pp.369-376, and J. N. Rosenau, 'Comparative Foreign Policy: One-Time Fad, Realized Fantasy, and Normal Field', op.cit., pp.34-38.

(7) This interpretation has been confirmed in discussions held with Professor Rosenau in November 1980.

(8) For Kuhn's initial development of the idea of normal science see T. Kuhn, The Structure of Scientific Revolutions, University of Chicago Press, Chicago, Ill. 1962. For a later development of his ideas see his papers, 'Logic of Discovery or Psychology of Research?' and 'Reflections on My Critics', in I. Lakatos and A. Musgrave (eds), Criticism and the Growth of Knowledge, Cambridge University Press, London 1970, pp.1-25 and 231-278.

(9) For a series of critical essays see Lakatos and Musgrave, op.cit.

(10) Rosenau's views on the nature of paradigmatic developments in foreign policy analysis are summarised in J. N. Rosenau, 'Muddling, meddling, and modelling: alternative approaches to the study of world politics in an era of rapid change', Millennium, Vol. 8 (2), 1979, pp.130-44. For a discussion of these views see S. M. Smith, 'Brother can you paradigm? A reply to Professor Rosenau', Millennium, Vol. 8 (3), 1980, pp.235-245.

(11) Waltz's views are outlined in K. Waltz, 'Theory of International Relations', in F. Greenstein and N. Polsby, Handbook of Political Science: Volume 8 - International Politics, Addison-Wesley, Reading, Mass. 1975, pp.1-85. See also K. Waltz, Theory of International Politics, Addison-Wesley, Reading, Mass. 1979, especially chapter one.

(12) See Rosenau, 'Puzzlement in foreign policy, op.cit. Rosenau, 'International studies in a transnational world, op.cit., and Rosenau, 'Muddling, meddling, and modelling: alternative approaches to the study of world politics in an era of rapid change', op.cit.

(13) See J. N. Rosenau, The Study of Political Adaptation, Frances Pinter, London 1981, Nichols Publishing Company, New York.

(14) The concern with global interdependence can be seen in Rosenau's collection of essays, J. N. Rosenau, The Study of Global Interdependence: Essays on the Transnationalisation of World Affairs, Frances Pinter, London 1980, Nichols Publishing Company, New York.

2 Theoretical review

Given that the aim of this study is to examine aspects of the foreign
policies of two states as a means of assessing the utility of one
form of macro foreign policy approach, this chapter seeks to provide an
overview of the major foreign policy models that aim to offer perspectives on the foreign policies of all states.   In other words, the concern of this chapter is to examine models of foreign policy that claim
to apply to the foreign policy of any state.   Fundamentally, it is
hoped that this review of the theory will indicate some of the shortcomings of most of the major models and approaches.

   An immediate qualification is necessary in relation to the choice of
approaches discussed.   Foreign policy analysis has not been noted for
its rigour in defining its approaches in terms of theories, models,
paradigms and the like.   Those approaches that are to be examined in
this chapter have been chosen primarily because they refer to the macro
nature of foreign policy; i.e. they seek to illuminate the basic characteristics of any state's foreign policy.   Therefore, a necessary
distinction will be made between those approaches to foreign policy
that seek to aid the understanding of individual decisions and those
that focus on a much more general level of explanation.

   The effect of this distinction is to preclude any detailed examination
of the approaches of Snyder, Bruck and Sapin (1954) (1) and Brecher,
Steinberg and Stein (1969) (2).   Nevertheless, it is necessary to point
out that these two approaches have been of considerable importance in
the study of foreign policy decision-making, although to date there have
been few attempts to operationalise either.   The Snyder, Bruck and
Sapin framework, although of considerable heuristic value, has only been
utilised in the Paige study of the Korean decision (3).   It may be
pointed out that the major weakness of the framework (as noted by
Frankel (4)) - that it omits any mention of the operational environment
- is rectified by the Brecher et al. framework.   Accepting the Sprouts'
distinction between the psychological and the operational environments,
the Brecher et al. framework offers a way of analysing the relationship
between the two.   However, as Dawisha (5) has pointed out, the Brecher
et al. framework still suffers from an inability to cope with the problem of dynamism; it is predominantly a static framework for the evaluation of decisions.

   Both of these approaches were originally considered as ways of examining the two foreign policies under discussion but were rejected for
differing reasons.   The Snyder, Bruck and Sapin framework was rejected
not only because it has serious theoretical shortcomings but also because it does no more than offer a checklist of all the possible relevant factors.   It appears to offer no indication of how to proceed to
examine two foreign policies - indeed, the title of the framework,
'State X as an Actor in a situation', indicates that the function of
the framework is to be 'crudely suggestive' of *possible* relationships
between *potentially* relevant factors.

The Brecher, Steinberg and Stein framework was not used because it is primarily a framework for the examination of specific decisions. It is clear, however, that Michael Brecher has utilised it in a most impressive examination of the nature of Israel's foreign policy.(6) Whilst there is no doubt in the mind of this author that this is a most fruitful piece of work, the sheer amount of work involved precludes any use of the framework as a means of comparing the general orientation of foreign policies. Thus, because the objective of this research was to examine the utility of a specific macro foreign policy approach in comparing, in very general terms, the two foreign policies under consideration, the Brecher, Steinberg and Stein framework did not appear to be the right tool for the job. The common feature of those approaches considered in this chapter is that each offers - or claims to offer - a means of comparing the general nature of the foreign policies of states.

This criterion also precluded a discussion of the other main area of theoretical work concerning foreign policy - that of the nature of foreign policy decision-making. The approach to foreign policy based on the process of decision-making, although clearly of considerable value in understanding the way foreign policy is made, does not concern itself with the questions that this study seeks to examine. Therefore, the work of Braybrooke and Lindblom, Hilsman, Verba, Jervis, Steinbrunner, and above all the seminal work of Graham Allison, (7) is not to be considered in this chapter. Despite the abundance of work on the nature of decision-making - especially the work related to the bureaucratic politics approach of Allison and Halperin - such perspectives did not appear to be relevant to the aim of this study. Whatever the nature of the decision-making process is, the main concern of this study is to offer a means of comparing the general nature of two foreign policies in terms of the behaviour of the states concerned. This outline of the approaches that were not considered in detail is deemed necessary because it illustrates the objectives of the theoretical approach of the study. It also indicates that the ultimate choice of approach was not a simple one but was one which was deliberately related to the nature of the case study. In addition to this consideration, the approach seemed of considerable value and claimed to be able to aid the understanding of the two foreign policies. To restate: the objectives of this study are primarily to examine the ways in which a specific theoretical approach aids the understanding of two foreign policies. Before discussing the approach that was finally adopted, this chapter outlines the other approaches examined and the reasons for their not being utilised.

A NATIONAL INTEREST

As has been noted by various authors, the primary feature of foreign policy is that it is the major connection between a state's domestic and external environments. As Frankel notes, foreign policy is the interface between domestic and international society - the feature which links formally sovereign states with other such units. Thus any approach to discussing the general nature of a state's foreign policy must offer some method of evaluating this connection. In this chapter, the approaches which will be considered are Rosenau's concept of linkage politics; Rosenau's work on pretheory; Holsti's analysis of national role; and Hanrieder's compatibility and consensus approach.

Before considering these approaches in detail it is necessary first to discuss the most commonly used concept in discussions of foreign policy - the national interest. In essence, it is believed that this concept is of very little use as an <u>analytical</u> term for the comparison of foreign policies. The term has suffered from a surfeit of usages and meanings since its initial usage in the 16th and 17th centuries. Although it is a term that is used in all areas of political debate, it is in foreign affairs that the term is used most frequently - often as a measure of a state's success in foreign policy. In addition to the common usage of the term in political debate, the term has been used by many writers as the basis of an explanation of international politics. This approach receives its most sophisticated treatment in the work of Hans Morgenthau (8) where the term becomes the cornerstone of his theory of foreign policy and international politics, bringing in the concomitant concept of the balance of power. Without outlining the details of the Morgenthau approach, it has served, in the Kuhnian sense, as the dominant paradigm for the study of international politics in the post war period. It and its state-centric assumptions have been the basis of a very large proportion of the writings on international relations. In an unpublished but succinctly titled paper, 'Color it Morgenthau', Handelman <u>et al</u>. (9) discuss the way in which the Morgenthau paradigm underlies even the most superficially different forms of analysis, such as the behavioural and quantitative literature. As they argue, systems analysis, integration theory, game theory, communications theory, and foreign policy analysis, among others, are often implicitly based on the Morgenthau paradigm. Again, in the Kuhnian sense, the same paradigm has set the limits to, and served as the measure of success of, the puzzles to be solved within the subject area of international politics.

Nevertheless, the concept of the national interest, which suggests that decision-makers think and act in terms of how various choices add to or detract from the national interest, appears to suffer from serious theoretical problems. James Rosenau, in an article reviewing the theoretical standing of the concept, starts from the perspective that the term has two distinct but related usages: as an analytical term used to 'describe, explain or evaluate the sources or the adequacy of a nation's foreign policy', and, as an instrument of political action where it serves as 'a means of justifying, denouncing, or proposing policies'(10). Although it is of use for practitioners since they can define their goals in terms of the national interest <u>because</u> it is value laden, this very fact means that the utility of the term is limited for analysts who seek to use it as a tool of rigorous investigation.

However, as Rosenau points out, the term is still very popular in academic discussions of foreign policy. He notes that there are two main groups among the analysts who use the concept. <u>First</u>, there are the <u>objectivists</u>, typified by Hans Morgenthau; these analysts argue that the best interest of a nation is a matter of objective reality and that by actually outlining this reality the analyst is able to use the concept of the national interest as a measure of the suitability of various policies. <u>Second</u>, there are the <u>subjectivists</u> who are less concerned with evaluating the suitability of various foreign policy proposals; they are concerned with using the term as a tool of explanation. They argue that by using the term they can discover the reasons why state decision-makers do what they do. Thus they deny the

8

existence of a reality that is easily discoverable and with which certain policies may, or may not, be in accord. Thus, the subjectivists analyse the various ways the national interest is defined by decision-makers and see this, and therefore the term, as the key to understanding foreign policy behaviour.

Rosenau states that, despite these different approaches, the term has proven fruitless and misleading. He gives several reasons for this failure: the concept of the nation is difficult to define; similarly there is the problem of specifying whose interests it encompasses; the elusiveness of criteria for determining the existence of interests; the absence of procedures for cumulating the interests once they have been identified; and, the uncertainty as to whether the national interest has been fully identified once specific interests have been cumulated or whether the national interest is greater than the sum of its parts.

More fundamentally, the objectivist school of the national interest suffers from the simple problem that whilst there may well be an objective reality (for example, a situation in which certain policies will actually aid the national interest) this is unknowable. Given that any conception of the national interest is rooted in values, then any notion of an objective reality can only be based on the values of the analyst involved - and normally this is with the benefits of hindsight. However, the objectivist school claims that the measure for the appropriateness of any policy is not value laden, rather it is the objective measure of a state's power. However, as has been pointed out by several writers, the concept of power is virtually as elusive as that of interest and the process of cumulating the various components of a nation's power clearly involves value judgements.

The subjectivist school, although they avoid the pitfall of arguing that the national interest has an objective reality, suffer from the initial problem involved in identifying the sources of the various conceptions of that interest - especially where there are no formal spokespersons. Furthermore, there is the additional problem that some definitions of the interest carry more weight than others; how this is to be accounted for is problematic, especially since the most tempting solution is to attach weights on the basis of the analyst's own assessments. As Rosenau points out, the most common way of settling this problem is to rely on the policy process to do it for the analyst - thus the analyst considers the decision-maker's conception of the relative weight of views of the national interest. Not only does this bring the analyst into problems over what happens when various decision-makers weigh the various conceptions in a different way but it also ignores the problems alluded to in Bachrach and Baratz's work on the conception of non decision-making (11). Any solution to the problem of which decision-maker's conception is correct must relate to the values of the analyst. The problem of analysing the foreign policy of an authoritarian society in such terms is obvious; the essential problem is that the national interest is defined by the political process.

Rosenau concludes that there can be little wonder that the national interest has not lived up to its early promise as an analytic tool since, 'all the approaches to it suffer from difficulties which defy resolution and which confound rather than clarify analysis'(12). Yet, as he points out, the term is still widely used in political debate and thus political observers must take cognisance of it.

In this connection, the most fruitful survey of the conception is that of Joseph Frankel in his monograph National Interest (13). Frankel aims to classify the term national interest into categories which allow the term to be examined and the various usages of it to be understood. He proposes the classification of the term into three categories: aspirational, operational, explanatory and polemical (although he points out that these classifications should best be seen as ideal types). Thus, despite the fact that there will be considerable overlap, Frankel argues that any individual usage of the term will fall predominantly into one of the proposed categories.

The aspirational level of usage of the national interest refers to the vision of the good life, to some ideal set of goals, which the state would like to realise if it were possible. Thus if some conception of the national interest is proposed on the aspirational level alone, it means that the policy is not being actively pursued, but indicates the general direction of policy desired. Given the opportunity, either by an increase in the state's capabilities or by a favourable change in the environment of the state (or by a combination of both), the policy may become operational. Frankel notes seven common features of conceptions of the national interest at the aspirational level: they are long term; they are rooted in history and ideology; they command the attention of the opposition, free from the restraints and preoccupations of governments, and the extremes in political parties; they provide a sense of purpose or hope in policy; they need not be fully articulated and coordinated and can be contradictory; they do not require any feasibility study and are rarely costed; they are determined by political will rather than by capabilities.

At the operational level, the concept of the national interest refers to the totality of the policies actually pursued. Frankel notes that they differ from the aspirational conception of the national interest in eight ways: they are usually short term interests, capable of achievement in the foreseeable future; they often stem from considerations of expediency or necessity; they are the predominant concern of the government and party in power; they are used in a descriptive rather than in a normative way; because of the necessity of implementation, contradictions are less easily tolerated than is the case with aspirations; they are translated into policies based on the prospects of their success and which can be costed; they are determined primarily by capabilities rather than by political will; they can be arranged into maximum and minimum programmes with the former representing the aspirational level of national interest.

As Frankel argues, the most significant factor for foreign policy is the interrelationship between the two levels. This relationship is modified by the nature of what Frankel calls the net achievement capability, i.e. the relationship between relevant goals, capabilities and constraints, which determines what the state can actually achieve in its external environment. However, as Frankel points out, this distinction between the aspirational and operational levels does not occur fully in real life, i.e. it is primarily an analytical distinction.

This confusion is compounded by the third level of use of the concept of the national interest. At this level, the concept of national interest is used to explain, evaluate, rationalise or criticise foreign policy; the main reason for using the term is to prove one's argument right and that of one's opponents wrong. The term is therefore not used as a means of describing and prescribing behaviour, although its usage might suggest this was the case. A further problem noted by Frankel is that of the difficulty in distinguishing between the use of the term at the explanatory and polemical level and its use in either the aspirational or operational level, as in, for example, the statements of government leaders.

As Frankel notes, the concept of the national interest is especially difficult for analysts to come to terms with. However, he concludes by examining the ways in which an analyst may distinguish between irregularities and conflicts within the perception of the national interest of any state and the problems encountered by the method of research. He argues that within a state a clear perception of national interest is likely when values are stable; when the net achievement capability is stable; and when the international environment is relatively comprehensible and manageable. Conversely, the perception of national interest will be unclear when there are contradictions within the value system; when the net achievement capability is disturbed; and when the international environment is intractable, especially if a state cannot comprehend it (for example, in a period of technological change).

The conclusion that follows from the reviews of the concept of national interest carried out by Rosenau and Frankel - supported by Robinson's review (14) - is that the term is of little use for the analysis of foreign policy. The analysis of Frankel clearly illustrates the variety of levels of usages of the term in political debate and, when this is compared with the analysis of Rosenau, it compounds the conclusion that not only is any objective analysis of national interest fraught with difficulties but so, also, is any subjective form of analysis. Frankel's work reinforces Rosenau's criticisms of any examination of the decision-making approach centred on the concept of national interest since it shows the way in which the concept is commonly, and normally unknowingly, used in a variety of analytical ways. Given the distinction made by Frankel of the three analytical levels of usage of the concept, and primarily because, as he points out, the actual use of the term tends to fall across these boundaries, any attempt by the analyst to discern the precise conception of national interest involved seems to be virtually impossible. Thus, although the term has been, and continues to be, used extensively in political debate it is so intangible and flexible to be meaningless in political analysis. In the Popperian sense, since there is no case that can be pointed to that could possibly falsify any usage of the term as used by any subjective analyst, then the concept is of little utility except in the purely negative sense of pointing to the shortcomings of a most commonly used term.

B NATIONAL ROLE

A concept that is related to that of national interest is that of national role; indeed the term has been widely used in both academic

11

and practical discourse. Underlying, for example, the balance of power approach to international relations, was an explicit division of states into one of three roles: aggressor states; status quo states; and, balancer states. If the states did not play the role postulated in the theory, imbalance, war and the transformation of the system would occur. Similarly, much of the academic work since the Second World War has been concerned either with the structural characteristics of the international system or with the foreign policy conceptions of states' decision-makers. Implicit in both these areas is a reliance on the concept of role: the non aligned; the Western bloc; the communist states; allies; satellites, etc. In the academic litera-ture as well as in the statements of political practitioners, the concept of role, or, at least, the vague characterisation of foreign policy as performing - whether at an aspirational or operational level - a role, appears to be widespread. When either academics or prac-titioners discuss the foreign policy of a state in terms of its being non aligned, an ally, an oil power, a communist state, a front line state or whatever, they are ascribing to the particular state a gener-alised form of behaviour, i.e. that in certain circumstances it will act or perform in a certain predictable manner.

The most extensive analysis of this concept of national role is that of K. J. Holsti (15), which appeared in the International Studies Quarterly in 1970. Holsti contrasts the widespread usage of the term role in international relations with its lack of definition. He points to the development of the term in many areas of the social sciences and yet argues that 'despite the large number of social sci-ence studies which employ the concept of the role, consensus on defini-tions or on the empirical referents of the concept does not yet exist. As with "power" or "interest" scholars tend to define the term to suit their research'(16). Nevertheless, Holsti examines the constituent parts of the concept and attempts to apply these to the use of the concept in the study of foreign policy.

After examining the literature on the concept and its use in the social sciences, Holsti divides the concept into four parts. These are: a) role performance - the attitudes, decisions and actions govern-ments take to implement b) their self defined role conceptions or c) the role prescriptions emanating from the external environment. Such activities take place within d) a position, that is, a system of role prescriptions. As he argues, any examination of the national interest as seen by the decision-makers totally misses out the nature of role prescription. But, as he points out, the major problem with foreign policy as role behaviour is that the setting or position of the action is very different from the societal or organisational setting in which the sociological analysis of role occurs.

Holsti modifies the formulation of the concept of role as used in the social sciences and changes the concept of position or setting to one of the international status of the national actor, to link the concep-tion of the role of the state held by its decision-makers with the prescription of the role enforced by the external environment. Funda-mentally, however, actual role performance in international politics is primarily determined by the policymaker's role conceptions of domestic needs and demands and critical events in the external environment. Thus, in Holsti's modified outline of role theory and foreign policy

FIGURE 2.1
ROLE THEORY AND FOREIGN POLICY

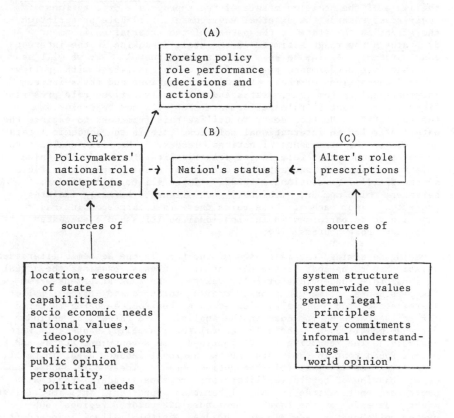

Source: K. J. Holsti, International Studies Quarterly, Vol. 14
(3), September 1970, p. 245.

(see Figure 2.1), the prescription of the state's role by the external environment, although relevant to foreign policy behaviour, is only of secondary importance to the policymakers' role conception, as is the status of the state in the international system.

Holsti therefore reformulates the components of role outlined above and redefines them as: a) National role performance - the general foreign policy behaviour of governments. b) National role conception - the image of the decision-makers of the appropriate orientations of their state towards the external environment. c) Role prescription - the effect on the state of the nature of the external environment. d) Status - the rough estimate of the state's ranking in the international system. Again, he sums up by stating that ' . . . we will assume that role performance results from, or is consistent with, policymakers' conceptions of their nation's orientations and tasks in the international system . . . Status and externally derived role prescriptions are relevant to role performance, but will not be explored further.' (17) He then seeks to utilise this framework to explore the nature of roles in international politics, both in the academic literature and in the statements of national leaders. He first analyses the use of the concept of role in the academic literature and finds nine role types 'implied, suggested or discussed in the disparate writings of the field': revolutionary leader - imperialist; bloc leader; balancer; bloc member; mediator; non aligned; buffer; isolate; protectee. For each of these roles there is a corresponding major function to be performed in international politics and a suggested set of primary role sources (18).

Having determined the main uses of the term in the academic literature, Holsti then turns and, in the bulk of his analysis, examines the actual national role conceptions of policymakers. He took statements from the presidents, prime ministers, foreign ministers and official policy statements by top officials, with at least ten sources being required for any state to be included in the analysis. A three year period was examined (1965-67) and only general foreign policy statements were analysed. The resulting study comprised some seventy-one states and Holsti found that in their statements, national leaders used, in total, some seventeen distinct role conceptions (19). These role conceptions were: bastion of revolution/liberator; regional leader; regional protector; active independent; liberation supporter; anti imperialist agent; defender of the faith; mediator-integrator; regional-subsystem collaborator; developer; bridge; faithful ally; independent; example; internal development; isolate; protectee.

From this survey the most immediate conclusion drawn was that the number of roles actually conceived by policymakers was almost double that found in the academic literature. Although there was some overlap there was a significant omission in that the term balancer - so vital to much of the balance of power theory - was missing in the empirical survey. However, the most interesting conclusion, and this is the one that both makes the study of Holsti so important and yet clearly illustrates the problem of utilising the national role approach, is that, whereas the academic literature ascribed one role to each state, the actual statements of policymakers showed that this was not the case. Thus, the average number of role conceptions per country was 4.6 - and even if those roles referred to only once are discounted

14

the average is still 3.2.   Holsti hypothesises that the more active
a country is in international affairs the more national role conceptions
will be perceived by its policymakers (thus, all of the major powers
have five or more role conceptions).   A further finding is that the
most frequently quoted role conceptions are those referring to the
region;   cold war conceptions account for only some twenty-eight per
cent of cases.

On the basis of this analysis, Holsti claims that the concept of
national role aids the study of international politics.   He argues
that the concept of role is the key to understanding foreign policy
behaviour because most decisions will be reasonably consistent with
role conception.   Thus, foreign policy analysis should concentrate on
explaining 'the origins, presence, and sources of change of national
role conceptions rather than single decisions'(20).   Such a focus
would, he states, avoid the danger of analysis becoming mere recon-
structed history.   It could also serve as a bridge between the study
of foreign policy and the wider focus of the international system,
which has been a troublesome divide for the development of a coherent
theoretical approach to international relations.

In a reply to the Holsti article, Carl Backman (21) argues that
Holsti's work has provided a much richer taxonomy of roles than suggested by the work of previous writers and that it organises and makes
sense of that which is already known.   Yet he doubts whether the theory
will lead to any new insights that suggest testable hypotheses, which
will, in turn, advance our knowledge.   The failure of any such application of Holsti's work would appear to confirm that reservation.   However, there seems to be a much more fundamental problem with Holsti's
approach that effectively makes it of little use for the comparative
analysis of foreign policy.   This problem can be stated simply and it
is that the whole approach is based on the assumption that statements
by policymakers are a reliable indication of intention and of actual
behaviour.   This seems to bring us back to the problems noted by Rosenau and Frankel in the analysis of the closely related concept of
national interest.   Put in the same language, if Holsti is accepting
that role prescription is weak (i.e. that an objective national role
exists) then how is the analyst to choose between the various role
conceptions offered by different policymakers?   The differentiation
between the aspirational, operational and explanatory/polemical levels
of national interest seems to be of equal relevance in the analysis of
national role.   How, therefore, does the analyst distinguish between
an aspirational role and an operational role, especially when these may
be confused by the use of the concept in an explanatory/polemical
sense?

If Holsti's answer to these objections would be to argue that the role
conceptions analysed were those outlined by the government leaders and
that the variety of role conceptions offers a meaningful way of discussing contradictions within the government over the desired role, then
this would seem to do no more than return us to the problems raised by
Bachrach and Baratz.   It would also cause problems in making any distinction between democratic and authoritarian regimes.   But again,
given that policymakers face at least two audiences - the foreign and
the domestic - at any one time, how reliable are statements of the
government's conception of role?   Since such statements can be

extremely flexible and would thus allow, for example, a liberator to both give and refrain from giving military support, then such a reliance on the concept would seem to be misplaced. This difficulty is compounded by the fact that statements may be either deliberately misleading or based on ignorance of their real nature by the decision-makers themselves. Whilst it would be imprudent to deny that role conceptions are a relevant variable for the analysis of foreign policy, it would appear unwise to make them the cornerstone, the dependent variable in Holsti's view, of foreign policy analysis.

C ROSENAU'S CONCEPT OF PRETHEORY

The third major approach to the problem of discussing the foreign policies of states is James Rosenau's concept of pretheory. It is necessary to make explicit the view of this writer that in moving from concepts of national role and national interest to the work of Rosenau, we are moving towards the form of analysis that appears to be the most relevant to the present study.

The work of James Rosenau has been of seminal importance in the study of foreign policy in the last fifteen years. His work has been severely criticised in academic circles. Yet it is believed that his work represents the form of analysis that would appear to offer the most stimulating and potentially fruitful path for the comparative analysis of foreign policy. The sections in this chapter that are concerned with the work of Rosenau will be critical indeed, but it is believed that therein lies one of the major advantages of his work - that it is so explicitly presented that it can be readily criticised.

The major aim of Rosenau's work appears to be that of producing concepts and frameworks that will allow the analysis of any state's foreign policy. He is not concerned with the in depth study of any one state's foreign policy, nor with the analysis of concepts as vague as national interest or national role. His work is aimed at producing a rigorous basis for the comparative study of foreign policy. Yet, herein lies one of the problems: by attempting to be so rigorous, so scientific, his work has to be judged, inter alia, by those criteria. By deliberately eschewing historical case studies and by stressing the rapidity with which conventional wisdom becomes obsolete, he is claiming that his frameworks and concepts have a timeless quality. In his intellectual autobiography (22) Rosenau remembers the feeling he had had of misleading his students in a discussion of the whys and wherefores of the Korean War, since he had given them 'no intellectual equipment with which they could 'probe the international scene long after Korea had moved off the public stage' (23). Such a rejection of the traditional tools of analysis clearly involves Rosenau in almost setting himself up to be criticised if his approach does not accord with the rigours of scientific enquiry.

The initial contribution to this approach by Rosenau is the now well known article (written in 1964, and published in 1966) 'Pretheories and Theories of Foreign Policy' (24). Rosenau starts from the belief that the subject of foreign policy - especially the effect of internal influences on external behaviour - has been both exhausted and neglected as a focus of inquiry. 'Even as it seems clear that everything worth

saying about the subject has already been said, so does it also seem
obvious that the heart of the matter has yet to be explored' (25).
Pointing to the vast amount of work that has been undertaken on the
subject of foreign policy since 1945, he argues that it is easy to
exaggerate the rate of progress. Although many relevant factors
have been identified, although the effects of internal and external
factors have been noted '. . . rare is the article or book which goes
beyond description . . . even rarer is the work that contains explicit
"if - then" hypotheses.' (26)   The rate of progress, he states, has
been very slow indeed.

The reason for this lack of progress is, he believes, not difficult
to discern and it is simply that foreign policy analysis is devoid of
general theory.   Whilst the field has many frameworks, concepts and
approaches that offer partial insights into foreign policy, there is
no scheme to . . . 'link up these components of external behaviour in
causal sequences' (27).   The field of foreign policy analysis lacks a
Rostow, or a Festinger, or an Almond; it has therefore been largely
historical and single country orientated.   Such an approach is incapable, Rosenau argues, of leading to general theory.   The primary
reason for this is that each single country study uses its own concepts
and approaches, so that comparative analysis is largely impossible.
Different questions are asked, different variables are analysed and are
treated in different ways.   Furthermore, by stressing the historical
and cultural/ideological factors that underlie any state's foreign policy, the analysts tend to treat each country's international situation
as unique.

Yet Rosenau feels that this situation is not the result of the inherent nature of the material . . . 'surely there is nothing inherent in
the nature of foreign policy phenomena which renders them more resist-
ant to theoretical treatment than the gross data that comprise . . .
other applied fields?' (28)   He contrasts the state of the discipline
with that of American political science generally and concludes that
the absence of theory cannot 'be readily justified or easily explained'
(29).   Rosenau sees two reasons for this shortcoming - one philosophical and the other conceptual.

The philosophical shortcoming arises out of the need, if any theoretical development is to flourish, for empirical materials that have been
similarly processed to be made available.   He analogises that it is no
more possible to build theory out of raw data than it is to build houses
out of fallen trees and unbaked clay.   He points out that similarly
treating the material does no more mean that the data has to be used in
one way than does the necessity of cutting timber to certain sizes and
baking clay in certain shapes require that only one form of building
can be built.   The overriding need is for a pretheory, 'which renders
the raw materials comparable and ready for theorising' (30).   Foreign
policy research has not carried out this processing.   This task does
not just mean that data should be collected in uniform ways, but it
means that the whole approach requires more order.

Rosenau proposes that the way to achieve this order is to outline the
main ingredients of any pretheory and then for him to organise them
into his own particular pretheory.   He claims that any pretheory of
foreign policy can be comprehensively derived from five sets of variables: individual; role; government; society; system.   The

individual variables refer to those characteristics unique to the
decision-maker.   The role variables refer to the behaviour of officials
that is generated by the roles they occupy and which would occur irrespective of the individual characteristics of the role occupants.   The
governmental variables refer to those aspects of a government's structure that limit or enhance the foreign policy choice made by decision-
makers.   The societal variables are those non governmental aspects of
a society which influence its external behaviour.   Finally, the
systemic variables are the non human aspects of a society's external
environment and the actions occurring abroad that influence the choices
made by government officials.

These are the ingredients of the pretheory, and, as Rosenau points out,
the main task of the pretheory is to assess their relative potencies.
Thus the task of constructing the pretheory involves assigning the
weight that each of the variables has in determining external behaviour.
The pretheory should indicate the variables that are most influential,
then those variables which rank next and so on; Rosenau points out that
' . . . there is no need to specify exactly how large a slice of the
pie is accounted for by each set of variables.   Such precise specifi-
cations are characteristic of theories and not of the general framework
within which data are organised.' (31)

Rosenau then suggests his own way of ranking the variables to form his
pretheory.   He does this by introducing three forms of distinguishing
between societies: large/small; developed/underdeveloped economy;
open/closed polity.   This pretheory is presented in Figure 2.2. It is
important to stress that Rosenau does not seek to justify or debate the
ordering of the variables, he merely wishes to indicate ' . . . what
the construction of a pretheory of foreign policy involves and why it
is a necessary prerequisite to the development of theory.' (32) Indeed,
because of the undeveloped nature of the subject, Rosenau accepts that
his rankings are idiosyncratic and can be neither proved nor disproved.
The actual task of theory would involve the assessment of the exact
potency of each variable; as Rosenau admits, his pretheory is little
more than an orientation.

The view that such an endeavour is a fruitless one is one that Rosenau,
correctly, assumed would be widespread amongst the historical, case
study analysts, yet his answer to that seems largely justified; it is
impossible not to have some pretheory whenever the task of tracing
causation is undertaken.   Any view that causation was not involved
would be equivalent to treating human activities as random, thus some,
however implicit, view of causation and therefore some, however uncon-
scious, pretheoretical stance is axiomatic to academic enquiry.

This very argument of Rosenau seems to be the turning point of most
subsequent debates on the nature of foreign policy analysis.   As he
points out ' . . . while it is thus impossible to avoid possession of
a pretheory of foreign policy, it is quite easy to avoid awareness of
one's pretheory and to proceed as if one started over with each situation'. (33)   The utility of explicit pretheory is that it will allow
the accumulation of similarly processed materials, which will provide
the basis for the comparison of foreign policies.   Even if the actual
pretheory involved was different (i.e. it ranked the variables in a
different manner) it would still allow the discernment of patterns.

FIGURE 2.2
ROSENAU'S ABBREVIATED PRETHEORY

An abbreviated presentation of the author's pretheory of foreign policy, in which five sets of variables underlying the external behaviour of societies are ranked according to their relative potencies in eight type of societies

Geography and physical resources	LARGE COUNTRY				SMALL COUNTRY			
State of the economy	Developed		Underdeveloped		Developed		Underdeveloped	
State of the polity	Open	Closed	Open	Closed	Open	Closed	Open	Closed
Rankings of the variables	Role Societal Governmental Systemic Idiosyncratic	Role Idiosyncratic Governmental Systemic Societal	Idiosyncratic Role Societal Systemic Governmental	Idiosyncratic Role Governmental Systemic Societal	Role Systemic Societal Governmental Idiosyncratic	Role Systemic Idiosyncratic Governmental Societal	Idiosyncratic Systemic Role Societal Governmental	Idiosyncratic Systemic Role Governmental Societal
Illustrative examples	US	USSR	India	Red China	Holland	Czechoslovakia	Kenya	Ghana

SOURCE

J. N. Rosenau, 'Pre Theories and Theories of Foreign Policy' J. N. Rosenau, The Scientific Study of Foreign Policy, Free Press, 1971, p. 113.

Having discussed this philosophical problem which prevents the emergence of foreign policy theory, Rosenau turns, in the second part of
the article, to consider the conceptual shortcomings that face the subject.   As he points out, even if explicit pretheories were utilised
all the problems would not be solved; it is a necessary but not a
sufficient condition.   The other main problem is that of the lack of
adequate concepts, since

> '. . . not only must similarly processed materials be available
> if general theory is to flourish, but researchers must also possess
> appropriate concepts for compiling them into meaningful patterns.
> Although rendered similar through the explication of pre-theories,
> the materials do not fall in place by themselves.' (34)

To return to his original analogy, buildings cannot be erected by wood
and bricks alone, certain engineering principles must be known; without
such principles the raw materials can be arranged in a variety of ways
that may well be totally unsound.

There are two main conceptual problems that, according to Rosenau,
are holding back the development of general theories of foreign policy
behaviour.   The first problem refers to the tendency of analysts to
distinguish rigidly between the national and international political
systems despite the evidence that this distinction is breaking down.
The second centres on the tendency to treat the political system as
functioning similarly over different types of issues.   Both of these
problems were the subject for later work by Rosenau - the former in his
work on linkage politics (35) (see below); the latter in his work on
foreign policy as an issue area (36).   With regard to the former problem, Rosenau claims that a new kind of political system has emerged -
the penetrated political system.

Most political scientists, he claims, use the words international and
national and deem the distinction to be relevant.   Rosenau believes
that the changes that have taken place in the twentieth century have
resulted in the self contained nation state becoming open to external
influences.   The result of this process he calls the penetrated political system, which is defined as a political system in which

> '. . . nonmembers of a national society participate directly and
> authoritatively, through actions taken jointly with the society's
> members, in either the allocation of its values or the mobilisation
> of support on behalf of its goals.' (37)

Rosenau admits that there are operational difficulties with the definition of the key terms in this statement, but believes that the concept
will be of considerable use in distinguishing between those forms of
society in which participation in decisions from the external environment does occur and those systems which still remain non penetrated.
As he points out, some systems may be penetrated over a single issue
whereas others are penetrated over many issues.   Such a conclusion
leads him to his second conceptual development, that of the issue area.

Given that some political systems can be seen as penetrated over some
issues and as non penetrated over others, he wishes to challenge the
assumption that political systems process different issues in the same

way.   Rosenau argues that different types of issue area elicit different motives on the part of different actors, i.e. different members of
the political system are activated in different issue areas.   However,
he claims that political scientists have been disinclined to recognise
this, and he sees this as connected to their reticence to recognise the
erosion of the national-international distinction.   It is also connected, of course, to the strong attachment to the thesis, most clearly
articulated by C. Wright Mills, of the power elite.   In short, he argues that further elaboration of the concept of the issue area is necessary and defines it as

> ' . . . (1) a cluster of values, the allocations or potential
> allocation of which (2) leads the affected or potentially affected
> actors to differ so greatly over (a) the way in which the values
> should be allocated or (b) the horizontal levels at which the
> allocations should be authorized that (3) they engage in distinct-
> ive behaviour designed to mobilize support for the attainment of
> their particular values.' (38)

Therefore, an issue area exists when an issue elicits a response from
the affected actors that results in the development of a vertical system of interaction to contrast with the horizontal organisation of the
political process.

   The next step is to outline a typology of the various forms of issue
area since if the term was merely used to refer to the debate over
a single matter then it would mean no more than that implied by the use
of the term issue.   Again, Rosenau recognises that any typology must,
at present, be largely arbitrary and therefore he aims to provide only
a single one;   he divides the behaviour associated with the authorit-
ive allocation of values into that occurring in one of four issue
areas;   territorial, status, human resources, and non human resources.
These refer respectively to the allocation of territorial jurisdiction,
the allocation of status in the political system, the allocation of
human resources, and the allocation of non human resources.   Such a
typology will, he states, allow the analyst to plot where issues arose -
i.e. at what horizontal political level (local, national, international
for example) - and to which level they extended.

   In the conclusion to the analysis, Rosenau states that the arguments
he has put forward have the clear implication that

> ' . . . the external behaviour of horizontal systems at the
> national level is likely to vary so greatly in scope, intensity,
> and flexibility in each of the four issue-areas that any theory
> of foreign policy will have to include if-then propositions
> which reflect these variations.   Similarly, theoretical account
> will have to be taken of the external behaviour of penetrated
> systems.' (39)

Furthermore, the combination of the two concepts of the penetrated
political system and the issue area means that any theory will have to
account for the difference between the degrees of penetration in the
various issue areas.   For example, the relative potency of the systemic
variables would appear to be of more importance in penetrated political
systems.

On the basis of this analysis, Rosenau deems it necessary to revise the crude pretheory outlined in Figure 2.2 above. He argues that it is necessary to subdivide each of the nation type columns into penetrated and non penetrated categories and to account for the different types of issue areas. This is outlined in Figure 2.3. As will be noted, the territorial and human resource issue areas have been combined by Rosenau, because the status and non human issue areas represent the two ends of the political spectrum in terms of the tangible/intangible nature of the ends and means; the other two issue areas are deemed to be a mix and therefore susceptible to similar analysis. Thus, whereas the status issue area is concerned with intangible means and ends and whereas the non human resource issue area is concerned with tangible means and ends, the human resource and territorial issue areas are a mix of tangible and intangible means and ends. Rosenau argues that the way a political system deals with tangible means and ends will differ from the way it deals with intangible means and ends and that both will differ from the third type of issue area.

This conception of pretheory as outlined in Figure 2.3 is a complex formulation. Rosenau does not believe that it is an easy task to build theory on the basis of it, but he believes that such a formulation, utilising the two concepts of the penetrated political system and the issue area, is necessary if theory is to be constructed. He accepts that the pretheory is only a starting point, that all it does is to outline and identify the materials out of which any theory must be constructed. However, as he makes clear, the framework does not predetermine the form of theory to be constructed; it does not dictate or limit the kind of theory that can be utilised. He writes that nothing in the framework ' . . . determines the design, elegance and utility of (the wide range of theories that can be built out of the materials).' (40). As he concludes, the nature of the theory developed depends on the analyst and this is why the task of theory building is so difficult.

It appears to be an impossible task to operationalise the Rosenau pretheory. It is difficult to square the undoubted heuristic value of the approach with the deafening silence resulting from its non application in empirical research. It has, however, provided the starting point for much of the comparative foreign policy research in the United States since its inception, but the tangible study based on its framework is missing. It does appear again in Rosenau's later work on adaptive politics, but it has certainly not fulfilled his claim of actually providing the pretheoretical basis for the development of comparative theory in foreign policy analysis. Whilst his claim that any pretheory of foreign policy must be composed of the five variables he lists involves the adoption of a clear and controversial stance, this has not been seriously discussed.

The major problem of the pretheory is then that it is extremely difficult to apply it to the actual task of constructing theory. The categories utilised are nowhere defined or justified: it would appear difficult to distinguish between many polities in terms of their being open or closed - indeed that would appear to be asking the wrong kind of question about a political system. It is difficult to utilise the distinction between a large and a small country except in the most extreme examples; there is a lamentable absence of empirical indicators. Similarly the developed/underdeveloped economic distinction would appear, especially after the oil crisis, to be a problematic one. The concept of the penetrated political system is dangerously near to being tautological since any conception of a totally closed society is extremely difficult to envisage. Likewise the typology of issue areas is based on a questionable assumption which, with the developments of, for example, Watergate, seems to be by no means an accepted one.

Naturally the actual pretheory outlined by Rosenau is highly debatable, although that objection does seem to be largely answered by Rosenau's explicit statement regarding the arbitrary nature of his intuitive listings. Perhaps a more basic reason for the lack of analysis based on the framework is that the subject area is, indeed, underdeveloped. Case studies and single country approaches have continued to be the main areas of research into foreign policy with the concomitant strengthening of the belief that general theories of foreign policy behaviour are impossible. This belief is certainly dominant in Britain and, with the exception of a relatively small group of academics centred around Rosenau, is still the overriding viewpoint that pervades the literature from the United States.

This situation is regrettable, but the nature of the subject area of foreign policy analysis appears to mitigate against the utilisation of other people's theoretical schemes. As the post behavioural revolution has come into full swing, perhaps the types of questions that the pretheory framework begs are no longer deemed the relevant questions to ask about foreign policy behaviour. That is not to deny the tremendous utility of the approach in the teaching of the subject but that, and the general unmanageability of the framework, would seem to go a long way towards explaining the lack of success of the approach.

Having noted the virtues and the problems of the framework, it is also necessary to point out why it will not be used in this study. The simple reason is that although it is attempting to locate the sources of any state's external behaviour, it does not offer any suggestions as to the nature of that behaviour. This is not, per se, a criticism of the framework, since the aim of the approach is to rank the various factors which may influence behaviour. Thus although the framework is utilised in the construction of the actual framework to be used for the examination of British and Dutch foreign policies, it cannot help with the analysis of the actual behaviour of those states. A final point to note is that there is a certain circularity, even virtual tautology, in the framework, in its stated objective. Hence, while on the surface the framework would appear to be useful in that it would suggest which variables should be analysed in order to explain British and Dutch foreign policies, it is precisely these variables which constitute the classification of political systems that the framework requires you to make initially.

In other words, to determine which variables an examination of Dutch and British foreign policies should concentrate on, an analyst would be required to choose what types of states these were; thus one might decide that Britain was, in 1945, an open, large, developed polity which was penetrated and that the Netherlands was, at that time, a small, rich, open polity. But is it not the case that the very ordering of variables - (systemic, societal, role, governmental, individual) - is what makes the country concerned a small, or large, open, developed polity? This

FIGURE 2.3 ROSENAU'S PRETHEORY

A further elaboration of the author's pretheory of foreign policy, in which five sets of variables underlying the external behavior of societies are ranked according to their relative potencies in sixteen types of societies and three types of issue-areas

Country	Economy	Polity	Penetration	Issue-area	1	2	3	4	5
LARGE COUNTRY	Developed Economy	Open Polity	Penetrated	other areas	so	r	sy	g	i
				nonhuman resource area	r	sy	so	g	i
				status area	r	so	sy	g	i
			Non-Penetrated	other areas	so	r	g	sy	i
				nonhuman resource area	r	g	so	sy	i
				status area	r	so	g	sy	i
		Closed Polity	Penetrated	other areas	r	i	g	so	sy
				nonhuman resource area	r	i	g	sy	so
				status area	r	i	g	sy	so
			Non-Penetrated	other areas	r	i	so	g	sy
				nonhuman resource area	r	i	g	sy	so
				status area	r	i	g	so	sy
	Underdeveloped Economy	Open Polity	Penetrated	other areas	i	r	so	sy	g
				nonhuman resource area	i	r	sy	g	so
				status area	i	r	sy	so	g
			Non-Penetrated	other areas	i	so	r	sy	g
				nonhuman resource area	i	r	sy	so	g
				status area	i	r	so	sy	g
		Closed Polity	Penetrated	other areas	i	r	sy	so	g
				nonhuman resource area	i	r	sy	g	so
				status area	i	r	sy	g	so
			Non-Penetrated	other areas	i	r	g	so	sy
				nonhuman resource area	i	r	g	sy	so
				status area	i	r	g	sy	so
SMALL COUNTRY	Developed Economy	Open Polity	Penetrated	other areas	sy	so	r	g	i
				nonhuman resource area	sy	r	g	so	i
				status area	sy	r	so	g	i
			Non-Penetrated	other areas	r	so	sy	g	i
				nonhuman resource area	r	sy	g	so	i
				status area	r	sy	so	g	i
		Closed Polity	Penetrated	other areas	sy	r	i	so	g
				nonhuman resource area	sy	r	i	g	so
				status area	sy	r	i	g	so
			Non-Penetrated	other areas	r	sy	i	so	g
				nonhuman resource area	r	sy	i	g	so
				status area	r	sy	i	g	so
	Underdeveloped Economy	Open Polity	Penetrated	other areas	sy	i	so	r	g
				nonhuman resource area	sy	i	r	g	so
				status area	sy	i	r	so	g
			Non-Penetrated	other areas	i	sy	so	r	g
				nonhuman resource area	i	sy	r	g	so
				status area	i	sy	r	so	g
		Closed Polity	Penetrated	other areas	sy	i	r	so	g
				nonhuman resource area	sy	i	r	g	so
				status area	sy	i	r	g	so
			Non-Penetrated	other areas	i	sy	r	so	g
				nonhuman resource area	i	sy	r	g	so
				status area	i	sy	r	g	so

i = individual variables, r = role variables, g = governmental variables, so = societal variables, sy = systemic variables.

Source: J. N. Rosenau, 'Pre Theories and Theories of Foreign Policy', in J. N. Rosenau, <u>The Scientific Study of Foreign Policy</u>, Free Press, 1971, p.149.

is not to claim that the two sections are mutually inclusive, but there does appear to be a very large degree of overlap; to restate, to decide on which type of state an actual state is, would appear to involve the prior consideration of what would be the ranking of the variables. For these reasons the pretheory framework was not utilised for this study, although again it is necessary to point out that it does have considerable heuristic value and is also an important component in the adaptive politics approach.

D ROSENAU AND LINKAGE POLITICS

The concept of linkage politics is closely related to the work of Rosenau on pretheory; indeed the approach may be most fruitfully seen as an attempt by Rosenau to deal with the first conceptual problem noted in his pretheory article - that of emerging linkages between national and international politics. The work really serves as the first attempt by political scientists to probe into the relationship between international and national politics. Despite earlier discussions of the problem, it was not until the mid 1960s that international relations scholars began to develop concepts about this relationship. The concept of linkage politics developed from a conference held in 1966, the papers of which were written up and published in a book, edited by Rosenau, and with the major theoretical statements contained in two papers by Rosenau (41).

The starting point for the analysis is the obvious fact of the importance of international affairs in domestic politics. Rosenau makes it clear at the outset that it is not simply the case that national-international linkages have been ignored by researchers. But, he states, despite much research into these linkages, the results have never been organised and examined systematically, because all the findings are derivatives of other primary concerns. They are also seen as results rather than as structural characteristics of the national and international systems; i.e. they are treated as the dependent variables rather than independent ones. He feels that

> '. . . in short, the problem with which we are concerned stems from a shortage of theory, not of empirical materials. What may be needed is the advent of an Einstein who, recognizing the underlying order that national boundaries obscure, will break through them and bring about a restructuring of the study of political processes.' (42)

Following a discussion of the problems involved in constructing a theoretical basis for examining this phenomenon, Rosenau turns to define the task. The aim is to

> ' . . . identify and analyze those recurrent sequences of behaviour that originate on one side of the boundary between the two types of systems and that become linked to phenomena on the other side in the process of unfolding.' (43)

The crossing of the boundary may be the result of direct interaction or by the processes of perception and emulation, therefore allowance needs to be made for both continuous and intermittent sequences. The basic

unit of analysis is called a linkage, which is defined as ' . . . any
recurrent sequence of behaviour that originates in one system and is
reacted to in another.' (44)   The initial and terminal stages of a linkage are referred to as an output and an input respectively.   Each is
classified in terms of whether it occurs in a polity or in its external
environment.   Such a classification results in the delineation of polity
outputs/polity inputs/environmental outputs/environmental inputs.   This
is refined by distinguishing between direct and indirect outputs/inputs;
where direct refers to foreign policy - the policy being deliberately
designed to bring about responses in other systems.   Indirect refers
to patterns of behaviour that are not intended to evoke boundary crossing responses, but do so through perceptual or emulative processes.

   Given this classification of inputs and outputs, the final dimension
of the linkage theoretical framework is that of the processes which link
inputs/outputs together.   Rosenau delineates three basic types - the
penetrative, the reactive, and the emulative.   A penetrative process is
defined as one where ' . . . members of one polity serve as participants
in the political processes of another' (45), i.e. they share the authority to allocate values in the penetrated polity.   A reactive linkage
is the opposite of the penetrative linkage;   it is the result of recurrent and similar boundary crossing reactions rather than the sharing of
authority.   Rosenau emphasises that

      ' . . . the actors who initiate the output do not participate
      in the allocative activities of those who experience the input,
      but the behaviour of the latter is nevertheless a response to
      behaviour undertaken by the former.' (46)

Whereas the penetrative process, virtually by definition, links direct
outputs and inputs, the reactive processes arise out of the joining of
both direct/indirect outputs to their respective inputs.   They are thus
considered to be the most frequent form of linkage.

   The third type of linkage process is a form of the reactive type.   The
emulative process is defined as being established when ' . . . the input
is not only a response to the output but takes essentially the same
form as the output.' (47)   It is assumed that emulative processes link
only indirect outputs and inputs since the behaviour is undertaken inde-
pendently of those who emulate it.   Frankel has suggested that

      ' . . . Rosenau's concept can do with an additional refinement
      by dividing this linkage into "emulative" where the polity reacting
      can expect to match the initiating State whereas in cases where
      the action is imitated without any expectations of matching, the
      process becomes "imitative".' (48)

Rosenau makes three points of elaboration concerning the formulation.
Firstly, the terminology is deliberately chosen so as to avoid terms
identified directly with the conceptual jails built either by national
or by international specialists.   Further, the terminology neither den-
ies nor exaggerates the relevance of national boundaries.   Finally, the
formulation is concerned only with recurrent behaviour not with single
events since only recurrent behaviour can serve as the basis for the
task of the study - that is, theory building.

FIGURE 2.4

ROSENAU'S LINKAGE FRAMEWORK

ENVIRONMENTAL ----→ POLITY Outputs and Inputs	The Contiguous Environment	The Regional Environment	The Cold War Environment	The Racial Environment	The Resource Environment	The Organisational Environment
Actors						
1 Executive Officials						
2 Legislative Officials						
3 Civilian Bureaucrats						
4 Military Bureaucrats						
5 Political Parties						
6 Interest Groups						
7 Elite Groups						
Attitudes						
8 Ideology						
9 Political Culture						
10 Public Opinion						
Institutions						
11 Executive						
12 Legislatures						
13 Bureaucracies						
14 Military Establishments						
15 Elections						
16 Party Systems						
17 Communications Systems						
18 Social Institutions						
Processes						
19 Socialization and Recruitment						
20 Interest Articulation						
21 Interest Aggregation						
22 Policy-Making						
23 Policy-Administration						
24 Integrative-Disintegrative						

SOURCE: J. N. Rosenau, 'Towards the Study of National-International Linkages', in J. N. Rosenau, The Scientific Study of Foreign Policy, Free Press, 1971, p. 325.

Given this basic formulation, Rosenau provides a framework of polity and environmental variables that might give rise to outputs and inputs. He does this by building up a 144 cell matrix (see Figure 2.4) comprising 24 polity variables (subdivided into actor/attitudes/institutions/processes) with sub-environments (contiguous, regional, cold war, racial, resource, organisational). The aim of his paper is made explicit with regard to this framework; he is not attempting to produce the definitive version. He stresses that his categories are imprecise, incomplete, impressionistic, and overlapping. His aim is to be suggestive, not exhaustive. What the paper has done is to build up a 3888 cell matrix (the 144 matrix x 3 (the types of linkages) x 9 (the basic interactions of polity/environmental outputs/inputs). There may be other possible frameworks but Rosenau notes six advantages of his.

First, it ' . . . prevents perpetuation of the analytic gap between national and international politics and compels thought about the way in which they are linked.' (49) Second, by subdividing polities and their environments, latent linkages may be discovered that a less explicit framework might miss. Third, by breaking down polities into many aspects the framework ' . . . inhibit(s) the tendency to treat national governments as having undifferentiated internal environments and thus to rely on the national interest as an explanation of international behaviour.' (50) Fourth, by identifying several international environments one can no longer presume that events abroad are constants in the functioning of polities. **Fifth**, ' . . . all of these **advantages** are further served by the distinction between direct and indirect linkage phenomena.' (51) The linkage framework thus calls attention to the actions of private persons or groups (businesses, religious organisations, unions, press, parties, interest groups, etc.). It also emphasises that there are many cases in which polities need to adjust to circumstances in their external environment that were not intended to affect them. Finally, the framework is an attempt to form a basis for the comparison of the relative potency of variables in the international behaviour of different polities.

Linkage politics is therefore the starting point for the modern study of the interaction of domestic and international environments. The general realisation by international relations scholars that foreign policy was an interface between two separate environments found coherence with Rosenau's early attempts to build up a matrix for the study of linkage politics. The size of the problem facing Rosenau in providing such a framework is shown by the fact that the rest of the papers in the book that he edited on this subject do not, with minor exceptions, follow on from his work.

As Rosenau states ' . . . the test of such a framework lies not in the advantages that are claimed for it, but in the theoretical questions that it generates.' (52) He claims, however, that there are several potentially innovative lines of enquiry suggested by the matrix (Figure 2.4); for example, he suggests that the framework would allow the examination of the origins, duration, flexibility, stability and functions of linkages, irrespective of the kind of political system that sustains them.

Furthermore, the impact of the cold war environment, for example, could be compared with that of the contiguous environment on the nature of political parties within the political system. Thus questions could be asked, such as: do the dimensions of the contiguous environment create more or less divisiveness within and among parties than do aspects of the cold war environment? Does the former tend to foster penetrative or emulative processes that divide parties and the latter reactive processes that unite them?

In addition to questions such as these, and he gives many more examples, he also states that the framework stimulates the asking of questions regarding the nature of processes within and between the columns. For example:

'Is the cold war environment more securely linked to, say, the structure of mass public opinion and the functioning of the systems of mass communications than to the various processes of governmental policy making?' 'Are some external environments likely to be linked to only a few selected aspects of polities, whereas with others linkage occurs across the entire range of polity activities?' 'Are some environments more likely to foster penetrative or emulative processes than others?'

A further line of enquiry that Rosenau claims is suggested by the framework relates to the subject area of comparative politics. For example:

'How widespread are the linkages to which the polity contributes outputs?' 'Are the polity's policy-making structures linked to the cold war environment whereas those of its interest articulation and aggregation are linked to the regional environment?'

Following from this, Rosenau claims that the framework leads to an examination of the degree to which similar types of polities have similar patterns of linkages. Again, to give examples:

'Do all democracies have a similar pattern of linkage to the outside world?' 'Are wealthy polities more successful in managing their direct linkages than poor ones?'

He gives further examples of the lines of enquiry which may be pursued on the basis of the framework.

Nevertheless, he concludes by asking, inter alia,

'is it irresponsible to raise questions that one neither answers nor provides the basis for answering? Is it self-defeating to propose research based on impressionistic and overlapping categories that have not been derived from a theoretical model and that may thus prove more misleading than helpful?' (53)

His answer to these, and other doubts he expresses, is that the utility of the framework in the examination of linkages will provide the measurement of success and failure. As has already been stated, the chapters in the remainder of the book did not really utilise the framework. As Dina Zinnes notes in a review of the book

' . . . while the book is unquestionably a stimulating inquiry into a series of questions that have largely been ignored to date, the volume does suffer from some important limitations.' (54)

29

She notes three major areas of confusion. First, although Rosenau sees
linkages as referring to either the effect of the international system
on its state members or the impact of state characteristics on the international system, most contributors examine the relationship between national attributes and foreign policy behaviour. This, she points out,
is an old and familiar theme, but it does not fit into the Rosenau conception of linkage. Second, in contrast to Rosenau's clear call for the
utilisation of the framework to obtain testable hypotheses, most contributors fail to do so. Zinnes claims that there are serious and distur-
bing problems over what constitutes a testable hypothesis and what constitutes logical argument. Third, although Rosenau claims that the
linkage framework can be used to probe into the linkage patterns of all
states, all the contributors select a certain set of countries for examination without explaining how or why those sets affect linkage patterns.

Zinnes raises the further objection that the contributors seem to see
the problem of linkage as a new one; she argues that it is not, and
claims that the book would have been more useful had it discussed previous approaches. Finally, she claims that Rosenau's argument itself
is difficult to follow and that for anyone wishing to utilise the approach there would be serious problems in constructing a research design
based upon it. Nevertheless, she believes that the subject is of considerable importance and that the problems of the book only illustrate
the degree of work required on the area of linkage politics.

Rosenau revisited the linkage politics approach in an article published
in 1973 (55). He points out that the approach

'arose out of a conviction that students of comparative and international politics were needlessly and harmfully ignoring each other's
work . . . to facilitate the convergence of the two fields it was
proposed that a "linkage" serve as the basic unit of analysis.' (56)

He admits that 'the initial effort to apply this framework systematically
to empirical materials fell far short of the claims made for it.' (57)
Although the contributors to the book spent two full days clarifying the
framework and reaching agreement on how they would all use it, the resulting essays

' . . . failed to yield comparable findings. The linkage dimensions
they were all to investigate turned out to have different meanings
for each of them . . . all in all, the editor of the essays was
compelled to conclude that the provision of a loosely designed,
atheoretical typology was a failure as a research strategy.' (58)

The end product, he admits, was painfully unproductive.

In this revisiting of the approach, Rosenau points to the major problem
of the framework - and this appears to be the basis of the problems found
with the approach - and that was that it was

' . . . simply a typology that was totally lacking in theory. The
cells were created by the convergence of national and international
variables, but there was no specification of the phenomena that
might be found in them . . . At the time, therefore, it seemed clear
that a different research strategy ought to have been used.' (59)

The framework, he admits, rather than stimulating enquiry, stifled it and, by so doing, demonstrated ' . . . through its very massiveness and lack of direction the wisdom of continuing to confine theory and research to a single analytic level.' (60)

Yet, as Rosenau goes on to point out in great detail, the concept did not die. He lists a series of studies based on the concept - involving some twenty academics utilising the 'linkage politics' approach. Many of these studies involve a conceptual revision of the original framework and Rosenau is forced to conclude that despite the widespread use of the approach ' . . . the empirical data thus far generated by the linkage framework have not been as innovative as the conceptual revisions.' (61) In many cases the approach has merely served as a new rhetoric with which to analyse old problems. Rosenau's conclusion is that it is too soon to reach a firm judgement about the theoretical utility of the linkage concept. On the one hand it has surmounted the common problem of failing to spark and guide further inquiry and it does have advantages over other concepts. On the other, he points out that it has not produced evidence that it lends itself to the derivation of interrelated propositions. On the basis of the evidence, he concludes, it is possible that the concept will either prove to be the basis of theoretical development or that it will merely lead to isolated insights.

Nevertheless, it might appear, on the surface, that the concept of linkage politics would serve as a useful starting point for the study of British and Dutch foreign policies and their interaction. The degree of penetration of the two states has immediate appeal as a tool of comparative study, as does the salience of various factors in the matrix formulation. Despite this immediate appeal, however, the framework of linkage politics is not to be used. Aside from the specific problems of Rosenau's formulation the main problems are methodological. The first major problem is that raised by Hanrieder in his article 'Compatibility and Consensus'. (62) As he points out, although it may be the case that there are advantages in linking international and national dimensions of foreign policy, there is also an advantage in keeping them apart, since both dimensions reach into different analytical environments. Whilst Hanrieder accepts that propositions derived from these two different analytical environments cannot be readily correlated since they are based on differing methodological assumptions and therefore on different data, he points out that if concepts of linkage between the two environments are to be established ' . . . they must be sufficiently isomorphic to assuage critics who contend - for sound reasons - that adding pears and apples makes good fruit salad - but bad theory.' (63) Thus, whilst it may be acceptable to contrast and juxtapose propositions that derive from the two levels of analysis it is much more difficult to formulate cumulative propositions for integrating the two levels of analysis. The tendency is thus to see the linkage as the fact that they are both political systems existing in parallel. Although Rosenau's work does attempt to avoid this parallel treatment, the danger is that the two environments will still be seen as parallel systems that are both conceptual and concrete entities, having distinct boundaries. The Rosenau matrix does suggest this conception of the relationship between the two environments.

However, this problem with the formulation could be eradicated by accepting that it served, for the purpose of research, as the most expedient way of progressing. The major problem with the framework is, however, that

of actually applying it.   As the evidence with respect to the actual
amount of work undertaken on the basis of the approach shows, there are
severe problems in translating a theoretical construct into a research
technique.   Hanrieder points out that although Rosenau sets out to
avoid the problems of parallelism by focussing as his basic unit of analysis on the process of interaction rather than on the source or the
target of that interaction, he does so only by using the concept of
linkage to connect such 'an extensive and variegated array of phenomena
that their cumulative quality is somewhat questionable'. (64)   The
usefulness of the framework in research is thus somewhat questionable
since the framework does not appear to be operational.   To say this
about the framework should not, however, be taken as dismissing the
work entirely.   Linkage politics - along with much of Rosenau's later
work - has served as a theoretical statement that on its own is an advance, but which also encourages more research into the subject matter
and leads to a development of theory (or pretheory) in the process.

    In sum, the linkage politics approach, although of heuristic value, is
of very limited use in the comparative analysis of foreign policy.   The
sheer size of the framework and its 3888 cells makes it unmanageable.
The categories are arbitrary and there is no specific definition of
what fits into them, what counts as significance, and how the cells
are interrelated.   There is no indication of how to utilise the framework, there is no procedure for identifying a linkage and no way of
relating such an observation to the process of constructing theory.   It
is more of a checklist than a framework, and, as such, offers little to
aid the comparative analysis of foreign policy.   Again it has to be
admitted that the approach has heuristic quality and that it does offer
an interesting way of asking questions, but it does not provide any
indication of how to carry out the research.   Are the cells of the
matrix to be ticked or ranked etc.?   What would ranking mean?   How
could it be measured?   How does the approach distinguish between types
of linkage?   Does a linkage merely represent a relationship?   How
does the analyst differentiate between the environments, the categories,
the forms of the linkages?   If this does not matter, then why stress
the differentiation?   If it does matter, what are the criteria for
differentiation?

    As with pretheory, the framework does not offer any indication as to
the nature of the foreign policy activity nor, fundamentally, does it
give the analyst any criteria for distinguishing the linkage analytically
from the series of issues that constitute state interaction.   To the
degree that it fails to rank and differentiate between linkages, it
falls into the problem of treating any linkage as of equal importance.
It seems clear that Rosenau would not aim to do this but his presentation offers no way of avoiding this conclusion.

E HANRIEDER - COMPATIBILITY AND CONSENSUS

An approach to the analysis of foreign policy which is linked with
Rosenau's work on linkage politics is Wolfram Hanrieder's compatibility
and consensus, initially published in an article in 1967 (65).   The
aim of Hanrieder's work is to develop concepts that ' . . . allow the
analyst to view foreign policy as a continuous process bridging the
analytical barriers between the international and the domestic political

32

system.' (66)   Hanrieder, in the first part of his paper, discusses both
the need 'for, and the failure of previous attempts to provide, concepts
capable of fulfilling this aim.

Although he claims that the salience of the interrelationship between
international politics and foreign policy has received increasing
attention, he believes that

' . . . it is questionable, however, whether the abundance of
literature on this matter has contributed appropriate analytical
frameworks to accommodate the concrete historical phenomena of
the interpenetration of international and domestic systems.' (67)

He cites two main reasons for this failure: first, the previous attempts
have been of a highly idiosyncratic nature.   Thus, although imaginative,
they are so individualistic that it is unlikely that other writers will
utilise them, preferring to develop their own frameworks.   In many
cases, and Rosenau is a clear target here, the theorist is unwilling to
follow up his conceptual framework with case studies.   Instead ' . . .
most proposals conclude with cordial invitations or urgent exhortations
to other analysts to substantiate empirically the **promise** of the new
analytical vista that has been opened up to the discipline.' (68)   This
situation may well be deplorable, but it is understandable since most
analysts are unwilling to become a researcher for someone else's theory.

The second main reason for the failure to bridge international and
national politics is that whilst there are advantages in combining the
two dimensions there are many reasons for keeping them apart.   This is
so fundamentally because the two subject areas deal with significantly
different analytical environments.   Given this factor, the development
of concepts and propositions in one analytical field may well appear
non cumulative in the other;   it is, he points out, the old problem of
adding pears and apples - it makes good fruit salad but bad theory.

Nevertheless, Hanrieder believes that there are

' . . . two concepts that permit the correlation of important
external and internal dimensions of foreign policy aims, and that
allow the analyst to view foreign policy as a continuous process
bridging the analytical barriers between the international and
the domestic political system.' (69)

Compatibility is designed ' . . . to assess the feasibility of various
foreign policy goals, given the **strictures** and opportunities of the
international system.'   Consensus is intended to assess ' . . . the
measure of agreement on the ends and means of foreign policy on the
domestic political scene.'   The two terms are further defined

' . . . By compatibility between the conditions of the international
system and foreign policy goals, I mean that a particular objective
has a reasonable chance of realization if implemented by a policy
that an outside observer would deem appropriate . . . the respective
degrees of compatibility between individual goals and the international system serve as the basis for evaluating the degree of
complementarity among goals.'

33

Consensus is further defined as ' . . . the existing measure of agreement on policy projects among the relevant elements of a national system's decision-making process.' (70)

Hanrieder claims that there are two major advantages in the application of these concepts to the study of the linkage between the external
and internal dimensions of foreign policy.   First,

' . . . with respect to highly individualistic conceptual schemes
that lack supportive case studies and fail to bridge the gap
between international and comparative politics, the organization
of data under the categories of compatibility and consensus seems
to offer a fruitful compromise.' (71)

He claims that even the most diverse studies of foreign policy can be
reformulated in terms of the two concepts, i.e. in terms of compatibility and consensus patterns.   In sum the first advantage of his approach
is that they can tap   ' . . . a large reservoir of existing studies
whose findings can be couched, and economically reformulated, in terms
of compatibility and consensus patterns.' (72)

The major advantage of the approach, however, is that both concepts
are standards of feasibility and are therefore not totally non-isomor-
phic.   Compatibility

' . . . is a standard of feasibility by definition because it
serves to assess the chances of success of foreign policy . . .
Consensus is . . . a standard of feasibility (as an) operational
consequence of psychological phenomena.' (73)

Thus, whilst each term refers to a distinct analytical environment the
isomorphic nature of the approach is maintained since both terms share
the attribute of being standards of feasibility.

Hanrieder then turns to extend the analysis by developing a framework
based on the two terms.   This is constructed by using a concept of
Rosenau's - that of the penetrated political system.   This is defined
as ' . . . one in which nonmembers of a national society participate
directly and authoritatively, through actions taken jointly with the
society's members, in either the allocation of its values or the mobilization of support on behalf of its goals.' (74)   Noting that ' . . .
penetrative processes may take place without the direct, personal or
authoritative participation of nonmembers of the national system . . .'
Hanrieder proposes an extension of the definition of a penetrated
political system.   Thus, a system is penetrated

' . . . (1) if its decision-making process regarding the allocation
of values or the mobilization of support on behalf of its goals
is strongly affected by external events, and (2) if it can command
wide consensus among the relevant elements of the decision-making
process in accommodating to these events.' (75)

Viewing the national and international systems as interpenetrated has
two analytical consequences.   First, the distinction between foreign
policy and domestic policy diminishes substantially.   Since external
events affect a wider range of value allocation then few allocations

34

can remain isolated from these external factors. Accepting an earlier categorisation by Hanrieder of policy goals with reference to three frames of values, then policy goals may be derived from internal, external, and systemic referents. These three types of goal referents overlap in the penetrated political system. The second analytical consequence is that the common factor of compatibility and consensus - the standard of feasibility - begins to coalesce. As the allocation of values in the national political system becomes strongly affected by external factors (i.e. as the system becomes highly penetrated), analytical concepts that relate goals to external factors (compatibility) overlap with analytical concepts that serve as domestic standards of feasibility (consensus). Thus the gap between the two analytical environments is bridged.

By measuring the degree of consensus, and by evaluating the degree of compatibility between a state's policy and the strictures of the international environment, Hanrieder claims that a typology may be constructed that relates states to penetration. Where consensus patterns correlate with compatibility patterns and there is wide consensus in value referents and on the goals and policies stemming from them, then the political system is highly penetrated. If there is wide consensus on goals and policies that are not compatible with systemic conditions, then a distorted perception of the international system exists. If consensus is lacking, then some decision-makers have a better chance than others of realising their policy proposals, thus the system is partially penetrated. It is claimed finally that

' . . . if the policy projects of all members of the international system were analyzed in this fashion . . . the resulting aggregate would automatically reflect the system's predominate patterns of power and purpose.' (76)

Again, as with linkage politics, this approach might appear to offer a sound basis for the examination of the foreign policies of Britain and the Netherlands. However, it is necessary to point out some serious problems with the analysis; several of these are brought out by Rosenau in a review article in the American Political Science Review (77). Two main criticisms are made by Rosenau: firstly, much in the article is unsubstantiated; for example, the reader is asked to assume that the concepts will somehow arrange data in a more meaningful way; the second, and major, criticism is that no clearcut definitions are given to compatibility and consensus. Compatibility is defined as the relationship between foreign policy goals and international conditions, but what are the dynamics of this relationship? How do you know if the goals and the conditions are compatible since no instances of compatibility/incompatibility are cited? Who is the outside observer? Consensus is defined as the existing measure of agreement in policy projects among the relevant elements of a national system's decision-making process. But what is meant by agreement? Is agreement between 10 per cent of the decision-makers sufficient, or 51 per cent, 99 per cent? Is agreement between 99 per cent of decision-makers better (in some way which would need definition) than agreement between 51 per cent? Does more agreement have different consequences? Probably the most serious problem is: 'How are the degrees of compatibility and consensus measured?'

Hanrieder, in claiming that the approach can serve as the common basis
for the analysis of foreign policy, is clearly proposing that the
approach can be operationalised.   Yet the problems of measurement
appear insurmountable.   Certainly, no meaningful measurement could
take place in closed political systems - according to Hanrieder's own
definition of consensus.   As Rosenau notes, the lack of definition of
when consensus begins - i.e. at what point is it significant - is a
primary obstacle.   Rosenau claims that any utilisation of the approach
would merely be an act of faith, since

> ' . . . the presentation is so continuously abstract and so lacking
> in concrete specifications that it is extremely difficult to
> evaluate the utility of the concepts of compatibility and
> consensus.   It is contended that great advantage would follow
> from the use of these two concepts, but there is no indication of
> why this is so.' (78)

On the use of his own concept of the penetrated political system, Rosenau claims that Hanrieder's reformulation, by defining it as existing
whenever a state is strongly affected by external events, has extended
the concept to cover all international phenomena, both political and
non political.

> ' . . . Hanrieder has substituted penetration for influence and
> equated politics with interaction.   His formulation encompasses
> the entire range of international relations and therefore distin-
> guishes none . . .   No distinctions survive his analysis.' (79)

It appears to be unnecessary to add any further criticisms.   Far
from providing the basis for the elimination of the deplorable idiosyncratic forms of analysis that preceded his article, Hanrieder has ended
up by adding one more set of concepts and definitions.   His claim that
his approach provides clear standards of feasibility disappears as
soon as the terms he introduces are analysed.   Whilst the approach
may be of use in the provision of metaphors for the discussion of
foreign policy, it is non operational.   However, in fairness to Hanrieder, his concepts can be justifiably accepted as indicators of the
domestic and external parameters of foreign policy in that they illustrate that there is a limit beyond which you cannot go in either area,
and that some compromise between what is feasible and what is acceptable
at home seems to represent the very essence of foreign policy decision-
making.

Rosenau, in his review of the article, does point to this important
feature of Hanrieder's approach: that is that it is concerned with the
process of adaptation, the process by which states adapt to their external environments.   The realisation that states are, in essence, adaptive entities represents the chronological development of the approaches
examined in this chapter.   It also leads us directly to the approach
that was tested against the foreign policies of Britain and the Netherlands.   For, by the late 1960s, comparative foreign policy analysis
had begun to be concerned with foreign policy as adaptive behaviour;
this approach, for a series of reasons, appears to have significant
advantages for the examination of foreign policy behaviour - most
saliently, it has the crucial attribute of being operationalisable.

Having, therefore, outlined the dominant approaches to comparative foreign policy analysis and, having listed the reasons why these approaches were not deemed to be suitable for this study, the approach that was used - the adaptive behaviour approach - can now be outlined.

NOTES

(1) For a full presentation of their approach see R. Snyder, H. Bruck and B. Sapin, Foreign Policy Decision Making, Free Press, New York 1962, pp.14-185.
(2) M. Brecher, B. Steinberg, J. Stein, 'A framework for research on foreign policy behaviour', Journal of Conflict Resolution, 1969, Vol. XIII, pp.75-101.
(3) G. Paige, The Korean Decision, Free Press, New York 1968.
(4) J. Frankel, The Making of Foreign Policy, Oxford University Press, London 1963, p.4.
(5) A. I. Dawisha, 'Foreign policy models and the problem of dynamism', British Journal of International Studies, Vol. 2, 1976, pp.128-137.
(6) M. Brecher, The Foreign Policy System of Israel, Oxford University Press, London 1972, and M. Brecher, Decisions in Israel's Foreign Policy, Oxford University Press, London 1974.
(7) D. Braybrooke and C. Lindblom, A Strategy of Decision, Free Press, New York 1963; R. Hilsman, To Move a Nation, Doubleday, Garden City, New York 1964; S. Verba, 'Assumptions of Rationality and Non-Rationality in Models of the International System', in K. Knorr and S. Verba, The International System - Theoretical Essays, Princeton University Press, Princeton, NJ 1961, pp.93-117; R. Jervis, 'Hypotheses on misperception', World Politics, Vol. XX, 1968, pp.454-79; R. Jervis, The Logic of Images in International Relations, Princeton University Press, Princeton, NJ 1970; R. Jervis, Perception and Misperception in International Politics, Princeton University Press, Princeton, NJ 1976; J. Steinbrunner, The Cybernetic Theory of Decision, Princeton University Press, Princeton, NJ 1974; G. Allison, Essence of Decision, Little, Brown, Boston, Mass. 1971; G. Allison, 'Conceptual models and the Cuban missile crisis', American Political Science Review, Vol. LXIII, 1969, pp. 689-718; See, for example: G. Allison and M. Halperin, 'Bureaucratic Politics: A Paradigm and Some Policy Implications' in R. Tanter and R. Ullman, Theory and Policy in International Relations, Princeton University Press, Princeton, NJ 1972, pp.40-79.
(8) H. Morgenthau, Politics Among Nations, 5th edition, Knopf, New York 1973.
(9) J. Handelman, J. Vasquez, M. O'Leary, W. Coplin, 'Color it Morgenthau; a data based assessment of quantitative international relations research', unpublished manuscript, Syracuse University 1973.
(10) J. N. Rosenau, 'The National Interest', in J. N. Rosenau, The Scientific Study of Foreign Policy, Free Press, New York 1971, p.239.
(11) P. Bachrach and M. Baratz, 'Two faces of power', American Political Science Review, Vol. LVI, 1962, pp.947-52; P. Bachrach and M. Baratz, 'Decisions and non decisions', American Political Science Review, Vol. LVII, 1963, pp.632-42.
(12) J. Rosenau, op. cit., p. 248.
(13) J. Frankel, The National Interest, Macmillan, London 1970.
(14) T. Robinson, 'A national interest analysis of Sino-Soviet relations', International Studies Quarterly, Vol. XI, 1967, pp.135-75.

(15) K. J. Holsti, 'National role conceptions in the study of foreign policy', International Studies Quarterly, Vol. XIV, 1970, pp.233-309.
(16) Ibid., p.238.
(17) Ibid., pp.244-5.
(18) See Table One, ibid., p.255.
(19) Ibid., pp.260-71.
(20) Ibid., p.306.
(21) C. Backman, 'Role theory and international relations', International Studies Quarterly, Vol.XIV, 1970, pp.310-19.
(22) J. N. Rosenau, The Scientific Study of Foreign Policy, Free Press, New York 1971.
(23) Ibid., p.IX.
(24) J. N. Rosenau, 'Pretheories and Theories of Foreign Policy', in R. B. Farrell, Approaches to Comparative and International Politics, Northwestern University Press, Evanston, Ill. 1966, pp.27-92; reprinted in Rosenau, The Scientific Study of Foreign Policy, op. cit., pp. 95-149; all references below are to the latter.
(25) Ibid., p.95.
(26) Ibid., p.99.
(27) Ibid.
(28) Ibid., p.104.
(29) Ibid., p.105.
(30) Ibid., p.106.
(31) Ibid., p.109.
(32) Ibid., p.112.
(33) Ibid., p.115.
(34) Ibid., p.116.
(35) J. N. Rosenau, Linkage Politics, Free Press, New York 1969.
(36) J. N. Rosenau, Domestic Sources of Foreign Policy, Free Press, New York 1967.
(37) J. N. Rosenau, The Scientific Study of Foreign Policy, op. cit., pp.127-8.
(38) Ibid., p.141.
(39) Ibid., pp.147-8.
(40) Ibid., p.148.
(41) J. N. Rosenau, Linkage Politics, op. cit.; the theoretical chapters are chapter one (pp.1-11) and chapter three (pp.44-63); reprinted in Rosenau, The Scientific Study of Foreign Policy, op. cit., pp.307-38, further references from this source.
(42) Ibid., p.310.
(43) Ibid., p.318.
(44) Ibid.
(45) Ibid., p.319.
(46) Ibid., p.320.
(47) Ibid.
(48) J. Frankel, Contemporary International Theory and the Behaviour of States, Oxford University Press, London 1973, p.43.
(49) J. N. Rosenau, The Scientific Study of Foreign Policy, op. cit., p.327.
(50) Ibid.
(51) Ibid. p.328.
(52) Ibid., p.330.
(53) Ibid., p.334.
(54) D. Zinnes, 'Linkage politics', Midwest Journal of Political Science, Vol. 14, 1970, p.344.
(55) J. N. Rosenau, 'Theorizing Across Systems: Linkage Politics

Revisited', in J. Wilkenfeld, Conflict Behaviour and Linkage Politics, McKay, New York 1973, pp.25-56.
(56) Ibid., p.42.
(57) Ibid., p.45.
(58) Ibid.
(59) Ibid.
(60) Ibid., p.46.
(61) Ibid., p.50.
(62) W. Hanrieder, 'Compatibility and consensus', American Political Science Review, Vol. LXI, 1967, pp.971-82; reprinted in W. Hanrieder, Comparative Foreign Policy, McKay, New York 1971, pp.242-64. References below are from the latter source.
(63) Ibid., pp.250-1.
(64) Ibid., p.252.
(65) Hanrieder, op.cit.
(66) Ibid., p.253.
(67) Ibid., p.248.
(68) Ibid., p.249.
(69) Ibid., p.253.
(70) All quotations from ibid., pp.253-54.
(71) Ibid., p.254.
(72) Ibid., p.255.
(73) Ibid., p.255-6.
(74) Ibid., p.257.
(75) Ibid., p.258.
(76) Ibid., p.264.
(77) J. N. Rosenau, 'Compatibility, consensus, and an emerging political science of adaptation', American Political Science Review, Vol. LXI, 1967, pp.983-88.
(78) Ibid., p.984.
(79) Ibid.

3 The theory of adaptive behaviour

Having, in the last chapter, outlined the major approaches for the
comparative analysis of foreign policy behaviour, and having offered
reasons why they were not suitable for the analysis of the two foreign
policies dealt with in this study, the theoretical perspective that
was used can now be outlined.   This is the adaptive behaviour approach,
which received its first outline in Ashby's Design for a Brain (1).   It
is closely related to the analysis of political entities as systems and
to the cybernetic approach to political activity.   Indeed, the concept
of adaptation is central to the structural-functional analysis of political systems.   Rosenau can be regarded as pioneering the development
of the concept and approach in the study of foreign policy, writing, as
he did, a series of conference papers on the subject in the late 1960s,
(2) and then a series of articles and a book in the early 1970s (3).
Rosenau starts from the premise that ' . . . the question of how and why
organisms adapt to their environments has long fascinated the minds of
men.' (4)   The environment of any organism, be it a single cell, an
individual, a small group or a large aggregate of people - is always
changing and thus poses a threat to the survival of the organism.   This
continually changing environment poses certain questions for the organism: can it adjust to the changes?   Can it take advantage of them and
prosper, or will it disappear?   What price will it have to pay for its
survival?   Are radical alterations necessary in its internal structure
or can the environmental demands be readily absorbed?   It is Rosenau's
contention that these questions are at the heart of the comparative
study of foreign policy.   Accepting that foreign policy is concerned
with complex systems involving perception, calculation and judgement,
Rosenau nevertheless believes that the biological analogy is apt since

> ' . . . the basic premise of the adaptive perspective (is) that
> all nations can be viewed as adapting entities with similar
> problems that arise out of the need to cope with their environ-
> ments.' (5)

With this basic concept of national states as adapting entities is
involved a distinction between the forms of adaptation.   Rosenau wishes
to divide adaptive behaviour into two types - that carried out by governments (foreign policy) and that carried out by a variety of private
individuals and groups in society.   Foreign policy is undertaken to
alter undesirable aspects of the international environment and preserve
desirable aspects and is thus necessarily calculated and goal orientated.
Whilst it is accepted that action may have unintended consequences that
may greatly affect the kind of adaptation, the action is purposeful.
Hence, although the action may be hasty, vague and long term, it is
based upon some conception of how events should evolve.   Since some
image of how the environment should be structured underlies foreign
policy acts, then foreign policy is a distinct form of adaptive behaviour.

The other form of adaptive behaviour is that undertaken by the variety
of individuals and groups in society who seek to adjust their own needs

to the changing environment.   Collectively, their behaviour constitutes
adaptive behaviour, but since it is the uncoordinated sum of private
decisions it is not purposeful.   Thus whilst non governmental adaptation has consequences for the decision-maker, it does not fall into the
purview of the student of foreign policy.

Since Rosenau considers foreign policy to involve ' . . . all the
attitudes and activities through which organized national societies seek
to cope with and benefit from their international environments', (6)
it is clear that the actor involved is the national society.   Rosenau
notes that the national actor may be identified by the existence of
four essential structures.   These structures are essential since they
are preconditions for survival.   These four structures represent

' . . . the patterns whereby the life and property of societies
are preserved and protected, their policy decisions made and
implemented, their goods and services acquired and distributed,
(and) their members' co-operation achieved and maintained.' (7)

These four structures, representing the society's polity, economy,
social structure and physical base, may vary in their levels of performance, but each is essential for the continued existence of the unit.
Hence, the object of foreign policy is to affect the actor's environment in such a fashion that environmentally determined variations in the
actor's structures are kept within the limits of change **that** ensure the
continuation of the actor.   Thus, foreign policy is primarily concerned
with factors salient to the actor with respect to its essential structures, since the basic purpose of foreign policy is to ensure the survival of the state.

Given that both essential structures and the environment of the actor
may vary in performance, then decision-makers always have some choice
over their actions.   Rosenau claims that there are four fundamental
strategies which they may follow.   The first is that of a promotive
foreign policy where decision-makers are unresponsive to changes in the
external environment and in essential structures, thereby being able
to promote changes at home and abroad.   A preservative foreign policy
may be followed, which is where decision-makers attempt to maintain an
equilibrium between changes in both the external environment and the
essential structures.   When decision-makers adjust external policies
and essential structures to the demands of the external environment
they are conducting an acquiescent foreign policy.   Finally, decision-
makers may pursue a foreign policy which is intransigent - one which
involves an attempt to alter the external environment to the demands
of the essential structures.

McGowan has stated that Rosenau's work rests on three empirical
hypotheses with an accompanying definition,

' . . . Definition: By foreign policy actors we mean national
societies characterized by structures - political, economic,
social and physical.   Axiom 1: Variations in the structures
of an actor are related to changes in the actor's external
environment.   Axiom 2: The continuation of an actor is the
consequence of variations in the actor's structures.   Axiom 3:
The actor's decision-makers undertake foreign policy in order to
ensure the continuation of the actor.' (8)

FIGURE 3.1

MCGOWAN'S MODIFIED PRETHEORY

The relationship between the type of society and the types of independent variables associated with foreign policy outputs

Geography and physical resources	LARGE COUNTRY				SMALL COUNTRY			
State of the economy	Rich		Poor		Rich		Poor	
State of the polity	Open	Closed	Open	Closed	Open	Closed	Open	Closed
Rankings of variables in terms of covariance with foreign policy patterns	So	I	I	I	Sy	Sy	I	I
	G	G	So	G	So	I	Sy	Sy
	Sy	Sy	Sy	Sy	G	G	So	G
	I	So	G	So	I	So	G	So
Illustrative examples c. 1972	USA	USSR	India	China	Holland	Greece	Gambia	Thailand

Modified from Rosenau (1966.48)

KEY

So = Societal, G = Governmental, Sy = Systemic, I = Individual

SOURCE

P. J. McGowan, 'Problems in the Construction of Positive Foreign Policy Theory', in J. N. Rosenau (ed) Comparing Foreign Policies, Sage/John Wiley, 1974, p.34.

Hence policies which maintain or increase the probability of actor survival are adaptive and policies which lessen its chances are maladaptive.

The main concepts involved in Rosenau's theoretical scheme have been described; it is now necessary to explain how Rosenau accounts for variations in the foreign policy strategies followed. The theoretical structure involved, McGowan believes, may be stated as follows

' . . . The type of actor influences the potency of source variables. Different source variables are associated with different foreign policy strategies. Finally, given an initial foreign policy strategy, the likelihood varies that a new policy strategy will be adopted.' (9)

(Here source variables refers to societal, governmental, individual and systemic factors of societies and actor type refers to large/small, rich/poor, open/closed variables of individual states.) The first element of this theoretical structure is discussed in Rosenau's earlier work on pretheory, outlined in the last chapter. As shown in Figure 3.1, it is predicted that in different types of societies different types of variables will account for observed foreign policy behaviour. Despite the criticism that the specific rankings of the importance of variables do not follow from Rosenau's theoretical framework and the weakness that no explanation is offered as to which variables within each cluster (i.e. which societal variables in particular) account for types of foreign policy behaviour, this conceptualisation not only represented a significant advance in the state of theorising but also has inspired a large number of empirical studies.

FIGURE 3.2

THE RELATIVE POTENCIES OF FOUR CLUSTERS OF INDEPENDENT VARIABLES
AS SOURCES OF FOUR TYPES OF FOREIGN POLICY STRATEGY

Relative potency of variable clusters	Acquiescent strategy	Intransigent strategy	Promotive strategy	Preservative strategy
High	Systemic	Societal	Individual	Systemic Societal Governmental
Low	Societal Individual Governmental	Systemic Individual Governmental	Systemic Societal Governmental	Individual

SOURCE

J. N. Rosenau, The Adaptation of National Societies, McCaleb-Seiler, 1970, p.16.

FIGURE 3.3
THE RELATIONSHIP BETWEEN FOREIGN POLICY STRATEGIES AND ACTOR TYPES

Likelihood of following a given strategy	Acquiescent strategy	Intransigent strategy	Promotive strategy	Preservative strategy
High	S R O	L R O	L R C	L R O
	S R C	L P O	L P O	S R O
			L P C	
			S P O	
			S P C	
	S P O	S R O	S R C	S R C
	S P C	S P O		
				L R C
	L R O	L R C		L P O
	L R C	L P C		L P C
	L P O	S R C	L R O	S P O
Low	L P C	S P C	S R O	S P C

KEY
L = large, S = small, R = rich, P = poor, O = open, C = closed.

SOURCE
P. J. McGowan, 'Problems in the Construction of Positive Foreign Policy Theory', in J. N. Rosenau (ed) Comparing Foreign Policies, Sage/John Wiley, 1974, p.36.

FIGURE 3.4
ESTIMATED PROBABILITY OF OCCURRENCE OF THE TWELVE TYPES
OF FOREIGN POLICY TRANSFORMATION

Transformation from:	Transformation to:			
	Acquiescent strategy	Intransigent strategy	Promotive strategy	Preservative strategy
Acquiescent strategy	-	Nil	Low	High
Intransigent strategy	Nil	-	Nil	High
Promotive strategy	Nil	·Nil	-	High
Preservative strategy	Low	Nil	Low	-

SOURCE

J. N. Rosenau, The Adaptation of National Societies, McCalcb-Seiler, 1970, p.20.

Rosenau related this framework to the four adaptive patterns of
foreign policy behaviour.   As is illustrated by Figure 3.2, Rosenau
posits that for each type of foreign policy behaviour, certain types of
variables will be more or less strongly associated with that pattern.
Finally, Rosenau has developed a series of theoretical relationships
that relate to changes in foreign policy behaviour.   Hence, assuming
an actor wishes to abandon a given strategy, which new strategy is he
most likely to follow?   Rosenau's answers are summarised in Figure
3.4.   The singularly most relevant outcome of this table is that
Rosenau clearly believes that there is a high probability of changing
to a preservative strategy and that there is a low probability of
changing from a preservative strategy.   If changing strategy is undertaken frequently, then given the balance of probabilities in Figure 3.4
the international system will move in the direction of all states pursuing preservative foreign policies.   Rosenau states

     ' . . . preservative adaptation may not be an immediate require-
     ment of national societies, but in the long sweep of history, it
     appears to be the ultimate outcome for most of them.' (10)

   In his critical evaluation of Rosenau's work on adaptive behaviour,
McGowan objects to Rosenau's conclusions as summarised in Figure 3.4.
If everyone behaves in a preservative fashion, where will the dynamics
of international politics come from?   He also claims that the Figures
3.1-3.4 are not consistent.   He claims that although Rosenau does
present falsifiable hypotheses, they are open to four criticisms:
first, they are not derived from his assumptions;   second, they are
only weakly related to one another;   third, Rosenau has ignored the
time factor;   fourth, certain presumed causes of behaviour are ignored.
These faults prevent Rosenau's work from being 'a general positive
theory of foreign policy.' (11)   But he points out, and this is why so
much time has been spent examining adaptive behaviour, Rosenau's work
is undertaken to enhance our understanding of foreign policy, and may
best be understood as constructing

     'an organizing theory whose purpose appears to be to unite within
     one framework currently disparate islands of theory and to provide
     a basis for understanding national foreign policy behaviour at
     the most general level possible.' (12)

Finally,

     ' . . . in comparison to other attempts to construct positive
     theories of foreign policy at a high level of generality, Rosenau's
     efforts have achieved an unmatched level of rigour and scope.   If
     general positive theories of foreign policy are our common goal,
     then Rosenau's work represents as far as we have as yet (1974)
     progressed.' (13)

   Since the development of the adaptive behaviour approach, McGowan has
attempted to make Rosenau's framework more exact by the use of simple
equations (14), whilst O'Leary (15) has pointed out that neither
Rosenau nor McGowan has discussed the ways in which the concept of
adaptation could be turned into a series of operational variables.
O'Leary attempted to extend the crude model into one that considered
subnational adaptation by considering the differing interests of groups

in the decision-making process (i.e. a combination of adaptive behaviour with the bureaucratic politics of Allison and Halperin).

The other major development of the approach has been that of Peter Hansen (16). He attempts to build a revised model of adaptive behaviour using the case study of Denmark and the European Community, by synthesising Rosenau's work on the approach with the theory of small state behaviour. This he does by developing an alternative classification for the independent variable - the genotype of states - using the measures of stress-sensitivity, and influence-capability.

Having outlined the basis of Rosenau's approach, it is now necessary to indicate how that approach is to be tested in this study. This test has been given an added relevance by the fact that Rosenau has recently claimed, in a review of the state of the theory, that ' . . . all the evidence points to the conclusion that the comparative study of foreign policy has emerged as a normal science.' (17) He claims that the great debates have faded into an obscure past. The task for foreign policy analysis is now to solve the puzzles emerging out of the ruling paradigm. Given that one of the key aspects of any normal science is its ability to develop cumulative evidence and approaches it seems appropriate to attempt such an endeavour.

The relationship between the empirical and theoretical sections of this study thus requires explanation. The aim of this study is not to provide new insights into the nature of British and Dutch foreign policies. The objective is to examine the empirical evidence in the light of the most recent approach to the comparative analysis of foreign policy behaviour. If foreign policy analysis has become a normal science, then the most recent paradigm - especially when developed by the author making that claim - should allow the examination of two states' foreign policies in a meaningful manner.

For the purpose of simplicity, the foreign policies of the Netherlands and Britain may be subdivided into three categories:

    those aspects in which they are different;

    those aspects in which they run in a parallel fashion;

    those areas in which they involve interaction.

Clearly such an analytical distinction is a gross oversimplification of reality but it is believed that such a distinction will not only allow the more straightforward arrangement of empirical material but will also allow the more thorough examination of the theoretical approach.

The empirical section of the study will, through giving brief accounts of the historical setting, examine the three categories of foreign policy behaviour: the differences through a brief survey of the Dutch and British attitudes towards European integration; the similarities by examining the attitudes of the two states to the issue of security; the interaction through a study of Anglo-Dutch relations over the Netherlands East Indies issue area. These examinations will be carried out ex vacuo from the theoretical material, since it is the general characteristics of the behaviour that will be compared to the theoretical

behaviour in the final chapters. It was debated whether or not to conclude each section of the empirical analysis with a comparison of the
behaviour with that predicted by the adaptive behaviour approach, but it
was decided against on the grounds that the task of comparison would
best be undertaken in a separate chapter.

It is necessary to restate the aim of the following chapters: their
primary role is to allow firm conclusions to be drawn regarding the
general nature of the two countries' foreign policie., so that this can
be compared with that behaviour predicted by the adaptive behaviour
approach.

Before turning to the generation of propositions regarding the foreign
policy behaviour of the two countries it is necessary to note the
problems involved in the operationalisation of the adaptive behaviour
approach. The initial difficulty in any attempt to utilise the approach is simply that of how to obtain theoretically derived predictions
of foreign policy behaviour. In all of Rosenau's published work on
the adaptive behaviour approach, there is little example of how to test
the approach. All that Rosenau presents is a series of tables that
relate source variables to actor genotype, source variables to adaptive
strategy, and adaptive strategies to actor genotype (18). Clearly a
major difficulty in this study was how to utilise these tables, which
contain the theoretical relationships inherent in the approach, to yield
testable propositions as to the foreign policy behaviour of any given
state.

It was clear at the outset of this study that the utility of the
adaptive behaviour approach was to be assessed inter alia by its ability
to predict successfully the foreign policy behaviour of states and
naturally the method of testing the approach must, therefore, be as
fair and as explicit as possible. Ideally the approach should be
tested according to criteria and methods laid down by the author of the
approach himself yet, as noted previously, such methods and criteria
were not available.

In the absence of any suggestions by Rosenau as to the operationalisation of the approach, it is necessary to offer a detailed account of
the methods of operationalisation utilised in this study since the
testing of the approach is the central aim of this study. As noted
previously, the theoretical relationships that are central to the
approach are contained in a set of tables and it is from these tables
that the actual predictions as to the foreign policy behaviour of the
Netherlands and Britain will be obtained below. However, it is necessary to point out that before deriving the specific foreign policy strategies there is a problem as to how to test any foreign policy strategy
derived from the theoretical approach. Given that, say, a state is
predicted as following an intransigent foreign policy strategy, how is
this to be tested? Again, as with the actual derivation of the theoretical predictions, Rosenau gives no examples as to how the predictions
might be tested. In this study, the method of testing has already
been mentioned; that is by dividing the foreign policies of the two
states under examination into three areas, parallels, differences and
interactions. This study will examine the foreign policies of the
two countries in three issue areas that provide one example of parallels, one of differences and one of interaction. These surveys of

47

empirical material will be utilised, in chapter seven, to yield foreign policy strategies in terms of the adaptive behaviour approach. These empirically derived strategies will then be compared with the theoretically predicted strategies and the result of this exercise will form the basis for the examination, in the final chapter, of the utility of the approach as a predictive model of foreign policy behaviour.

This method of operationalising the approach has been utilised because it appears to this writer to be the only possible way of fully testing the approach, although it is accepted that there are possible objections to the method used. It might be objected to on the grounds that the three case studies chosen were not sufficient in number to test fully the approach. To such an objection the reply of this writer would be that the case studies have been chosen specifically to cover as much of a spread of the two states' foreign policies as possible. By dividing the foreign policy behaviour of the two states into parallels, differences and interactions, and by choosing an empirical example of each, this study is attempting to offer as extensive a test of the approach as possible. Thus, the aim of the study is to examine a single example of each of the three foreign policy relationships contained within a dyad. Nevertheless, it is necessary to point out that such a test is only one out of a whole range of possible empirical tests and, therefore, any conclusions derived from the test must be seen as being based on a very small sample. Again, it is an axiom of this study that inductive case study testing of the approach is the only feasible way of assessing its validity and utility as a general model of foreign policy behaviour.

A further objection that can be made to the method of testing utilised in this study is that the empirical and theoretical foreign policy strategies are derived from different forms of analysis and refer to different analytical material, and, as such, are not strictly epistemologically comparable. This objection would conclude that the method of testing the approach, by deriving strategies from empirical material and then placing these in the terminology of the adaptive behaviour approach, was open to the charge of not being a correct or acceptable test of the approach since there would be many instances in which the judgement of the writer could lead to conclusions which were not derived from the theoretical analysis. This is an objection which has been of considerable importance during the research. It is clear that there are many instances in the following chapters in which the judgement made by this writer, concerning which empirical data to include, how to sum macro foreign policy behaviour, and, especially, how to translate broad conclusions as to the foreign policy strategies of the two states into the four adaptive strategies suggested by Rosenau, could lead to erroneous results. In other words, there is a danger in any attempt to test the approach, such as in this study, that the strategies derived empirically will not be comparable to those derived from the theoretical analysis due to the intervening variable of the judgement of the writer concerning key parts of the operationalisation of the approach.

In the light of this possible objection it must be emphasised that the method of testing used in this study is both made as explicit as possible, so that any inconsistencies may be observed, and is undertaken in the light of this problem. Indeed, it is accepted that a non recognition of this problem would seriously degrade any conclusions derived

from the study.   Specifically, in answer to this possible objection,
the method of testing the approach used in this study can be defended
and justified on the grounds of explicitness and the possibility of
retesting.   In each of the three empirical case studies, the aim has
been to give a summary of the macro level of foreign policy behaviour.
In chapter seven then, these empirically derived strategies are compared, as explicitly as possible, with the theoretically derived strategies.   By this explicit method of translating the empirical material
into the terms of the adaptive strategies and, thereby, comparing them
with the theoretical strategies, it is argued that the possible deficiencies of the utilisation of empirically (and therefore external to the
theory) derived strategies are reduced to a minimum.   Such a procedure
allows any reader to replicate the process by which the empirically
derived strategies are obtained.   As such, any objection to the findings of this study on the lines that its conclusions were derived from
criteria external to the theoretical approach being used (and thus that
the study did not constitute a meaningful test) would have to show
deficiencies in the process of testing.   In other words, since the
method of testing is made explicit, then such an objection can only
hold if deficiencies can be found in one of the following areas: the
accuracy of the empirical surveys; the translation of the empirical
findings into the adaptive strategies; and the comparison of the
empirically derived and the theoretically derived adaptive strategies
in chapter seven.   If no such deficiencies can be found, then it is
believed that the method of testing represents a fair and theoretically
sound means of assessing the utility of the approach.

A final possible objection to the method of testing the approach
utilised in this study would refer to the use of case studies of issue
areas.   It might be argued that since the approach deals with macro
foreign policy behaviour, any division of that behaviour into issue
areas will seriously detract from the findings, since the problem of
combining the results of the various case studies of issue areas imposes
onto the material an artificial, external means of cumulating and en-
grossing foreign policy behaviour.   It is accepted that the method
of testing employed in this study does represent a simplification of
reality and that it does impose artificial, analytical issue areas on
reality, yet it is necessary to restate that Rosenau's approach does not
offer any suggestions as to how to examine macro foreign policy behaviour.   Thus, given that some method of testing the approach has to be
utilised, then the use of case studies of issue areas appears to be the
most acceptable way of proceeding despite the problems noted above.
The only other alternative available would be to examine, in some way,
the macro level of foreign policy behaviour in total, without splitting
it into issue areas.   Such a method of analysis would aim at answering
the broad question of which adaptive strategy did Britain or The Netherlands pursue from 1945-63.   Whilst it is accepted that the analytical
division of the empirical survey into issue areas may involve the imposition of an external framework on reality, it is argued that the problems associated with studying the two foreign policies at a general
level are much greater and that they would seriously weaken the conclusions of any such study.   This is because the subjective elements in
testing the approach noted previously would appear to be a much greater
intervening variable in such a method of testing.   Not only would considerable subjective analysis have to be used to answer questions as to
the macro nature of the two foreign policies, but also it would require

a width of analysis that would be impossible in a study such as this. Such a study would certainly require much more time, which would appear to rule out any comparative analysis. Furthermore, it is strongly argued that any general foreign policy strategies arrived at by such a study would be extremely subjective in terms of which issue areas were dominant, and would be achieved by precisely the inductive issue area analysis (albeit more extensive) that the initial criticism would be levelled against. Such factors, primarily the subjective cumulation of various strands of policy, derive from the fact that foreign policy is a series of discrete events in a continuous world, and as such, the only way of building up a picture of a state's foreign policy is through inductive issue or issue area analysis. For these reasons the general macro level approach was deemed to be both full of potential pitfalls and incapable of providing an acceptable test of the approach.

Finally, before turning to the generation of propositions, it is necessary, having discussed the problems of operationalising and testing the adaptive behaviour approach, to mention the nature of the sources used in this study. With the exception of chapter six, which deals with an example of interaction between the two countries' foreign policies, the bulk of the material used in the empirical sections of this study is of a secondary source nature. It is incumbent on this writer to justify the use of such source material and to note the problems of explanation that arise from it. The overriding reason for the utilisation of secondary sources is that of the nature of the study. Given that the central aim of this study is to examine the utility of the adaptive behaviour approach, then the requirements of such an examination necessitated a wide-ranging survey of the two countries' foreign policy behaviour. To test the approach in accordance with the procedures noted previously, examples of parallel foreign policy behaviour, divergent foreign policy behaviour and interacting foreign policy behaviour were necessary. Furthermore, the wide time span of the survey was demanded by the requirement of tracing adaptive strategy transformation. For these reasons it was decided to concentrate upon secondary sources. However, the choice of these secondary sources involved a deliberate and conscious attempt to obtain a representative and authoritative set of data for the British sections of the study; for the Dutch sections every English language source that appeared to be relevant was used.

There are also certain objections which could be made to the choice of sources for this study. In addition to specific criticisms of the omission of certain secondary works, there is an important overall objection that arises from the use of secondary sources per se, namely that the picture of reality described in the empirical sections of this study does not justify the emphasis placed upon the evaluation of the theoretical approach found in the conclusion. In other words, since the theoretical approach is to be tested by comparing its predictions with those obtained from the empirical surveys, should not that empirical material be as accurate a picture of reality as possible? Such an objection would conclude by contending that the empirical sections should be based on primary sources not secondary, thereby presenting a more reliable explanation of the foreign policies of the two countries. In reply to such an objection this writer would argue that it is largely peripheral to the main aim of this study, with the proviso that the picture painted of reality can never be totally accurate. This argument requires clarification; without going into detail on the methodology

of explanation, the problems hinted at by the objection are not deemed
to be conclusive in this study.   The aim of the empirical sections is
to provide a macro level view of the <u>behaviour</u> of the two states in their
foreign policy.   The aim is neither to provide an explanation of how
the decisions were taken nor to give an account of the perceptions of
the individuals taking those decisions.   Similarly, as noted in chapter
two, the form of decision-making analysis undertaken by Snyder, Bruck
and Sapin, Paige, and Brecher <u>et al</u>. is deemed to be outside of the
confines of this study.   This study is concerned with behaviour, that
is the dependent variable in the analysis.   It is accepted that if a
detailed explanation, in historical terms, of any specific decision
included in this study was the focus of analysis, then the methodology
utilised would have to be different.   In essence, therefore, the
methodology of this study is deemed appropriate to the focus of that
analysis, and in this context the use of secondary sources is justified.

A similar argument is advanced to meet the possible objection that
interviews were not utilised in the study.   Whilst on the surface this
study might appear to be an excellent case for the employment of interviews with some of the major participants in the foreign policies of
the two states, this research technique was not used for the simple
reason that such evidence would be essentially peripheral to the subject
of this study.   Thus the views of participants in the decision-making
processes of the two states would be unlikely to shed much light on the
behaviour of those states.   Again, it is fully accepted that a full
historical account of any such particular decision could not be written
without such interviews, but that is not the aim of this study.   In
addition, of course, there are a whole set of methodological problems
associated with the use of interviews, e.g. reliability, memory, ana-
chronism, teleology, the tendency to see personal viewpoints as proved
correct <u>etc</u>.

In conclusion then on the use of sources in this study, it is believed
that the reliance on secondary sources is totally justified both by the
size and time requirements of the study and by the methodological considerations of the area of focus of the enquiry.   It is accepted that
the picture of reality painted in this study may fall short of total
accuracy and that, therefore, the conclusions of the thesis are degraded
by this inevitable proviso.   However, it is believed that the inaccura-
cies in the empirical overviews have been reduced to a practical minimum
by cross-checking sources and by the full use of footnotes and references.
As mentioned previously, this study is very consciously concerned with
the possible problems of utilising these different modes of enquiry,
especially with comparing empirically derived foreign policy strategies
with theoretically derived strategies.   Again, it is believed that
such problems of evidence and explanation as apply to these two modes of
enquiry are offset by the explicit and thorough method of presenting the
material and the development of hypotheses.

Whilst, therefore, the empirical material contained in this study is
historical and is used to obtain, inductively, empirical foreign policy
strategies, the theoretical section of the study is firmly based on a
notion of parallel politics.   Thus, in contrast to the voluntarist
view of foreign policy presented in the empirical chapters, the theoretical underpinnings of the approach being tested are based on a determinist viewpoint.   According to this determinist notion of parallel politics, states may well follow similar foreign policies, but will do so

not because of the free will of their decision-makers, but because of the genotype of state involved. Hence, the adaptive perspective views the parallels, differences and interactions in states' foreign policies as due to the form of adaptive strategy adopted by the state genotype. Thus, the dependent variable according to this perspective is the adaptive foreign policy strategy adopted by the state, with the independent variable being the national genotype: the intervening variables being what Rosenau calls the source variables of foreign policy.

Having discussed in some detail the problems of operationalising the approach and of the evidence used in the testing of it, it is now necessary to indicate how the propositions regarding the foreign policy behaviour of the two states were generated. As noted in the previous paragraph, the adaptive perspective of foreign policy views the dependent variable as being the adaptive strategy pursued by the state. As noted in the discussion of the adaptive behaviour approach, the task of foreign policy - the function which it performs for the organism of the state - is that of adapting the external environment so as to ensure the continued survival of the four domestic essential structures (polity, economy, social structure and physical base). Rosenau argues that the adaptive strategy followed by a state is related, by the five source variables, to the independent variable of the genotype of the state. Thus, to determine the predicted form of foreign policy strategy for Britain and the Netherlands it is necessary to operationalise the Rosenau framework by following through the tables which contain the relationships between the independent, intervening and dependent variables.

The first step in obtaining the predicted foreign policy strategies is to determine to which national genotype the two states belong. All that Rosenau gives as guide lines for demarcating the genotypes are the dicotomous terms of large-small, rich-poor, open-closed, as developed in the pretheory article. The operationalisation of these dichotomous terms was achieved by using Rosenau and Hoggard's listing of the genotypes of 130 countries presented as an appendix to their article, (19) based on operational definitions outlined in that study (20). Indeed, the 1974 Rosenau and Hoggard article represents the first attempt to operationalise the measures; in the 1970 Adaptation of National Societies paper, Rosenau notes that 'specific hypotheses relevant to these questions cannot be developed here'. (21) It was, in fact, left to McGowan to bring together the relevant elements from Rosenau's work (22). A further check on the operationalisation of the dichotomous terms was the listing of genotypes published in Jenkins and Chittick (23).

On the basis of the operational definitions given by Rosenau and Hoggard, the three national attributes are dichotomised on the following lines. Societies with a population of over 23,376,000 (1963 data) are deemed to be large; those with populations below this figure are deemed to be small. Societies with a GNP per capita of over $402 (1963 data) are deemed to be rich; those with a GNP per capita below this are deemed to be poor. Societies with a free press are called open; those which do not have this attribute are called closed.(24) Clearly this dichotomous treatment of these attributes may be criticised, but the important point is that the operationalisation of the attributes of the two states under consideration in this study is carried out according to the criteria utilised by the author of the approach to be tested.

Given these operational measures, the two states were classified according to national genotype, a classification which was supported by checking in the Rosenau and Hoggard, and Jenkins and Chittick listing of genotypes.

Britain
with a population of over 23,376,000, a GNP per capita of over $402 and a free press was designated as a large, rich, open polity. This was supported by the Rosenau and Hoggard listing (25) and the Jenkins and Chittick listing (26).

The Netherlands
with a population of below 23,376,000, A GNP per capita of over $402 and a free press was designated as a small, rich, open polity. Again this was supported by the Rosenau and Hoggard listing (27) and the Jenkins and Chittick listing (28).

With the establishment of the national genotypes of the two states, the next step in the generation of propositions regarding the foreign policy strategies adopted by the states was to relate the national genotypes to the ranking of source variables as shown in Figure 3.1. According to this table, the listing of the source variables of the two states was:

Britain
as a large, rich, open polity the ranking of variables was societal, governmental, systemic, individual.

The Netherlands
as a small, rich, open polity the ranking of variables was systemic, societal, governmental, individual.

Following this, the source variable rankings were compared with the listings of rankings associated with the various adaptive strategies as shown in Figure 3.2 above. The results obtained from this comparison were combined with the results obtained from the relationship between actor genotypes and adaptive strategies as contained in Figure 3.3. The results were:

Britain
according to Figure 3.2, a country with the ranking of source variables such as that attributed to Britain, fits most neatly into the intransigent strategy. Figure 3.3 indicates, as supporting evidence, that a large, rich, open polity is the most likely genotype to follow an intransigent strategy.

The Netherlands
according to Figure 3.2, a country with the ranking of source variables such as that attributed to the Netherlands, fits most neatly into either the preservative or acquiescent strategy. The decisive factor in determining the strategy to be adopted by the Netherlands is that in Figure 3.3, the genotype of small, rich, open is most likely to follow an acquiescent strategy.

Therefore, on the basis of this procedure of operationalising the approach, the initial strategies for the two countries can now be stated:

53

Britain would initially pursue an <u>intransigent</u> foreign policy strategy whilst the Netherlands would initially pursue an <u>acquiescent</u> strategy.

Finally on the Rosenau approach, the adaptive perspective indicates that states' foreign policy strategies will be transformed over time; a relationship contained in Figure 3.4. From this figure it is clear that in both cases the foreign policy strategies will be transformed into <u>preservative</u> strategies.

Hence, the propositions generated from Rosenau's approach with regard to the foreign policy strategies to be adopted by the two states under consideration in this study can now be stated formally.

<u>Proposition One</u> Britain will initially pursue an <u>intransigent</u> foreign policy strategy that will be transformed over time into a <u>preservative</u> strategy.

<u>Proposition Two</u> The Netherlands will initially pursue an <u>acquiescent</u> foreign policy strategy that will be transformed over time into a <u>preservative</u> strategy.

In chapter seven these deductive predictions as to the foreign policy behaviour of Britain and the Netherlands will be compared with strategies obtained inductively from the empirical survey that follows. This comparison will be used to form the basis for the evaluation of the adaptive behaviour approach in the final chapter.

NOTES

(1) W. Ashby, <u>Design for a Brain</u>, 2nd edition, Wiley, New York 1960.
(2) See J. N. Rosenau, 'Foreign policy as adaptive behaviour', <u>Comparative Politics</u>, Vol. II, 1970, pp.365-87, see p.367.
(3) See J. N. Rosenau, 'Adaptive politics in an interdependent world', <u>Orbis</u>, Vol. XVI, 1972, pp.153-173; J. N. Rosenau, <u>The Adaptation of National Societies</u>, McCaleb-Seiler, New York 1970; J. N. Rosenau, 'Adaptive Strategies for Research and Practice in Foreign Policy', in F. W. Riggs (ed) <u>International Studies: Present Status and Future Prospects</u>, American Academy of Political and Social Science, Philadelphia, Pa. 1971, pp.218-245; J. N. Rosenau, P. Burgess and C. Hermann, 'The adaptation of foreign policy research', <u>International Studies Quarterly</u>, Vol. XVII, 1973, pp.119-44; J. N. Rosenau, <u>op.cit</u>.
(4) Rosenau, 'Foreign policy as adaptive behaviour', <u>op.cit</u>., p.365.
(5) <u>Ibid</u>., p.366.
(6) <u>Ibid</u>.
(7) Rosenau, <u>The Adaptation of National Societies</u>, <u>op.cit</u>., p.21.
(8) P. McGowan, 'Problems in the Construction of Positive Foreign Policy Theory', in J. N. Rosenau, <u>Comparing Foreign Policies</u>, John Wiley, New York 1974, pp.31-2.
(9) <u>Ibid</u>., p.33.
(10) Rosenau, <u>The Adaptation of National Societies</u>, <u>op.cit</u>., p.20.
(11) McGowan, <u>op.cit</u>., p.38.
(12) <u>Ibid</u>., p.41.
(13) <u>Ibid</u>., p.38.
(14) See P. McGowan, 'Adaptive Foreign Policy Behaviour', in J. Rosenau, <u>Comparing Foreign Policies</u>, <u>op.cit</u>., pp.45-54.

(15)   See M. O'Leary, 'Foreign Policy and Bureaucratic Adaptation', ibid., pp.55-70.
(16)   P. Hansen, 'Adaptive Behavior of Small States - the Case of Denmark and the European Community', in P. McGowan (ed), Sage International Yearbook of Foreign Policy Studies, Vol. II, Sage, Beverly Hills, Ca. 1974, pp.143-174.
(17)   J. N. Rosenau, 'Restlessness, Change and Foreign Policy Analysis', in J. N. Rosenau, In Search of Global Patterns, Free Press, New York 1976, p.369.
(18)   See Figures 3.1, 3.2 and 3.3 above.
(19)   J. N. Rosenau and G. Hoggard, 'Foreign Policy Behavior in Dyadic Relationships: Testing a Pretheoretical Extension', in Rosenau (ed), Comparing Foreign Policies, op.cit., Appendix A, pp.146-49.
(20)   Ibid., pp.121-2.
(21)   J. N. Rosenau, The Adaptation of National Societies, op.cit., p.16.
(22)   See P. McGowan, 'Problems in the Construction of Positive Foreign Policy Theory', op.cit., pp.34-36.
(23)   J. Jenkins and W. Chittick, 'Reconceptualizing Foreign Policy Behavior: the Problem of Discrete Events in a Continuous World', in R. Merritt (ed), Foreign Policy Analysis, Lexington, Lexington, Mass. 1975, p.81.
(24)   J. N. Rosenau and G. Hoggard, op.cit., pp.121-22.
(25)   Ibid., p.146.
(26)   J. Jenkins and W. Chittick, op.cit., p.81.
(27)   J. N. Rosenau and G. Hoggard, op.cit., p.147.
(28)   J. Jenkins and W. Chittick, op.cit., p.81.

4 Dutch and British policies towards European integration

This section will outline Dutch foreign policy over the process of European integration by considering the attitude of the Dutch Government to the major proposals for European integration between 1948 and 1963. Specifically, the section will be concerned to show the type of European integration desired by Dutch Governments.

Dutch Governments in the immediate post war period were concerned with three main areas of the international environment - the problem of the Dutch East Indies; the 'quest for security'; and the process of recovery internally. Combined with this was the clear impact of the Second World War, which illustrated to the Dutch Government the shortcomings of a disunited Europe. These factors had the effect of emphasising in Dutch governmental statements the desirability of four power agreement over the nature of post war Europe. With the 'loss' of the Dutch East Indies, another factor emerged that influenced the position of the Dutch Government towards Europe.

The 'loss' of the Dutch East Indies entailed a complete restructuring of the Dutch economy. Given the similar losses of overseas territory by other European countries, something had to replace the economic features of the former colonies. Soviet actions in sealing off Eastern Europe economically from the West exacerbated this situation. The Marshall Plan and its stress on the fact that the emphasis must come from Europe itself, acted as the catalyst for this feeling.

With this process of recovery occurring in Europe, there was a strong movement aiming at European unity as represented by the many organisations created to further this aim. These organisations met at a Congress held between 7 and 8 May 1948 at the Hague. This Congress of Europe declared that

> ' . . . the time has come when the European nations must transfer and merge some portion of their sovereign rights to secure common political and economic action for the integration and proper development of their common resources.' (1)

It also demanded

> 'the convening, as a matter of urgency, of a European Assembly chosen by the Parliaments of the participating nations designed, . . . to advise upon measures to bring about the necessary economic and political union of Europe.' (2)

Following this Congress, the five governments of the Brussels Pact met and, in October 1948, set up a Commission to examine the possibilities of European integration in social and economic fields. The Dutch Government did not object to the establishment of this Commission, but it made no proposals for their representatives on the Commission who, therefore, made their own proposals. The Dutch Government preferred a functional approach to integration, whereby the process would be one of international, intergovernmental, specialised authorities dealing

with one sector of joint concern, which, although containing some supranational elements, would not require the same degree of agreement in
the wide range of issues as would be required by the political integration of the federal approach.   The Commission created by the Brussels
Treaty powers finally proposed the establishment of a Council of Europe.
This body, the statute of which was formally signed on 5 May 1949, comprised an Assembly (without legislative power) and a Committee of
Ministers to ensure national control of the activities of the Council
(this being the result of primarily British and Scandinavian pressure).

In the Netherlands, the attitude of the Government was restated in
February 1949.   The Government was still in favour of a policy of slow,
but certain, progress; it still felt that needless duplication of international organisations should be avoided; it still could not envisage
the establishment of a federal state and thus felt that the Council of
Europe should not be invested with binding powers, yet the Government
welcomed the Council as a possible forum for public opinion (3).   In
line with this position, the Dutch Government opposed British suggestions that the members of the Consultative Assembly should be appointed
by national governments and should vote en bloc according to instructions.

Discussion on the Statute of the Council of Europe occurred in the
States-General during June and July 1949.   The general feeling was one
of satisfaction that a European organisation had been established, but
it was felt that the organisation was little more than a modest beginning.   The most notable criticism was that the Consultative Assembly
was subordinated to the Ministerial Committee and that it could not,
therefore, be a forum of public opinion.   Thus, many members felt that
the statute did not go far enough - yet it was generally accepted that
the statute was a compromise and that there were dangers involved in
granting supranational powers to any body, the members of which did not
seem willing to accept the implications of such a state of affairs.

The Government's reply to these criticisms was that the statute was
a compromise and that whilst, in the Netherlands there was a strong
commitment to far reaching proposals for federalism, these had to be
balanced against the position of a state such as Britain.   The Dutch
Government would be prepared to amend the statute to increase the powers
of the Assembly.   Such a position was in marked contrast to the position adopted only six months earlier.

The next major proposal for European integration was the Schuman Plan
of May 1950: Schuman announced that the French Government proposed 'to
place all Franco-German coal and steel production under a common High
Authority, in an organisation open to the participation of the other
countries of Europe' (4).   This pooling would

   'mean the immediate establishment of common bases of industrial
   production, which is the first step toward European Federation
   and will change the destiny of regions that have long been
   devoted to the production of war armaments of which they themselves
   have been the constant victims.' (5)

However, as Schuman later admitted, the primary motive was not economic,
but political, 'to end Franco-German hostility once and for all'. (6)

The Dutch reaction to this proposal was determined by their commitment
to a customs union, and once the larger neighbouring powers moved in a
similar direction, this had a joint effect since the Dutch could not
afford to stay outside any such organisation and this was also an opportunity that the leadership and the proponents of closer European unity
welcomed. In a very short period of time, the six nations that took
part in the negotiations were able to agree on a treaty setting up a
European Coal and Steel Community (ECSC); this established a common
market for coal and steel; set out a series of rules for the conduct
and regulations of the common market; and created a series of institutions to run the Community. Although the French made the acceptance
of supranationalism a condition of entering into the negotiations, this
was modified during them. Indeed, the Dutch Government took part in
the negotiations on the understanding that it could not at the start
be committed to all the purposes of the Plan. The Dutch Government
was especially concerned about giving a carte blanche to the High Authority. They, therefore, stressed the necessity for the establishment of
a Council of Ministers, to which the High Authority had to refer certain
proposals; more importantly for the Netherlands, the Council of Ministers had to ensure that the High Authority did not act in the other
areas of national economic policy. Having obtained this agreement, the
Dutch Parliament ratified the treaty with very little controversy and
the Community came into being in August 1952.

Given that the ECSC was only concerned with coal and steel products,
a further Dutch reaction to it was the proposal for a European organisation of agricultural markets - the Green Pool. This proposal was
announced by the Dutch Minister for Agriculture, Sicco Mansholt, in
November 1950 and it called for an agricultural community to be established on the lines of the ECSC. Despite meetings on the proposal,
which continued until July 1954, the project was essentially unfeasible
due to the vast differences between the countries involved. The plan
involved British participation, although this was especially difficult
to achieve since the British agricultural system was based on a system
of subsidies. The supranational element of the plan was another stum-
bling block to British participation; in fact they proposed an intergovernmental body to replace the supranational element and finally
proposed, and kept to the proposition, that the body to discuss agriculture should be a Ministerial Committee within OEEC - a proposition
which was accepted at the final meeting of the Committee in 1954.

The ECSC represented, in many ways, a decisive turning point in the
post war process of European integration since Britain refused to join
the organisation. However, this was not the only measure for integration being proposed at that time and, with the exception of the European Payments Union which developed out of OEEC, the British position
was one of 'with but not of Europe'. Thus, the British response to
such plans as the Stikker Plan, the Pella Plan and the Petsche Plan -
all of which were raised within the OEEC in July 1950 - was unfavourable.

As British hesitation and concern about joining in any form of supranational European venture grew, the impetus increased on the Continent
and, following ideas for 'Fritalux', 'Finebel', and a French-Italian
Customs Union, the ECSC form of organisation was proposed for a European
Defence Community (EDC). The Dutch Government felt that military
integration should at least be accompanied, if not preceded, by further

economic integration (7).   Thus, Foreign Minister Beyen proposed a six
power customs union to the Foreign Ministers' Conference of the EDC
countries in February 1953.   The plan was for a gradual reduction in
tariffs leading to a Customs Union; a gradual reduction in import
quotas; and free movement for labour.   However, although the plan was
accepted by the Foreign Ministers, it was referred to a group of experts
and was not revived.

The other major initiative for European integration that occurred
through the negotiations for EDC was the proposal for a European Political Community (EPC).   This proposal was the result of many interacting forces: pressure from European federalists; concern over the lack
of supranationalism within the ECSC; and, a desire to ensure political
control over the European army envisaged in the EDC.   A draft treaty
was drawn up by an ad hoc assembly of the ECSC under the chairmanship of
Spaak but the treaty was shelved by the Foreign Ministers.   By the
time the French National Assembly rejected the EDC the Foreign Ministers
had not produced a firm draft for the EPC, although it was clear that
the Community would be one of sovereign states with supranational power
limited to that of treaties in force and any agreed in later treaties.
With the defeat of the EDC, the plans for the EPC were shelved, since
the two were very closely linked.   The policy of the Dutch Government
to the EPC proposal is difficult to assess.   On the surface it was
summed up, by the Economist, as being one of 'pressing forward, in
spite of several disappointments, with the project'. (8)   However,
the Dutch Government's concerns over the EDC give an indication that the
EPC, although to be welcomed as a further step on the path of European
integration, would have to be carefully considered if it ever came to
be ratified.

The attitude of the Dutch Government towards EPC was one of promoting
it at a superficial level whilst having doubts about its desirability.
In the same way that the Government had expressed concern about the
Statute of the Council of Europe and had expressed the view that the
Brussels Treaty Organisation was not to be seen as a supranational body,
the Government, in contrast to many members of the Parliament and much
public opinion, rejected federalist solutions (9).   As noted above,
Stikker and the Government preferred functionalist solutions to the
all embracing federalist alternative.   Although Stikker claims that
the 'distinction between a functionalist and a federalist was often
only a matter of championing a slower or a quicker pace of integration'
(10), the differences appear to be more fundamental.   The Dutch felt
that it should proceed primarily via economic integration: political
and military integration could follow once the economic and social conditions required has been established.

With the fall of the EDC and thus the EPC, the situation in Europe was
one of deep pessimism with regard to the prospects for European integration.   The initiative of the British Government, which resulted in
the WEU and the admission of Germany into NATO, did, however, relieve
some of the fears, but as Camps points out

   'anyone who . . . predicted that the Six would soon be actively
   engaged in the creation of two new Communities might reasonably
   have been dismissed as a light-headed visionary'. (11)

However, there existed a strong desire, and considerable political will, on the Continent for further integration in Europe and the relaunching of Europe occurred.

Following discussions between Monnet, then head of the High Authority of the ECSC, and those interested in the relancee (the relaunching of Europe), and after a favourable statement on future integration by the new French Prime Minister, Edgar Faure, the Benelux Governments announced that they would call a Conference on European Integration and they finally presented a memorandum on the subject to a meeting of the Foreign Ministers of the ECSC countries held in June 1955. This meeting, at Messina, resulted in the setting up of a committee under the chairmanship of Spaak, which was to examine how ends were to be achieved. The aims were outlined in the resolution issued at the end of the meeting. It called for

'. . . a fresh advance towards the building of Europe. (The six Governments) are of the opinion that this must be achieved, first of all, in the economic field . . . the establishment of a European market, free from all customs duties and all quantitative restrictions, is the objective of their action in the field of economic policy.' (12)

This was to be combined with the study of proposals for atomic energy cooperation and integration in various sectors of the European economy. Furthermore, the resolution accepted the Benelux position that Britain be invited to participate in the negotiations. As will be discussed below, the British Government withdrew from the Spaak Committee in November 1955 and this was according to Camps, '. . . a critical turning point in the development of relations between the Six and the United Kingdom'. (13)

From this point the Six continued alone. The Spaak Report was presented to the Foreign Ministers in April 1956 and came out in favour of a scheme which represented a compromise between the competing desires for further sector integration and those proposing a general common market. Thus, a separate institutional development was proposed for the peaceful uses of nuclear energy (Euratom), whilst an economic common market was also proposed. Accepting the report as a basis, the Foreign Ministers charged the Spaak Committee with the job of drawing up the necessary treaties. Despite some problems in the negotiations, which will be discussed below, the treaties establishing the EEC and Euratom were signed at Rome on 27 March 1957.

The attitude of the Dutch Government towards the relaunching of Europe generally and the specific proposals which resulted in the formation of the two Communities will now be outlined. In general terms, the Dutch attitude towards the relaunching of Europe was one of intense interest and promotion.

The Dutch conception of the preferable form of integration was, in part as the result of the activities and success of Benelux, for a functional development of an economic union. The Netherlands, after the loss of the Netherlands East Indies, was increasingly dependent on the international economic environment generally and on Europe's economic market specifically. In any economic crisis the Dutch Government feared that the old beggar-my-neighbour policies might return and thus

their narrow economic base might provide insufficient stability.   Since
the Netherlands would be affected more sharply than most because of its
high dependence on international trade, the Dutch Government was concerned to enlarge economic units and press for more liberal international
trade policies.

In the initial discussions over the possibility of relancee, which
took place during the winter and spring of 1955, whilst Spaak and Monnet
preferred further sector integration, Beyen (the Dutch Foreign Minister)
favoured abandoning the sector approach and, instead, proceeding by the
creating of a general customs union.   After the announcement by the
Dutch Government that the Benelux countries would hold a conference on
the subject of further integration (itself an expression of concern
that bilateral French-German discussions might result in a united front
proposal for integration), the Benelux countries issued a memorandum
containing their suggestions for further integration.   In comparison
with the resolution issued at the end of the Messina talks, the Benelux
memorandum placed more emphasis on institutional development - stating
that

> ' . . . the establishment of a European Economic Community,
> necessarily presupposes the establishment of a common authority
> endowed with the powers necessary to the realisation of the
> agreed objectives.' (14)

The Benelux memorandum called for the participation in the discussions
of any country that had signed a Treaty of Association with the ECSC;
the only country that had done so was the United Kingdom.   Shortly
after the Messina discussions, the Dutch Foreign Minister, Beyen, visited London as the emissary of the Six and offered the British participation on any terms it chose (15).   As mentioned above, and as will be
discussed in the next section, the British Government withdrew from the
discussions by the groups of experts in November 1955.   Beyen again
visited London and despite initial optimism following his talks with
Butler (Chancellor of the Exchequer), a statement issued by the British
Government effectively ended any attempts to improve the relations
between Britain and the Six.

During the detailed negotiations over the formation of the two Communities that followed the British withdrawal, a major strand of Dutch
policy was to tie together the proposals for Euratom and the EEC since
it was feared that the French Government might accept the former and
reject the latter.   Within the negotiations for the Communities the
major problem for the Dutch Government concerned agriculture - a problem in which they found themselves in opposition to the French Government.   The Dutch, in line with their support for the idea of a Green
Pool, supported a free market for agricultural goods within the community whereas the French proposed a system of intricate controls - especially minimum prices and long term contracts.   The Dutch Government
saw minimum prices as protectionist and long term contracts as involving
the danger of French control of the German market and fundamentally
felt that the French were seeking to use the Community organisations
to do what they could not - organise domestic agriculture.

The resultant mood in the government and business circles was that
the Netherlands might be better off in the Free Trade Area proposed
by the British Government in January 1957 rather than in the Common

Market, which was seen as being less of a method of integration than
an organisation for the consolidation of national interests. (16) This
position appears to have been more of a negotiating tactic than a reali-
stic policy alternative for a variety of reasons. The British plans
were then at a vague stage in comparison to the projects for the EEC
and Euratom; but more fundamentally the Netherlands could not stay
outside the Common Market and still stay inside Benelux with the other
two partners in the Common Market.

   In the ratification debate, although the outcome was never in doubt,
serious misgivings about the proposed Communities emerged. Camps sees
these misgivings as being more widespread and genuinely felt than in
any other signatory (17).   Nevertheless, the Dutch States-General ratified the two treaties on 5 October 1957 by 114 to 12 with 24 abstentions;
in the Upper House the process was not completed until December and, as
in the Lower House, there was no real doubt over the outcome.   Thus,
'rather more for political than for economic reasons' (18), the Dutch
ratified the treaties - and were, rather surprisingly, the last to
complete ratification.

   Following the establishment of the two Communities on 1 January 1958,
the major position to be formulated was that with regard to the attempts
by the British to form some sort of association with the new Communities.
The British Government issued a White Paper in February 1957 in which
it outlined its proposals for the establishment of a European Industrial
Free Trade Area.   This proposal would embrace the Six and the other
eleven members of the OEEC, and would involve the removal of internal
barriers to industrial trade.   It stated that agriculture 'must be
excluded' and it rejected any common external tariff with each member
able to maintain existing preference agreements.   Nor would there be
any harmonisation of social and economic policies and no common political
supranational institutions were involved.   Initially, the Dutch Government, along with the German Government, supported the possibility of
the Six forming some sort of wider association with the rest of the
OEEC countries.

   Yet the economic and political advantages for the Dutch of a wider
Free Trade Area were to be balanced against the political consequences
and potential of the movement that had culminated in the creation of
the EEC and Euratom.   Despite the concern felt by the Dutch Government,
at the time of ratification, about the shortcomings of the new Communities, there was the important consideration that the EEC represented a
considerable political advance in Europe.   The very fact that two years
of negotiation had resulted in a firm structure gave the Six a feeling
of common purpose and cohesion.   Thus, the Dutch Government could not
consider any agreements that would hinder the progress of the EEC into
an economic union.   In addition to this, the British position with
regard to agriculture was unacceptable for the Dutch Government, although
they differed, notably with the French, over the preferred set of arrangements for agriculture.   In the final resort the Dutch, like the other
members of the Six,' . . . agreed that a clear priority should be given
to maintaining the integrity of the Treaty of Rome'. (19)

   Dutch policy towards the proposals for an EFTA was thus an attempt to
balance the economic and political benefits to be obtained from British
and other OEEC countries' membership of a wider Free Trade Area, with

the strong desire to strengthen and maintain the commitment to integrate in Europe as represented by the three Communities. Although British policy changed on certain key points during the negotiations, the fundamental difference between the positions of the outer six and the Six was that the British Government was proposing not a Customs Union but a Free Trade Area. The French Government was totally unwilling to enter into any Free Trade Area which gave similar trade benefits as those within the EEC, yet had less far reaching commitments to common policies and tariffs. A common feeling amongst the Six was that such an agreement would give the British economic advantages due to their preferential arrangements with the Commonwealth as well as comparative cost advantages due to the absence of any common social and agricultural policies. In addition to these problems there was the strong feeling that the existence of the Free Trade Area would make the further integration of the EEC more difficult.

In the November of 1958 the negotiations for a Free Trade Association broke down. However, negotiations continued, notably at the Consultative Assembly of the Council of Europe, and at a special committee of the Council of Ministers of the Six. The Dutch, during these negotiations, were still attempting to find some means by which an association could be made between the Six and the other countries of the OEEC. However, as the economic advantages of the EEC and the ECSC came to be realised and as the US overtly moved to support a united Europe, the possibility of reopening negotiations for a European free trade agreement seemed less likely. When the Outer Seven decided, in July 1959, to form EFTA this had the effect of making the divide between the Six and the Seven more permanent.

By 1960 then, the Dutch Government was firmly involved and committed to the further development of the European Communities. From 1957 to 1960 the Dutch had played a dual role but by 1960 the Dutch

> ' . . . had to lower their sights. Giving up . . . the idea
> of a European solution which would merge the common market
> in something different and bigger, they have settled down to
> working within the common market and improving it as best as
> they can.' (20)

The prospect of British membership, although desired, was by 1960 considered a long way off and thus Dutch policy concentrated on achieving their major objective - the liberalisation of trade - within the Community.

The various strands of historical experience and political predispositions that have been mentioned above seem to come together most clearly in one area of debate within the European Community - the debate over political union, which Bodenheimer in her extensive study of the negotiations has called a 'microcosm of European Politics' (21). An important preliminary consideration concerning political union is that it is to be distinguished from the earlier plans over the EPC; whereas EPC envisaged some form of supranational organisation, political union was concerned with a particular form of institutional arrangement that, through consultation, would facilitate the adoption of common policies among the Six. On 5 September 1960, De Gaulle stated that, following discussions with the other members of the Six, he proposed an extension of cooperation between the Six into the political field. He envisaged a Council of the Heads of Governments to act as the principal organ of cooperation, to be served by a Secretariat located in Paris. There would also be an Assembly of delegates from national parliaments and four commissions to promote cooperation in the fields of defence, economics, culture, and politics.

The plan outlined by De Gaulle was discussed at the Little Summit held in Paris on 10 and 11 February 1961. At this, and the subsequent meetings to discuss European Political Union (EPU),

> ' . . . the debate . . . may be viewed as a confrontation between the two extreme positions - the French and the Dutch. For on almost every issue, the French conception of Europe has been most clearly and most consistently resisted by the Dutch.' (22)

Dutch policy, during the initial phase of the negotiations, was one of attempting to obtain an invitation to the British whilst, as long as this was not accepted, weakening and delaying any agreement. With regard to the former, Luns stated at the Little Summit that it was a condition for Dutch cooperation (23). With regard to the latter aim - that of delaying and weakening any agreement - the Dutch rejected the French plan as presented in February at the Summit.

The decision of the British Government to seek membership of the European Community, announced in the House of Commons on 31 July 1961, reinforced the dual approach of the Dutch to obtain British participation in the discussions and delay any outcome until Britain was included. The evidence suggests that Dutch policy was, essentially, 'no British - no political union'. After that date accession negotiations took place with the Six, and the issue of political union and that of British membership of the Communities became intertwined. The Dutch position with regard to British membership could not, as indicated above, be more clearcut. It was the most consistent advocate of British membership and thus of British participation in the discussions over political union. Thus, following De Gaulle's veto in January 1963, political union could not have been further away.

The Dutch were the only government to insist consistently on British participation, yet alone they were unable to have the desired effect. This indicates a reason for the difference between their declaratory interest in supranational institutions and their policy over political union. Although it is stated that supranational institutions impose the same constraints on the larger nations as have always been practical limitations on the ability of small states to act, the Dutch Government felt that supranationalism could not override the effects of differences in state power.

The position of the Dutch Government over supranationalism within any scheme for political union was that, as experience within the EEC had shown, bargaining power was clearly different between, say, France and the Netherlands. In a supranational political union, with matters of a higher priority being dealt with, this tendency would be exaggerated. For the Dutch Government the more secure guarantee of their interests as a small nation was British participation to counteract French and German influence.

The debate over political union is also a strong example of the way in which the Dutch commitment to NATO was wedded to the other main pillar of post war Dutch foreign policy - European integration. At one level the Dutch Government was the only member of the Six that stated that defence should not be considered within the proposed political union. It also insisted - and was consistently defeated - on statements that the Atlantic Alliance was to be respected by the new institutional framework.

The other level of Dutch policy over the Atlantic Alliance was seen in its insistence on British membership. Bodenheimer in her exhaustive study of the Dutch attitude to the negotiations sums up this level by arguing that,

> ' . . . it becomes clear that the real "cornerstone" of Dutch policy, the national interest which has inspired their campaign to bring Britain into Europe and which underlies their whole attitude toward political union, is the preservation of the Atlantic Alliance.' (24)

This being the fundamental aspect of Dutch policy, the attitude towards political union was in essence one of British membership to guarantee the cohesion of the Atlantic Alliance. The question of supranationalism was largely irrelevant if the policies of the nations involved were to lead to a weakening of that Alliance.

As noted above, the British application for membership was effectively vetoed by De Gaulle at his Press Conference on 19 January 1963. The Dutch position was the most extreme; they suggested that the other five states might draw up a treaty with Britain and invite France to adhere to it (25). But, it soon became obvious that neither Germany nor Italy was willing to sacrifice progress in the area of European integration for British membership.

Dutch policy towards European integration was, therefore, based on the interaction of a series of principles: the necessity of British membership of the Communities; the overriding necessity for free trade, which resulted in some ambivalance over the protectionist implications of economic integration; the fear of domination by their larger neighbours; and, the concern for the maintenance of the Atlantic Alliance.

BRITISH POLICY TOWARDS EUROPEAN INTEGRATION

British policy towards Europe in the immediate post war situation appears to be best explained by three factors. At one level, as Frankel points out, the historical experience suggested that Britain would seek to establish a balance of power in the new European situation and would then withdraw from European affairs (26). At another level, the reasons for British aloofness from involvement in Europe were to be found in the striking contrasts between the situations of the continental powers and Britain. Whereas all the continental nations had been either defeated or occupied, Britain had emerged from the war victorious. Britain had survived intact; her political and economic structures although under strain had not faced the same obvious dislocation as had those of the continental powers. At a third level, British aloofness from Europe can be seen as a consequence of the nature of Anglo-American relations. Frankel argues that the British felt more at home with other English speaking people who shared a common cultural background and a stable democratic system of government (27). In contrast to the severance of links suffered by the the continental powers, the Atlantic link had been strengthened during the war.

The combination of these factors resulted in a situation in which the dominant conception of post war British Governments with regard to foreign policy was the Three Circles approach. Although outlined by Churchill in 1948 and Nutting in 1950, the conception seems to have been shared by the leadership of both parties although for different reasons (28). The doctrine of the Three Circles was that Britain was involved in ' . . . the three great unities of the world. The unity across the Atlantic, the unity within the British Commonwealth and Empire, and the unity with Western Europe.' (29) Although the doctrine had the implication that the key of British policy was to avoid a commitment to one element of the circles which involved a severance of links with another circle, the position accorded to the European element was one of a lower priority than that accorded to either the US or the Commonwealth.

In this context, the famous speech of Churchill in Zurich in September 1946, when he called for the building of a United States of Europe, requires examination since it was considered at the time to be an important impetus to the development of European integration. Churchill called for the building of

> 'a kind of United States of Europe . . . which could give a
> sense of enlarged patriotism and common citizenship to the
> distracted peoples of this mighty continent . . . Therefore,
> I say to you, "Let Europe arise!"' (30)

However, it is important to note that the form of Europe that Churchill envisaged was one that was later summed up as one in which Britain would be 'with, but not of'. He continued

> 'in all this urgent work France and Germany must take the lead
> together. Great Britain, the British Commonwealth of Nations,
> Mighty America, and I trust Soviet Russia . . . must be the
> friends and sponsors of the new Europe and must champion its
> rights to live and shine.' (31)

Britain was, therefore, to be a sponsor, not a participant, in this kind of United States of Europe. The statement indicates that Britain, as a member of the Big Three, could not participate and that the Commonwealth relationships were of primary importance. The fact that Britain was to be a sponsor of this new Europe indicates that it was primarily seen as an object of foreign policy rather than as a partner.

During the period of the Labour Government, it was heavily criticised by the Conservatives for failing to advance the European cause as, for instance, in the case of the Hague Congress of European movements when the British Labour Party boycotted the meeting. In contrast to the grandiose statements made by Churchill, the Labour Government was unwilling to accept participation in any European integration that involved any surrender of control over national policy to a supranational authority. This was especially important in a Europe that, after 1948, was dominated by non socialist governments. The primary concern of the Party was to carry out the proposals for social change at home, and any European commitment which would affect the ability to carry out these proposals would be avoided. A further reason for the position of the Labour Government was that any movement towards European unity could result in the withdrawal of US aid and thus continued US participation in Europe would best be achieved by frustrating the movement for European unity. However, as Lieber points out (32), the attitude of the Conservatives was little different from that of the Labour Government. The form of unity envisaged by Churchill was more a spiritual form of unity than a constitutional one.

Thus, the broad strand of thought that dominated the thinking of the majority of British politicians towards European unity was one of little interest. Cooperation with Europe was desirable and necessary but integration would not only have involved making a definite choice of circles (and to the least dominant of circles) but would also have involved undertaking open-ended commitments that would affect the domestic policies of the Labour Government.

Given this general position towards European integration, the actions of the British Government over specific proposals become clearer. Following the Hague Congress of May 1948, which called for the establishment of an economic and political union, the Consultative Council of the Brussels Treaty powers commenced negotiations that resulted in the formation of the Council of Europe. In these negotiations, Britain, supported by the Scandinavian powers, led the opposition to the creation of a political framework. The British representatives argued for governmental control over the proposed organs. Thus, although Britain finally agreed with the proposal for a Consultative Assembly, it did so in return for acceptance that the Assembly could not consider defence questions. Furthermore, the British originally insisted that the members of the Assembly were to be appointed by national governments and were to vote in accordance with the wishes of their governments; a compromise was finally agreed whereby each government could decide on its own form of appointing members to the Assembly.

Bevin summed up the British view of the Council of Europe in the House of Commons in 1950

' . . . the original concept of the Council of Europe was that
this body should afford, in the first place, a forum for European
opinion . . . which could be taken into account by governments
through the Committee of Foreign Ministers . . . As to the Consultative Assembly, it was never considered that it should be a
parliament, that it should have in any sense legislative powers.'(33)

Bevin had explained British policy towards European integration in more general terms in September 1948,

' . . . I feel that the intricacies of Western Europe are such that
we had better proceed . . . on the same principles of association
of nations that we have in the Commonwealth. Britain has to be

67

in both places: she has to be and must remain the centre of the
Commonwealth and she must be European. It is a very difficult
role to play. It is different from that of anyone else and I
think that adopting the principle of an unwritten constitution,
and the process of constant associations step by step, by treaty
and agreement and by taking on certain things collectively instead
of by ourselves, is the right way to approach this . . .
problem.' (34)

The Conservative Party, although they made much political capital out
of the Labour Government's reluctance to become involved in any European
integration - a position which resulted in considerable hope being placed
on a change of policy when they came to power in 1951 - made their
position clear soon after their electoral victory. At a meeting of the
Consultative Assembly of the Council of Europe, the chief British dele-
gate stated that it was unrealistic to expect Britain to join a European
federation.

With the developments of the Schuman and Pleven Plans - which will be
discussed below - the members of the Council of Europe and the Six were
drifting apart. It is interesting to note that the British plan for
bridging this gap, the Eden Plan, envisaged the Council of Europe becoming the parent body for all existing and future European communities.
Thus, Britain could, through the Council of Europe, keep involved with
the new Communities without becoming committed to any supranationalism.
The plan shows, however, that the attitude to European integration was
one held by both leaderships and that statements in opposition provide
little indication of policy when in government.

The major initiative of integration in Europe in the late 1940s and
early 1950s was, however, the Schuman Plan for a European Coal and
Steel Community. As noted above, the basic strand of British policy
towards integration in Europe was one of at best encouragement in functional integration, at worst one of antipathy. Frankel claims that
the attitude of the British Government over the Schuman and Pleven Plans
was based on two assumptions: that neither plan would succeed; and
that if they did, Britain would be able to join at a later stage (35).
The Schuman Plan, which led to the creation of the European Coal and
Steel Community (ECSC), has been seen as the issue which marked the
parting of the ways between Britain and the Six.

The British reaction, although, on the surface, a matter of dispute
between the Labour Government and the Conservative Party, is seen by
Lieber as the best illustration of the ' . . . underlying kinship of
Labour and Tory attitudes' over European policy (36). After consultation with the French Government over the terms of participation, the
British Government decided not to take part in the Conference to draft
the treaty. Unlike the Dutch, who attended the Conference in order to
find a 'way in' by obtaining concessions, the British were - according
to Nutting - trying to find a way out. In a statement to Parliament,
Attlee explained the British response to the Schuman Plan. He pointed
out that the French had required that Britain accept two principles as
preconditions for negotiation: the pooling of resources, and the
creation of a high authority whose decisions would be binding. In the
words of a Government statement, 'HM Government do not feel able to
accept in advance, nor do they wish to reject in advance, the principles
underlying the French proposal.' (37)

Although the non Socialist nature of Europe was a relevant factor in the considerations of the Labour Government it masks the more fundamental reason for the rejection. This was the nature of the preconditions required for taking part in the negotiations. Northedge states that

' . . . no British government was able to accept the principle of supranationalism by which the control of basic industries would have moved out of British hands.' (38)

Camps writes that

'the Front Bench of the Conservative Party was as opposed as the Government to any yielding of powers to a "supranational" organization.' (39)

When they returned to power in November 1951, the Conservatives did not take long to confirm their basic policy agreement with the previous Government. In a statement to Parliament on 12 November 1951, Nutting called for a closer association and endorsed the friendship between Britain and the ECSC; the British Government did not offer to participate fully. This makes it difficult to accept Nutting's arguments in Europe Will Not Wait, in which he states that

'Great Britain's rejection of the Schuman Plan marked the most vital turning point in Anglo-European relations since the Second World War.' (40)

The Conservative Government did reconsider the question of joining the ECSC and rejected the possibility, preferring instead to negotiate an association agreement with the ECSC (41). Furthermore, the October 1951 General Election did not see the question of European unity as a major aim of Conservative foreign policy. According to David Butler their manifesto did not even mention the Schuman Plan or the question of supranationalism (42).

The associated proposal for a Green Pool received a similar response from the British Government (43). The British reaction to this proposal was to suggest, at the first meeting of the nations involved, that an intergovernmental body be constructed to deal with the issues; therefore, the British position was one of rejecting supranationalism and proposing that the subject be discussed on the much wider basis of the OEEC.

The proposal for a European Defence Community again illustrates both the bipartisan nature of policy towards European integration and the superficial nature of the differences between the statements of both parties. In contrast to the rejection of the plan for EDC by the Labour Government, the Leader of the Opposition, Churchill, had been the first European statesman to air the idea. At a meeting of the Assembly of the Council of Europe in August 1950, Churchill moved a resolution for 'the immediate creation of a European army under a united command in which we should all bear a worthy and honourable part.' (44) As Nutting points out, the statement by Churchill, in contrast to the rejection of the proposal by the Labour Government, could only mean 'that, under Churchill at least, the British would throw in their lot and merge their army with Europe'. (45) Thus, when Eden announced in

Rome, at a meeting of the NATO Council, that Britain would not participate in the EDC ' . . . the effect on the mercurial atmosphere of the
Strasbourg Assembly was nothing short of shattering'. (46)

Given the British policy of non participation in the EDC project, the
question of the British position over the EPC proposal did not arise
although it is clear both from British arguments over the Council of
Europe, ECSC, the Green Pool and the later position over the Fouchet
negotiations, that that proposal would not have been accepted at any
price as long as supranational elements were present.   The Eden Plan
can be pointed to as the type of arrangement that Britain envisaged for
the management of the communities.   This stance reflects the dominant
considerations at the end of the 1940s, that attempts at integration
were unlikely to succeed and that, if they did, Britain could always
join in the projects later, although from a position outside rather than
inside the Communities.   British policy towards unification proposals
in the period up to 1955 was one of encouragement and a willingness to
participate in those which involved intergovernmental cooperation such
as the Council of Europe, OEEC and WEU.   With supranational proposals,
British policy was based on the principle that these were not only undesirable but were unlikely to be successful.

Up to 1955, therefore, British policy towards European integration was
one of never seriously considering any radical departure into European
integration.   Despite claims to be pro European, British policy was one
of objecting to each supranational initiative and even those who were
deemed pro European, and proposed entering discussions, did so on the
basis of trying to move Europe away from supranationalism towards intergovernmental cooperation.   The major disagreements were not between
parties but within them.   As Lieber concludes, ' . . . The dominant
sentiment was one of great hesitation toward any sort of European venture.' (47)   In retrospect, it is clear that the major initiative
towards European integration, in terms of achievement, was, however,
the proposal for a European Common Market, which resulted in the Treaty
of Rome.   The British Government was not represented at the Messina
meeting, according to Nutting,

> 'because (it) did not want to be there and did not really
> believe that the ambitious schemes that were to be considered
> would ever see the light of day.' (48)

Following the Messina meeting, the Dutch Foreign Minister, Beyen,
visited London and according to the Economist offered Britain an invitation to the Committee which was to draft the terms of the treaties
(49).   Macmillan, in the Government's formal reply, accepted the
invitation on the understanding that the Government was anxious to ensure
that the work of the OEEC should not be duplicated; there were, however, 'special difficulties for this country in any proposal for "a
European common market"'. (50)   During the discussions, the position
of the British Government was basically that the objectives sought at
Messina might better be pursued by strengthening the OEEC and that
little new organisational machinery need to be created.   The British
representative then withdrew.

One reason for this withdrawal was that the relationship between the
Six and Britain appeared to be moving to a satisfactory basis with the
signing of the Association Agreement between Britain and the ECSC and

the development of WEU.   Again, other, wider concerns were assuming
greater importance.   Camps concludes that

> ' . . . there is little to suggest that at any time during 1955
> any real consideration was given by the British to joining
> some form of Common Market.' (51)

The Euratom proposal appeared more salient and, although the qualms
over supranationalism still applied, participation in the proposal was
objected to on the grounds that Britain had little to gain from it,
being clearly ahead in the field of atomic energy.   With the withdrawal
from the Committee, British policy appeared to shift to that of discour-
aging any European integration in the economic field by pointing out
that any Common Market plans might lead to conflict with OEEC.   The
British Government preferred to start negotiations over an industrial
Free Trade Area in Europe.

The matter was debated in the House of Commons at the end of November
1956 (52) and, despite certain reservations, the Labour Party welcomed
the decision to proceed with negotiations for a Free Trade Area;   no
vote was taken.   Given this posture towards a Customs Union, the
Government proposed a Free Trade Area excluding agricultural produce.
The positive reasons for this proposal were the manifold advantages of
participating in a larger market;   the negative reason was that it would
prevent British and Commonwealth goods being discriminated against in
the large, and growing, market of Western Europe.   Camps points out
that the debate was

> 'remarkable for the **absence** of controversy and the unanimity of
> view on both sides of the House that the course of action outlined
> by the Government was, broadly, the right one.   There was
> general acceptance of the need to do something, wide support for
> the Government's view that a customs union was "out" and that
> agriculture must be excluded, and almost no questioning of the
> negotiability of the Government's proposals.' (53)

The proposal for a Free Trade Area was unacceptable to members of the
Six on both economic and political grounds.   At the economic level,
Britain stood to gain by a Free Trade Area since it did not involve the
removal of Commonwealth preferences or the harmonisation of economic and
social policies (of course, Britain was also attempting to exclude
agriculture from such a Free Trade Area).   At the political level, much
had been achieved during the negotiations for the EEC and Euratom and
it was felt that the proposal for a Free Trade Area would undermine
these efforts.

The Free Trade Area proposal could only have been successful had it
offered the Six either the prospect of a similar economic union to
that proposed under the Treaty of Rome and thus not containing the
possibility of the area superseding the EEC, or it could be made a
different form of arrangement which would not detract from the efforts
of the Six.   The British, however, wanted on the one hand to avoid any
supranational or common agricultural, external, economic and social policies as envisaged in the Treaty of Rome.   On the other, the British
Government had developed the idea of a Free Trade Area to prevent British goods being discriminated against within the EEC - thus, that Free
Trade Area had to be concerned with the same range of products as those

71

involved in the EEC.   Hence, when the British Government was ready to make concessions, the increased cohesion within the Six resulting from the signature and ratification of the Treaty of Rome combined with the delicate situation within France made the realisation of these impossible.

In the debate in the House of Commons held in December 1959 to approve the establishment of the EFTA, there was little discussion on the nature of the EFTA.   Most discussion was concerned with the possibility of future association between Britain and the Six and it was felt that the EFTA would not complicate any such association agreements.   However, the Labour Party felt that the EFTA was a second best plan that was clouding the issue of obtaining a wider European Free Trade Area; they, therefore, abstained on the vote.   Nevertheless, the issue of British policy towards Europe did not receive political treatment between 1956 and 1960.   As Lieber points out, the negotiations were carried out by economic ministries, notably the Board of Trade.   At another level, the subject was not a matter of public debate - in the 1959 election the matter was raised by less than one per cent of Labour candidates and eight per cent of Conservative candidates (54).   Neither did the Press treat Europe as a major political issue nor were there specialised pro and anti European groups.   At a final level, the issue was not a contentious one in Parliament with the major differences being within rather than between the Labour and Conservative Parties - only the Liberals attempted to make the issue 'political'.   Lieber sees this 'non politicised' status of the European question as reflecting a predominant consideration that Europe was primarily an economic, and low priority, issue (55).   Fundamentally, he argues that the non politicised nature of the issue stemmed from the fact that the Conservative and Labour Parties had essentially similar policies which existed not through calculation but out of an instinctive revulsion for European entanglements.

The final area of this survey is the important change in British policy towards Europe represented by Macmillan's announcement in the House of Commons on 31 July 1961 that Britain was to seek membership of the European Community.   A full scale debate on the proposal was held on 2 August 1961 (56).   The important point is that, again, there was little criticism of the move by the Opposition.   Although many concerns were expressed with regard to the relationship with the Commonwealth, the motion to proceed with negotiations was passed by 315 to 5.   The history of the negotiations is not the concern of this work, nor is the effect of De Gaulle's veto on British membership. The crucial point is that by July 1961 Britain had radically changed the foundation of its policy towards Europe.   From July 1961, the non politicised nature of previous debates over Europe vanished.   The Labour Party finally came out against joining the EEC at the Annual Conference in October 1962, where Gaitskell argued that membership would end a thousand years of history, and, of course, the position of the parties over Europe has been a salient issue in British politics since then.

The reasons for this radical change may be divided into economic and political considerations.   The Six had, by 1961, achieved considerable economic progress - the EEC had been seen to work; indeed, it was acquiring its own momentum.   The economies of the Six were growing rapidly and the tariff reductions were being accelerated (57). In contrast, the British economy was suffering from serious difficulties with a low growth rate and a series of balance of payments problems culminating in the sterling crisis of 1961. An economic cold shower was seen as being necessary to prevent the stagnation of British industry. At the political level, the effects of the Suez expedition and the realisation that, following the termination of the Blue Streak project, Britain could no longer go it alone in high technology weaponry meant that the perception of Britain's place in the world had to change. The collapse of the 1960 Summit Conference tended to make Macmillan's policy of promoting detente seem unrealistic. Added to these factors, the Commonwealth was, in the words of Lord Harlech, now 'a broken reed' following the crisis over South African membership. Finally, the special relationship appeared to be being eroded with the election of Kennedy and the stress placed by the US Government on the desirability of a united Europe. In this situation, Europe appeared to be a more important issue area - witnessed by the fact that the responsibility for the relations with the Common Market moved from the Board of Trade to the Foreign Office in 1960. Lieber, following a series of inter-views, believes that it was these political factors that were preponder-ant in the decision of the Macmillan Government to seek membership (58). Nevertheless, by July 1961 a decision that would have seemed impossible eighteen months earlier was taken and, despite later shifts and debates, the fundamental attitude of British Governments towards Europe had been transformed.

CONCLUSION

The discussion of the forces underlying Dutch policy towards the issue of integration isolated two main catalysts for their stance. The loss of the NEI, and thereby of a considerable economic asset, meant that some economic outlet had to replace this. On the political front the severe illustration of the failure of the policy of neutrality in-dicated to the Dutch leadership that some form of arrangement had to develop to prevent further war. Given the effect of the war on the Dutch economy and its pre-war linkage - in terms of trade - with other European countries, notably Germany, Dutch recovery was seen as being fully dependent on that of the rest of Europe. The Marshall Plan re-presented the catalyst to combine these economic pressures with those more political desires for some form of organisational development of integration.

With regard to the Commission set up by the Brussels Treaty powers to examine the possibilities of integration in social and economic fields, the Dutch Government made no proposals but did not object to the work of the Commission. In contrast to the federalist forces that largely dominated these discussions, the Dutch Government preferred a functional approach to the problem. The Council of Europe was seen, therefore, as a body for the airing of public opinion and not as the basis for some European federalist state; although, as the United States indicated its support for the project, the Dutch Government's position evolved to one of more open support for the enterprise.

With regard to the functional developments in European integration, although officially favouring such developments, the Dutch Government's

policy was again qualified.   It only entered into discussions regarding
the Schuman plan on the condition that it would not be seen as being
committed to all the stated purposes of the plan.   In the discussions
on the project, the Dutch Government stressed that the supranational
authority of the proposed Community should not be allowed to interfere
in other areas of the economy.   As noted above, during the debates on
the EDC the Dutch Government's major concern was to obtain from the
United States and Britain guarantees that they would treat events within
the EDC as being of significant interest.   The concomitant proposal for
a European Political Community (EPC) found the Dutch Government officially welcoming the move as one more step on the road to European integration, yet still preferring primarily a functional, but essentially an
economic, path to integration.   As with the attitude over the Brussels
Treaty, the Council of Europe and the ECSC, the Dutch Government was
unwilling to accept any supranationalism uncontrolled by national
governments.   It is no coincidence that during the discussions over
EDC and EPC the Dutch Government proposed further economic integration
in the form of a customs union among the six.   Underlying the Dutch
attitude to integration, therefore, appears to be the strong conception
that economic integration should precede political and military integration.

   The debate over the establishment of the European Economic Community
(EEC) and Euratom sees these factors again dominating Dutch policy.
The Dutch preferred the creation of a customs union, and one that included Britain.   Given that British participation was ruled out, the
Dutch Government pressed for supranational control of the new Communities
rather than control (and thereby possible domination) by national
governments.   During the attempts by the British Government to form
some kind of Community linking the Six with the rest of the OEEC, the
Dutch Government, although initially welcoming the move, saw little
advantage in such a Community.   It would not include agriculture -
which would be totally unacceptable for the Dutch given their reservations over the EEC - and it did not offer any benefits that could possibly justify jeopardising the concrete achievement represented by the
Treaties of Rome.

   The discussion of the Dutch attitude towards the negotiations for a
European Political Union illustrates the main strands in Dutch policy
towards European integration.   Essentially, Dutch policy towards the
proposal was to obtain an invitation to the British and, if this was
not accepted, to weaken and delay any agreement.   The former became
a condition of continued Dutch participation and the latter was designed
as a delay until British participation was ensured.   Despite a clear
indication by the British Government that their preferred view of any
such political union would be Gaullist, the question of British participation was still the cornerstone of Dutch policy.   Essentially,
therefore, the Dutch position was one of 'no British, no political
union'.   The French veto of British membership of the Communities
illustrates the importance of the issue to the Dutch - on the one hand
they proposed going on without France and negotiating an agreement with
Britain.   Yet, on the other, the fact that they were isolated in a
Community that did represent concrete achievements in European integration meant that such a policy was impossible.

   In summary, therefore, Dutch policy towards European integration,
although motivated by a genuine desire for trade liberalisation, was

founded on a policy which saw the Atlantic Alliance as the cornerstone of Dutch foreign policy. European integration was, therefore, seen as primarily concerned with economic, functional integration rather than with large scale, federal or supranational political integration. The issue of British participation reflected both the desire to prevent domination of European Communities by France and Germany and the strong belief that Britain would balance the continental outlook of, primarily, France with an Atlanticist orientation. As the debate over European Political Union well illustrates, it was this conception of foreign policy that predominated over concerns as to the precise form of integration to be adopted.

The nature of British policy towards European integration during the period under consideration underwent a fundamental development, from the 'with but not of' stance that dominated the first fifteen years after the war, to the tentative move towards Europe made by Macmillan in 1961. Naturally, such a contrast is an oversimplification since there were elements of dissent in the initial stance whereas the decision to apply for membership was extremely controversial at the time and is still a major political issue.

The policy of the British Government towards Europe at the end of the Second World War was the result of the interaction of three major factors: the traditional British policy of withdrawal from European affairs in the face of a balance of power situation on the Continent; the striking contrast between the defeated and occupied continental powers and Britain, who had emerged from the war unoccupied and 'victorious'; and, the British conception of, and reliance upon, the special Anglo-American relationship - a relationship that had been strengthened during the war. The dominant conception of Britain's position in international politics was summed up by the Conservative conception of the three circles. Within these three circles, the relationship with Europe was of the lowest priority. In reality, the leadership of both parties shared a very similar conception of Britain's relationship with Europe. Whilst Churchill might attack the Labour Government, the view of Britain's relationship with Europe that he held was more of a spiritual than a practical one; it was more cooperative than integrative: Britain was with Europe but not of it.

With this general conception of Britain's relationship with Europe underlying the superficially differing views of the parties in the Commons, the continuity of British policy towards Europe, despite the change of government in 1951, becomes more understandable. With regard to specific measures of European integration, British policy stemmed from this general conception. Thus, in the negotiations over the Council of Europe, the British Government attempted to ensure control by the member Governments over the proposed institutions.

British reaction to the proposal of Robert Schuman for a European Coal and Steel Community (ECSC), although on the surface a matter of interparty dispute, does, according to many observers, illustrate the high degree of agreement between the leaderships of the two parties. The Labour Government's refusal to participate in the talks - on the grounds that the prior requirements laid down by the French were unacceptable - was echoed by the Conservative Government's decision, soon after taking office, not to offer to participate fully. British policy towards the

EDC was continuously to refuse to participate despite Churchill's pioneering call for the creation of a European Army in 1950. Eden's proposals for the Western European Union (WEU) represented British thinking on Europe, as did the association agreement signed with the ECSC and the Eden Plan over the Council of Europe. British policy was to associate itself with the developments without actually participating - thus keeping her position at the centre of the three circles.

This attitude was clearly dominant at the time of the negotiations for what has become the major measure of European integration - the European Economic Community (EEC). At the Messina talks, British policy was made clear; it was felt that the proposals detracted from the work of the OEEC and that Britain would have difficulty in joining any such supranational organisation. When discussions moved on to the detailed plans, the British representative withdrew from the meeting. British policy was formally stated in February 1957 when it was announced that Britain was proposing negotiations over a Free Trade Area, in industrial goods, within the OEEC; again in domestic debates this was an uncontroversial issue.

After the signing and ratification of the Treaties of Rome, the probability of the British proposals being successful was very low. Fundamentally, this low probability arose from the fact that Britain was proposing not a customs union, but a free trade area. As such it had very little indeed to offer the Six economically and it would undermine the political and social ramifications of the Euratom and EEC projects.

The official 'reversal' came on 31 July 1961, when Macmillan announced his Government's intention to seek full membership of the European Economic Community. From this date, Europe became a politicised issue. It is not intended to suggest that 31 July 1961 marks a total break in previous policy; nor is it suggested that from that date on the issue was dealt with and seen in the same light as had characterised the continuity of policy before 1961. Yet, although the Labour Party finally came out against joining the European Economic Community, it is clear that it was this decision, of Macmillan, in 1961 that represented the turning point in British policy towards Europe. The reasons for the decision were both economic and political; economically, the stagnation and balance of payments problems suffered by the British economy could be contrasted with the growth visible amongst the Six. Politically, the results of Suez and the effects of the American-Soviet nuclear arms race meant that Britain's place in the world was no longer as it was. With independence being planned or having taken place in many colonies, with the Commonwealth undergoing severe internal battles, with Britain visibly unable to mediate between the super powers at a new peak in the Cold War, and with the strain in the special relationship represented by Kennedy's election, Europe appeared a more important and more appealing area for British action.

British policy towards European integration therefore underwent considerable change; although it appears, now, to have been less of a dramatic turnaround than it appeared at the time. From the very strong policy of 'with but not of' that dominated the early years of European integration, British policy continued, with a marked sense of consistency, either to attempt to water down any measures for integration that appeared likely to succeed, or to ignore what was occurring on the Continent in the belief that it would be ultimately unsuccessful. Nevertheless, as the success of the EEC became so marked, in contrast to the problems of the British economy, and as this form of policy had clearly failed, the situation had to be reviewed. In the light of the changing international and internal environments, membership of the EEC appeared to offer a solution to two sets of problems - those of Britain's position in the world and those of British economic capability.

NOTES

(1) D. Stikker, Men of Responsibility, Harper and Row, New York 1966, p.161.
(2) Ibid., pp.161-2.
(3) S. I. P. van Campen, The Quest for Security, Martinus Nijhoff, The Hague 1958, p.118.
(4) F. Willis, France, Germany and the New Europe, Oxford University Press, London 1968, p.80.
(5) Ibid.
(6) Ibid.
(7) P. Calvocoressi, Survey of International Affairs 1952, Oxford University Press, London 1955, pp.114-16.
(8) The Economist, 18 December 1954.
(9) S. J. Bodenheimer, Political Union: A Microcosm of European Politics, A. W. Sijthoff, Leyden 1967, p.165.
(10) Stikker, op.cit., pp.188-9.
(11) M. Camps, Britain and the European Communities, Oxford University Press, London 1964, p.20.
(12) Messina Resolution, Appendix A, ibid., pp.520-1.
(13) Ibid., p.45.
(14) Quoted ibid., p.24.
(15) The Economist, 25 June 1955; Financial Times, 23 June 1955.
(16) The Economist, 9 February 1957, p.484.
(17) Camps, op.cit., p.91.
(18) The Economist, 19 October 1957, p.236.
(19) Camps, op.cit., p.133.
(20) The Economist, 30 April 1960, p.432.
(21) Bodenheimer, op.cit.
(22) Ibid., p.152.
(23) Ibid., p.154.
(24) Ibid., pp.161-2.
(25) Although Camps points out that this position and those positions following were not the official 'stated' viewpoints. Camps, op.cit., pp.485-6.
(26) J. Frankel, British Foreign Policy 1945-73, Oxford University Press, London 1975, pp.234-5.
(27) Ibid., p.235.
(28) R. J. Lieber, British Politics and European Unity, University of California Press, Berkeley, Ca. 1970, pp.17-20.
(29) Nutting, House of Commons, 20 November 1951. Quoted ibid., p.17.
(30) D. Calleo, Britain's Future, Hodder and Stoughton, London 1968, p.42.
(31) Quoted Lieber, op.cit., p.17.
(32) Ibid., pp.19-20.
(33) H. Heiser, British Policy With Regard to Unification Efforts on the Continent, Sijthoff, Leyden 1959, pp.37-8.
(34) Weekly Hansard, House of Commons 101, 15 September 1948, Clmn. 106.

(35) Frankel, op.cit., p.237.
(36) Lieber, op.cit., pp.20-21.
(37) Quoted Heiser, op.cit., p.41.
(38) F. Northedge, Descent from Power, Allen and Unwin, London 1974, p.157.
(39) Camps, op.cit., p.11.
(40) A. Nutting, Europe Will Not Wait, Hollis and Carter, London 1960, p.34.
(41) Camps, op.cit., p.11.
(42) D. Butler, The British General Election of 1951, Macmillan, London 1962, p.47.
(43) Heiser, op.cit., ch. 4.
(44) Quoted Nutting, op.cit., p.35.
(45) Ibid., p.35.
(46) Ibid., p.41.
(47) Lieber, op.cit., p.27.
(48) Nutting, op.cit., p.83.
(49) See The Economist, 25 June 1955.
(50) Quoted Camps, op.cit., p.30.
(51) Camps, op.cit., p.48.
(52) See the extensive review of the debate, ibid., pp.105-110.
(53) Ibid., p.109.
(54) Lieber, op.cit., p.148.
(55) Ibid., pp.150-1.
(56) Camps, op.cit., pp.358-66.
(57) Northedge, op.cit., pp.337-8.
(58) Lieber, op.cit., p.163.

5 Dutch and British policies towards West European security

Fundamental to any understanding of Dutch foreign policy since 1945 is a recognition of the importance of the Second World War in altering Dutch perceptions of the policy appropriate for a small European power. The key aspects of Dutch foreign policy to be examined are those concerned with this shift, this form of adaptation to the new international environment.

The prevailing stance of Dutch foreign policy in the inter-war period was that of neutrality; for years the Netherlands had attempted to ensure security by the policy of neutrality.   In the view of Jacquet

> 'On the morning of May 10th 1940 the Netherlands' people awoke and saw with their own eyes that Dutch neutrality, which had existed for about a century, did not exist anymore.   It were (sic) the German paratroopers who brought the message.' (1)

The immediate question, in the light of the rather obvious failure of that stance, was what was to be the stance of the Dutch Government vis-a-vis neutrality in the new Europe.   Van Campen argues that 1945-50 was the period during which the new orientation of Dutch foreign policy finally overcame the old one (2).   As Van Campen points out, the inevitable effect of a policy being held for such a long time was that certain trends of thought continued long after the disappearance of the policy that contributed to their rise.

The fundamental problem, then, was: could the policy of neutrality offer real security in the post war world?   The issue appears to be less clearcut than might be imagined.   Not only had the policy of neutrality been handed down for generations - almost as a heritage - but it had been tested during the First World War and had succeeded, and in the idealistic period of collective security between the two World Wars it became cloaked with the sentiments of elevated idealism.   Thus, the argument advanced by many that the German attack on 10 May 1940 brought the policy of neutrality to an end, appears to be a simplification.   The complication is caused by the Dutch conception of neutrality which is linked closely to the concept of the balance of power.   Neutrality failed because the balance of power mechanism failed and thus the question was not primarily which policy should the Dutch adopt in the post war environment but what would be the nature of that environment.   The important variable that intervened in the conception of neutrality in comparison with the Dutch experience in World War One was that of occupation. Thus, whereas the events of 1914-18 had been regarded by large sections of the Dutch population as confirmation of the success of the policy of neutrality, the invasion put an entirely different conception on the policy.

As Stikker points out in his memoirs, the Dutch initially based their post war policy on collective security in the United Nations (3). The reliance on the United Nations was well in line with traditional Dutch faith and interest in the principles of international law and organisation, especially since the United Nations embodied the principle of universal cooperation, which in 1945 was still conceived as the most promising road to maintaining security. However, the Dutch Government's views on the United Nations - as expressed in two documents - one on Dutch suggestions on the Dumbarton Oaks proposals (dated January 1945) (4), the other a series of amendments to the proposed United Nations Charter at the San Francisco Conference (5) - were mixed. The Dutch Government called for the inclusion of a standard of international behaviour in the Charter, the observance of which would be ensured by

'the appointment of an independent body of eminent men . . . known for their integrity and their experience in international affairs . . . to pronounce upon decisions of the security council . . . from the point of view of whether or not the council's decision is in keeping with the moral principles above referred to.' (6)

The Dutch Government also wished to protect the small nations by ensuring that 'consent of half of the smaller states represented on the Security Council be required for decisions being taken.' (7) Fundamentally, the Dutch Government proposed that

'care should be taken not to repeat the mistake made in the Covenant of the League of Nations by virtue of which every member-state was pledged to apply, if required, armed force against adversaries unknown in advance, in the company of unknown partners and in unknown circumstances.' (8)

Thus, each state should be allowed to decide whether or not to participate in the application of armed force.

The Dutch Government was also concerned by the existence of the veto; they saw no point in having a general veto power for great powers since that

'would mean that any power having the right of veto could prevent the discussion of any matter raised, with the result that there would be no international forum left.' (9)

As the final Charter shows, the Dutch were not successful in their attempts to obtain these amendments. The debate in the States-General over Dutch membership of the United Nations saw the view commonly expressed that the United Nations would not prove to be a League of Nations with teeth. Van Kleffens argued that, whilst he accepted that there were structural problems with the United Nations, there was no alternative to it. Without a universal organisation like the United Nations, the Dutch Government feared universal anarchy. Thus, the Dutch Government had tried its best to obtain their preferred form of organisation - but they would rather have agreement on some form of international cooperation than no agreement at all. The Charter of the United Nations was, therefore, the best that could be obtained; it did embody the principle of universal cooperation without which the small states of the world would be endangered by the same forces of international anarchy that had engulfed the Netherlands in 1940.

Dutch policy towards the United Nations was motivated primarily by a desire to ensure stability in the post war world. This stability was fundamentally to be obtained through determination;

> ' . . . one thing is certain: a set of rules, however carefully devised and however perfect on paper, will never by itself suffice to maintain international peace and security. The best organisation is useless if the will of its members to wield it for the good of the world is lacking. Nothing but that determination can support the scheme and make it work as it should; without it, it will come crashing to the ground.' (10)

The important point with regard to this statement is that it was clearly based on the idea that the great powers (the United Kingdom, the US, France and the USSR) would be in agreement since 'nothing will help the world if the great powers are not in agreement'. (11)

Although the Netherlands Government was initially concerned with the nature of the post war world, the major problems facing the Government were those concerning domestic reconstruction. Of fundamental importance in this reconstruction was the position of Germany as a trading partner. In the realm of trade from 1930 to 1939, between 20 and 30 per cent of Dutch industrial imports came from Germany and about 15 to 20 per cent of Dutch industrial exports went to Germany - with Germany also a market of major importance for Dutch agriculture. Thus, there were for the Dutch two related problems that arose out of the four power occupation of Germany. First, the economic status of Germany, its economic relations with other countries, and the problem of reparations. Second, Germany's future political status, and the organisation of preventing renewed German aggression.

With regard to the problem of the economic position of Germany there was no single economic Germany - the Dutch had to deal with four separate zones. In addition to the level of interdependence in trade, the Dutch had much investment in Germany and also were heavily involved in providing shipping and other services. Given that the immediate policy of the four occupying powers was to limit the use of foreign exchange, the Netherlands was discriminated against in matters of trade. In the area of reparations, the Dutch Government felt entitled to reparations on a large scale. In a statement issued on 28 October 1944, the Dutch Government claimed the right to obtain territory in lieu of reparations (12). In 1945 they claimed 45,000 million fl. in reparations from Germany (13).

At the end of 1946, the States-General debated - surprisingly, for the first time - the general principles of foreign policy. Reflecting the developments noted above over the United Nations, the Government stated that the policy of neutrality was firmly rejected as the necessary condition for that policy - equilibrium - was no longer in existence. The Government proposed that it be replaced by support for collective security measures. Universal cooperation was the Government's first objective but this was to be backed up by collective security when necessary. Yet even this was to be channelled via the United Nations. With regard to regional blocs, the Government stressed the necessary distinction between economic/cultural blocs, and security blocs; the former, in the form of voluntary associations, were desirable and here the Government pointed as an example to the Benelux arrangement.

However, as far as security was concerned, the Government pointed out that their attitude to regional security blocs would depend on how the German problem was solved. Reflecting what appears to be a paradox in Dutch foreign policy, the Government wanted two conditions fulfilled vis-a-vis the German settlement: first, German aggression should be made impossible once and for all; second, the German economy should be allowed to re-establish itself gradually. If these conditions were fulfilled, the Netherlands would be the neighbour of a militarily weak yet economically viable Germany and thus the Netherlands would not require a West European bloc which, as a matter of principle, the Dutch Government felt was not desirable, since blocs tended to lead to the formulation of other blocs thereby further deteriorating the international climate. Furthermore, the Government stated that they felt that the prospects for cooperation in Western Europe were bleak. Cooperation between France and Germany was impossible - at least in the short term. Neither did the Dutch Government see the inclusion of Germany in any western bloc as desirable nor did they believe that any federal or supranational European organs were possible without the USSR or Great Britain since Europe would be in danger of domination by either France or Germany. Fundamentally, Dutch foreign policy, in general, was therefore formulated in a series of contingent possibilities - the independent variable being the nature and extent of great power agreement.

The events of 1947 showed that the possibility of great power agreement was increasingly unlikely. Van Campen cites the two major instances of this: first the breakdown of the four power conferences on the future of Germany; second, General Marshall's speech at Harvard (5 June 1947), which proposed what came to be known as the Marshall Plan and established the Organisation for European Economic Cooperation. The major political effect of the Marshall Plan was the overt split that it caused between the great powers. The speech of Marshall at Harvard was followed by a three power conference between Bevin, Bidault and Molotov in Paris on 27 June 1947. This resulted in a Soviet refusal to take part in the programme and was followed by the refusal of its East European satellites.

In November 1947, the States-General again discussed foreign affairs. The Government made it clear that universal cooperation was their primary objective and that they welcomed close cooperation - citing Benelux as the cornerstone of their foreign policy. However, the Government also pointed out that this position could only be maintained as long as the international situation did not show fundamental changes. Thus,

> 'should, contrary to our hopes, the division of Germany into
> western and eastern parts, assume a more or less definite
> character, the Government would feel impelled to reconsider
> their whole policy in Europe.' (14)

Nevertheless, the Government still refused to discuss alternative policies, persisting in a negative attitude towards European federalism or a Western European bloc. Although the Government preferred unity to chaos, and although they admitted that national solutions alone were not enough, a Western European bloc with a political character was seen as harmful to hopes of international cooperation. The Dunkirk Treaty (a bilateral defence agreement between France and Britain, signed

in March 1947) was also raised in the debate.   The Government stated
that it did not want to partake in a series of bilateral treaties,they
preferred regional treaties as outlined in article 52 of the United Nations Charter.   Furthermore, the Government again stated that it wished
to wait until the political character of Europe had revealed itself.

The collapse of four power cooperation over Germany meant that a
divided Germany was now looking likely, and, given the developments
vis-a-vis the Cold War that occurred in 1947, the probability was that
the western powers would deem their sectors of Germany to be of crucial
importance in the formation of a barrier to communism.   Essentially,
'Western' Germany assumed an importance in a wider political problem and,
given the nature of the Truman Doctrine, announced on 12 March 1947,
it was improbable that Dutch demands for territory would receive support
from a US concerned to prevent Soviet aggression in Western Europe.
The Dutch Government also had to take into account the economic situations of both the US and Britain, the former involved in a massive aid
programme, the latter in a severe economic position.   Thus, once the
political crisis of the Cold War set in the chances of Dutch policy
being supported by the US and Britain were greatly diminished.

For Dutch foreign policy the events concerning the breakdown of the
four power agreement over Germany combined with the general concern
during the first few months of the Cold War, resulted in a substantial
reappraisal of the fundamental tenets of that foreign policy.   On
22 January 1948, the British Foreign Secretary spoke in the House of
Commons and announced that he was proposing talks to

'develop our relations with the Benelux countries in concert with
(our) French colleagues . . . I hope treaties will be signed
with our near neighbours, the Benelux countries, making, with our
treaty with France an important nucleus in Western Europe.' (15)

Within a week of Bevin's speech the Governments of the Benelux countries met to discuss it at a conference in Luxemburg on 29-31 January.
At this meeting they agreed on the principles of a common policy - a
policy held by them throughout the negotiations.   The Benelux nations
proposed a regional multilateral agreement under articles 51, 52, 53
and 54 of the United Nations Charter - arguing that whilst other powers
might react strongly to bilateral agreements, no one could argue with
pacts as already envisaged in the United Nations Charter.   The Dutch
preference was for a regional system aimed at the consolidation of
Western Europe, directed against no power in particular, and which,
stressing the need for economic consolidation, would require German
participation.

However, when the French and British proposals were received, they
showed a large area of disagreement between them and the Benelux proposals since the French and British envisaged a series of bilateral treaties similar to the Dunkirk Treaty.   The Benelux proposal involved a
much wider interpretation of Bevin's statement than that held by the
British and French Governments.   Nevertheless, it was the multilateral,
regional proposal of the Benelux countries that was finally accepted and
Van Campen argues that this was the result of events in the global situation - especially the Soviet-inspired coup in Czechoslovakia of February 1948.   This made the British and French Governments move towards a

regional conception of defence.

The treaty was fully discussed in the States-General and, according to Van Campen, three main lines of opposition were expressed (16). Although the Government stressed the security aspect as the reason for breaking with neutrality - in that since the United Nations could not guarantee Dutch security it was the duty of the Netherlands Government to protect the country - there was a body of thought that objected fundamentally with the breaking of the policy of neutrality.

This first line of opposition rejected the pact because it broke with the policy of neutrality. The break with the old policy was to be considered a matter of profound regret and it was pointed out that neither the Scandinavian countries nor Switzerland had broken with the policy. It was feared that the prospects of the Netherlands being involved in war was greatly increased by the signing of the pact. The second line of argument was that of those agreeing with the treaty in principle but opposing certain terms of it. The treaty was criticised because it did not involve the dissolution of the Dunkirk Treaty. The main criticisms, however, were those concerned with any alliance with Britain and those concerned with the vagueness of the treaty. With regard to the former, it was pointed out that Britain was involved in an anti-Dutch policy in the Netherlands East Indies.

The third main bloc in the States-General was composed of those who saw the treaty as merely the beginning of a process that would eventually lead to some form of supranational organisation, and as such they warmly welcomed the pact, seeing it as the basis of a federal Europe. The Government's reaction to this was that this position was incompatible with the policy of universal cooperation, which was a more preferable policy to follow. Yet the debate finally resolved to support this conception of the Brussels Pact and the Government accepted this resolution.

With the ratification of the Brussels Treaty, formal Dutch foreign policy takes a definite turn: up to that point foreign policy was clearly in a period of transition, waiting to see how events unfolded. But with the obvious breakdown of the hoped for great power agreement over the post war world, Dutch foreign policy shifted towards a strong linkage with other western powers. The Brussels Treaty signified the transformation of Dutch foreign policy from an overt stance of independence and trying to be on good terms with every state to being tied closely to the wider Western European context.

During the discussions on the nature of the military organisation of the pact, which was a problem for Britain, France and the Netherlands - all with large troop commitments overseas - the USA and Canada were represented and the possible expansion of the pact became an important consideration. The position of the US was of crucial importance to the position of the Brussels Treaty Organisation in the same way that the Marshall Plan and the commitment of the US involved therein was crucial to the economic recovery of Europe. The aims of the pact were clearly in accord with the broad outline of American foreign policy as stated by President Truman in March 1947. Thus, it was of little surprise when the US invited representatives of the Brussels Pact powers and Canada to discussions in Washington on 6 July 1948. These discussions led to a draft treaty to include the US and Canada, which was approved in principle by the Brussels Pact Consultative Council in October.

At the end of the year, the Government stated the general principles of Dutch foreign policy and these illustrate the changes in foreign policy during 1948.   In response to the then clear split between the western powers and the USSR, the Government pointed out that its major preoccupation was closer association with other Western European powers.

The breakdown of the four power conferences on Germany in 1947 had the effect of forcing the three western occupying powers to decide whether to go on alone or persist with attempts at four power cooperation in the face of what appeared to be Soviet stonewalling.   Their decision was to go ahead on their own without the USSR in solving a number of urgent German questions and they met in London in February 1948, and, since this took place simultaneously with the negotiations for the Brussels Treaty, the Dutch, along with other Benelux nations, called for full participation.   Eventually, the Benelux nations were admitted to what became the six power conference which met from 23 February to 1 June 1948.

The conference, which was seen openly as the last chance for the Dutch Government to press its claims in the areas of reparations, territorial settlement, and the political and economic organisation of Germany, was almost a total failure for the Dutch.   As Van Campen notes, this failure, and indeed the whole progress of the conference, was due to the prevailing world situation (17).   It was, he claims, the decisive factor in forming the outcome of the conference.   What is meant by the world situation was the overt split between East and West, which resulted in fundamental differences emerging among the western great powers.   The first position was that represented by the US and this was one which the Dutch almost totally supported: the breach with the Soviet Union imposed the duty on the western powers of bringing and keeping Germany into the western orbit.

At the opposite extreme were the French, who argued that, although there was a rift between East and West, this should not allow the west to forget that there was another potential aggressor - Germany.   The main result of the conference was the proposal to draw up a constitution that would enable a West German Government to assume, initially, responsibilities compatible with minimum requirements of occupation, and, ultimately, full governmental responsibilities.

The Dutch attitude to the outcome of the conference was one of disappointment.   The Government stated that the conference was so unsuccessful for the Dutch because the US and Britain felt that the Dutch claims for reparations and territorial adjustments were politically inopportune and economically undesirable since the burden of paying reparations would either be carried by the occupying powers or by the Germans with money obtained from Marshall Aid (the European Recovery Programme).

However, there were positive results too - the Netherlands obtained some form of contact with the occupying powers over policy towards Germany.   The Dutch were to have a say over future developments regarding the Ruhr and foreign investments in Germany.   On 12 June the Benelux Governments stated that they approved the recommendations on Germany.

Thus, in 1948, Dutch policy towards Germany moved considerably from that of late 1947 - although the Government stressed that territorial and economic claims would be retabled at any peace conference. Yet it is clear that the Dutch Government was aware of the effect of the changing global situation on the settlement of the German question.

As mentioned above, in October 1948 the Consultative Council of the Brussels Pact approved the principle of a defensive pact for the North Atlantic area. Following a series of negotiations, which began on 10 December 1948, an agreed text was prepared and signed on 4 April 1949. Although in a wider context the North Atlantic Treaty may be seen as a major turning point - in that it involved for the first time in peacetime a European commitment by the USA and, as such, can be seen as one of the key dates of the Cold War - Van Campen argues that it was merely a logical development for Dutch foreign policy. In other words, it was the natural continuation of the reorientation that began with the Brussels Pact. Certainly, the debates in the States-General were clear in regarding the North Atlantic Treaty as a legitimate development in Dutch foreign policy, seeing it as a necessary measure to ensure national security in a situation where the expansion of the Soviet Union appeared threatening.

In the debate on the Treaty in the States-General, there was not much opposition to the concept of the Treaty per se, but there was considerable discussion over the issue of the Netherlands East Indies. Again, the question was asked as to whether the Netherlands should be combining with states such as the USA, Britain and Canada. Were not their actions in embargoing arms supplies incompatible with membership of a 'friendly' organisation generally and, for the US, was the action compatible with article 3 of the treaty, which stated that the US would deliver munitions and raw materials to European powers to aid them to resist armed attack? (18)

Stikker replied to such criticisms by stating that he did not feel there was any contradiction between these embargoes and membership of the North Atlantic Treaty and, rather illuminatingly, he stated that it was not the policy of the Government to make their ratification of the Treaty dependent upon the repeal of these embargoes (19).

Having outlined the evolution of post war Dutch foreign policy with regard to the major security factors it is now proposed to turn to discuss the major developments in Dutch security policy since 1950. It is a basic argument of this section that Dutch foreign policy had, by 1950, adopted an orientation that was both an obvious change from the old policy of neutrality and also represented the orientation that Dutch foreign policy followed for the remainder of the period under consideration. This section will, therefore, examine the debate over the European Defence Community (EDC) and the Dutch attitude to its security commitments from 1950 until 1963.

The issue of the EDC arose out of a reappraisal of western defences and Soviet intentions following the outbreak of the Korean War. In the west this was seen generally as a Russian-inspired move. It brought Europe to its feet with the immediate reaction being that in Korea - a divided country like Germany - a communist incursion had occurred despite US nuclear strength. This led the US Government to propose a package deal including the rearming of Germany, which was no longer seen by the US Government as a threat but rather as a solidly anti-communist state - in comparison to France with its large Communist Party.

The Dutch reaction to the American position was that an independent German army was not the best way forward. France, however, was the only nation unwilling to accept German rearmament in principle. The French alternative was the Pleven Plan for a European Defence Community, proposed by the Prime Minister on 24 October 1950. This proposed a United European Army, including Germans, under a European Minister of Defence responsible to a supranational council of ministers - thus rearming Germans without rearming Germany.

When the European Army Conference began in Paris on 15 February 1951, the Netherlands attended as an observer only. However, when

> 'there seemed to be a glimmer of hope . . . (the Dutch Government) decided, partly out of the desire to keep in step with our Benelux partners, that we would participate actively in the conference.' (20)

This 'glimmer of hope' in October 1951 followed the decision by the US Government to support the concept of a European Army - reflecting a general desire in the US Government to see Europe more closely unified, and a specific need to rearm Germany. Nevertheless, the Netherlands Government seems to have been motivated more by a desire to keep in step with Benelux than by any conviction that the plan was likely to succeed. This is backed up by the fact that, even with the US agreement to the concept of a European Army, the Netherlands Government was still 'too doubtful that the project would be anything but a waste of time to change its status as an observer only', (21) especially since the British Government, whose attitude was of crucial importance to the Dutch, had indicated that they would not participate.

However, the negotiations on the EDC did reach agreement on a European Defence Force in November 1951. The Netherlands were concerned especially over the issue of the budget and the nature of control over the army. The Dutch Government insisted that the budget should not be controlled by a European parliament but by national governments. They were also unwilling to accept supranational control over their troops - preferring a council of defence ministers rather than supranational authority (22). This reflected a general desire of the Government to proceed gradually with integration. This reflected a fear that the Benelux nations might be constantly outvoted by Italy, Germany and France and that this might weaken their ties with Britain and the US. Thus it was feared that France or Germany might dominate the Defence Community in a way that they could never do within an Atlantic alliance or in a European alliance including Britain. There were also strong feelings in the Netherlands Government that economic union should precede military union - especially a military union which was fraught with difficulties in organisation. Yet the Dutch had abandoned neutrality and did realise that their own defence and that of Europe required German participation.

Following constitutional amendments, ratification was virtually completed in the Netherlands by the end of 1952. However, from the date of initialling the treaty the prospect of the EDC being the solution to the problem of German rearmament decreased. The US was initially involved in a presidential election and thus was unwilling to push the matter; France was involved in Indo-China and thus stalled over ratification, partially because of the fear that whilst they were occupied elsewhere, the EDC could be dominated by Germany.

Thus, by 1954, the Benelux nations and West Germany had ratified the EDC Treaty. In France, the Government of Mendes - France finally put the treaty to the vote on 30 August 1954 without recommending its passage and it was defeated on a procedural question by 319 to 264. The result of this was that the EDC was finished.

Although the defeat in the French National Assembly was not a total surprise, the impact of it was twofold. First, to provide a severe psychological upset for the Europeans who had built high hopes on the EDC; second, it removed an entangling impediment from the scene - because of its existence, no progress towards the rearmament of Germany could occur, yet at the same time it was increasingly unlikely from 1952 onwards that it would be ratified. The result of this situation was that Eden convened a conference in London on 28 September 1954 with the US, Canada, France, Germany, Italy and the Benelux countries as participants, along with Britain. The results of the conference were the Paris Agreements signed on 23 October 1954. Under these agreements, Germany was to enter NATO as a sovereign nation and Germany and Italy were to join the Brussels Treaty, which was to be renamed the Western European Union (WEU). The major difference from the EDC negotiations with regard to the British position was that the British Government offered an undertaking not to withdraw its forces assigned to the Continent against the wishes of its partners. This was a solution that satisfied the Dutch Government and the WEU came into existence after being ratified by the members on 5 May 1955.

The Dutch attitude to western security has been summed up by a government official, quoted in Russell's penetrating study of this relationship, who states that 'the Dutch have no foreign policy: we have only NATO' (23). Russell's main thesis is that such a statement is as misleading as are the Government's statements of the principles on which Dutch foreign policy is based, i.e. international legal order, Atlantic solidarity, and European integration. Russell argues that the Dutch position vis-a-vis NATO is the result of the nature of the international political system combined with 'the internal features of the Netherlands (which) suggest the desire to pursue an Atlanticist policy'. (24)

Therefore, the Dutch attitude to NATO is that 'the European countries in NATO should declare their readiness to leave their nuclear defence entirely to the US' (25). This involves a Dutch policy against, in principle, both the French 'force de frappe' and the British 'independent' nuclear deterrent.

In the post war period then, the Dutch policy of orientation towards the USA and NATO was at first ' . . . not only a natural one, but almost the only option Dutch governments had . . . in a period of an almost completely bipolar world' (26). In an appraisal of the role of a small state in an alliance, Jacquet argues that, in these circumstances, the United States was the natural and accepted leader of the Western alliance - being the ideological leaders, having a nuclear monopoly and superior economic and financial resources (27). Since then the Dutch priority for Atlantic cooperation has been based on the conviction that ' . . . Dutch interests are best guaranteed by a world power that is at the same time strong and unbiased in European affairs' (28).

In more recent pronouncements, the Government has stated that the development of NATO was the only course available to the western nations after the Second World War; i.e., despite the common historical, political and cultural ties of the NATO countries, the activities of the Soviet Union were the direct cause of the North Atlantic Treaty.

It is the conclusion of this survey that Dutch foreign policy in the realm of security in the period under consideration was one of firm allegiance to NATO. As the Brussels Treaty merged its military responsibilities into NATO, and as the WEU ensured German rearmament within NATO, this allegiance was strengthened.

To understand British foreign policy in the immediate post war period it is necessary to realise that the policies - as in the Dutch case - did not simply emerge in 1945. As Frankel points out ' . . . policies are, of course, continuous, and Britain in 1945 was not starting with a tabula rasa in a new postwar world' (29). He suggests 1942 as a convenient starting date for an examination of post war foreign policy since it is then that the Government first became engaged in planning for the post war period. As Lord Gladwyn points out in his memoirs, there was a long and detailed debate within the Foreign Office as to whether Britain could continue her world role after the war. Whilst some officials felt that this was undesirable and that Britain should step down and see the responsibility pass to other powers, the effect of this decision would have been to relegate Britain to second rank status. Since this would involve the prospect of domination by one or more of the newly emergent great powers, the choice was to try and continue the world role even if this meant concentrating on a role of mediation and conciliation. At this early stage the preferred strategy for the post war period was the four power plan which was based on the assumption that the big three (Britain, the USA, the USSR), and France would be willing to cooperate in worldwide commitments to keep the peace. A secondary assumption was that the primary objective of such a cooperative venture would be to prevent the re-emergence of Japan and Germany. The

' . . . most promising strategy was to draw a clear boundary between Eastern Europe, where Russia would, inevitably, have the dominant influence, and Western Europe, led by Britain, and, with the assistance of the Americans, to maintain a balance between the two.' (30)

Yet the exact pattern of alignments in British post war policy were by no means clear - in 1942-43 the Soviet Union was still a possible post war ally and stated American policy over the colonies clearly made an American alignment questionable.

With regard to the United Nations, British policy as outlined in the four power plan was for a continuance of consultation among the big three plus France rather than for a universal organisation, which was deemed unlikely and probably undesirable (31). However, given the feeling in the United States Government for a new universal organisation to replace the League (due to its association with failure, and Russian

89

reaction following being expelled from it in 1939) the British committed
themselves to a universal organisation in the Moscow Declaration of
the Four Nations on General Security on 30 October 1943. This was
further extended in the Teheran Declaration of December 1943.

British policy with regard to the actual negotiations over the subs-
tance of the United Nations can be summarised as an attempt to continue
the great power cooperation of the war whilst preventing the incursion
of the United States into the sensitive question of the British Empire.
The British were, therefore, eager to support the plans of the US
Government ' . . . if only because it would bind the US to participate
in world affairs as she had omitted to do in the years between the
wars' (32).   Indeed, the basic concern of British policy over the post
war environment was expressed in 1943 by Eden in a cabinet paper that
stressed the need for the great powers to agree on a common world policy
and being prepared to act together to enforce it;

> 'failing this we shall be confronted by the prospect of a world
> in precarious balance, with the great powers, each with its circle
> of client States facing each other in a rivalry which will merge
> imperceptibly into hostility' (33).

At the Dumbarton Oaks conference, the British representatives succeeded
in leaving undecided the work of the United Nations on colonial issues.
In the Charter, the United Nations was barred from encroaching on the
Empire by the provisions concerning domestic jurisdiction (Article 2)
and non self-governing territories (Article 73).   Furthermore, the
existence of the veto allowed Britain to protect this sensitive issue
area.

In a general election immediately after the end of the war the Labour
Party achieved a massive victory - gaining some 48 per cent of the total
vote and a lead of 247 seats in the House of Commons.   This victory was
expected to bring a vast change in British foreign policy.   However,
in Bevin's first speech to the House of Commons as Foreign Secretary
he denounced 'socialist foreign policy, as fantasy' (34).   In fact,
by October 1945, Bevin and Attlee had, according to Gordon, rejected
any hope of an accord with the USSR.   As McNeil writes ' . . . Whatever
their differences over domestic matters, Bevin and Churchill saw nearly
eye to eye with respect to British foreign policy' (35).

Combined with this change of British Government, the economic situation was the other major domestic factor in British foreign policy in
the immediate post war period.   Northedge in his study of British
foreign policy discusses these problems under the chapter heading 'The
Bankrupt Estate', and comments

> ' . . . the domestic cupboard was bare, the population down-at-heel
> and much industrial property superannuated' (36).

This economic situation, says Frankel,

> 'constituted the major restraint on her freedom of manoeuvre both
> at home and abroad' (37).

On top of these problems, which the new Government had only had a short time to consider, came the sudden cancellation of the American lend-lease supplies on 1 August 1945.

With regard to British policy towards the occupation of Germany, the British zone of occupation comprised the most highly industrialised areas, - notably the Ruhr. These regions were the most devastated regions. Given the lack of agreement on how the four occupation zones were to be organised, the previous economic whole was now divided so that the industrial regions in British hands were cut off from their agricultural suppliers in the Soviet zone. Given the domestic problems for the British Government, the necessity of feeding the 20 million or so Germans in their occupation zone constituted a severe drain on British resources - in 1946 some £80 million was spent by the British in the zone of occupation. Thus, British policy towards French and Soviet claims for reparations was primarily determined by a desire to see an economically viable Germany develop to aid European recovery generally and alleviate the costs to Britain of occupation specifically.

On 4 June 1946 Bevin reviewed foreign affairs and stressed the necessity of agreement and cooperation between the great powers but added that, because of the current situation ' . . . we cannot be forced to acquiesce in an indefinite stalemate' (38). The possibilities in international affairs were: a balance between states of equal strength; the domination by one power or by two blocs of powers - both of these were not considered feasible and thus he proposed a united effort by the four powers with the cooperation of smaller allies. In the United Nations the British would act as an intermediary between the USA and the USSR. This situation is summed up by Gordon as the Government's 'two-sided predicament'. It perceived a Soviet threat and could do little about it alone, yet the US Government seemed unwilling to play the role the Labour Government desired of it.

Fitzsimons asserts that 1947 was the 'decisive year' for British foreign policy (39). The winter of 1946-47 was an exceptionally heavy one that resulted in coal supplies to industry being cut by 50 per cent. This was followed by an exceptionally dry spring. On one level this severe winter was important in emphasising the need for massive capital inputs to allow recovery. Thus, the British Government leapt at Marshall's speech and held talks with France on 17 and 18 June which, following the Soviet rejection of the programme, was followed by a conference chaired by Bevin, to draw up the European response to the proposal as demanded by Marshall.

At another level, the winter of 1946-47 precipitated a crisis in British thinking with regard to their overseas commitments. Plans were in hand to give independence to large areas of the Empire but more fundamentally a reappraisal was necessary concerning British commitments in Europe. As Wheeler-Bennett and Nicholls point out, the situation was especially desperate with regard to Greece where the ruling military government was being supported, against a communist rebellion, by the British to the tune of some $275 million for 1947. On 21 February, the British Government informed the American Secretary of State that Britain could no longer provide economic aid to Greece and Turkey. The reaction in the US was the announcement of the Truman Doctrine on 12 March 1947, which pledged American aid for 'free peoples who are resisting attempted subjugation by armed minorities and by outside

pressure'.   The Truman Doctrine and the Marshall Plan represented the
firm emplacement of British foreign policy in the US orbit.

The continuing economic problems also had their effects in British
policy towards Germany.   The main requirement for British policy was
to see European and world economic recovery and this necessitated the
recovery of Germany.   For Britain, therefore, the choice was either to
let the USSR have vast reparations and share control of the Ruhr in
return for the treatment of Germany as one economic unit, or the Western
powers building up a Western Germany and thus divide Germany.   Britain
and the USA had already agreed to combine their zones of occupation as
from 1 January 1947.   At the Moscow and London conferences of the
Foreign Ministers in 1947, the differences between the US-UK views on
economic and political issues and those of the USSR were wide and both
meetings failed to resolve these issues.   With Marshall Aid, the
western zones were included in the sphere of the aid.   By this time
what Fitzsimons calls 'the logic of disagreement' between the USSR and
the other great powers was complete, and what Northedge calls 'the parting of the ways' was in full swing (40). This 'logic of disagreement' led
to the establishment of a separate German state in 1949.

Following the signature of the Dunkirk Treaty between Britain and
France on 4 March 1947, and following the 'parting of the ways' of 1947,
Bevin, speaking in the House of Commons on 22 January 1948, called for
West European union.   He started by outlining the three principles of
the Government's foreign policy

' . . . The first is that no one nation should dominate Europe.
The second is that the old fashioned conception of the balance
of power as an aim should be discarded if possible.   The third
is that there be substituted four power cooperation and assistance
to all the states of Europe, to enable them to evolve freely each
in its own way.' (41)

Bevin then recited the list of disagreements with the Soviet Union and
concluded that the third principle was impractical.   These developments

'point to the conclusion that the free countries of West Europe must
draw closely together . . . I believe the time is ripe for a
consolidation of Western Europe.' (42)

However, as discussed above the resultant treaty turned out to be a
multilateral one.   The Berlin crisis - itself a response to the increasing western cooperation and integration of their economic zones - acted
as an impetus for the transformation of the Brussels Pact into the North
Atlantic Treaty (NAT).   British policy towards the NAT was pragmatic
since four power cooperation had clearly failed and the United Nations
was of little use in maintaining security; thus, the NAT was 'a practical way of dealing with a practical question' (43).

Thus, by 1949, Britain was committed to the defence of West Europe by
the Brussels Treaty and to the defence of the Atlantic Community by the
NAT; the major tenets of security policy were set.   Although continuing
to act as an independent great power in areas such as the possession of
nuclear weapons, the basic orientation of British foreign policy towards
security was set with the signature of the NAT.   However, although

British defence policy in the 1950s represents a closer alignment with the US position over security despite the occasional differences - notably the Suez issue - one area that seems especially pertinent to the subject of this study is that of the British attitude towards the European Defence Community (EDC).

The British attitude to the EDC is somewhat complicated by the fact that it was Churchill who, in August 1950, speaking at the Consultative Assembly of the Council of Europe, proposed a

'unified European army subject to proper European democratic control and acting in full cooperation with the US and Canada'. (44)

However, when the Pleven Plan was announced, the position of the British Government was that the plan duplicated the existing NATO structure. Bevin, speaking in the House of Commons on 29 November 1950, stated that the Government would prefer to see NATO built up as the only organisation in the military sphere (45). The British Government was unwilling to submit its forces to the proposed supranational controls. However, Bevin argued that although the British Government felt that the proposal was misguided, they would not stand in the way - and indeed they attended the discussions as observers.

As Stikker argues, the return of the Conservatives to power in 1951 was expected at least to 'result in full British participation in the Paris Conference' (46). However, the Conservative Government put forward the same reservations as had the Labour Government. As Eden argued in a memorandum to Churchill on 1 December 1951, ' . . . I have never thought it possible that we could join such an army' (47). He concluded that

'(a) we should support the Pleven Plan, though we cannot be members of it . . . (b) If the Pleven Plan does collapse we should try to work out a more modest scheme with our allies, based upon the technical military arrangements agreed upon, but without elaborate political superstructure.' (48)

This rejection of the prospect of British membership of the Community was combined with a desire to 'do anything which might assist in the creation of a European army, short of British participation' (49).

The reasons for British non participation in the EDC were summed up by Eden in a speech at Columbia University in January 1952 when he stated that 'This is something which we know, in our bones, we cannot do . . . for Britain's story and her interests lie far beyond the continent of Europe.' (50) These reservations were expressed more succinctly by Churchill in the House of Commons in May 1953

' . . . We are not members of the EDC, nor do we intend to be merged in a Federal European system. We feel we have a special relationship to both. This can be expressed by prepositions, by the prepositions "with" but not "of" . . . we are with them but not of them. We have our Commonwealth and Empire.' (51)

British policy was, therefore, based on the doctrine of the 'three circles', as stated by Churchill at the Conservative Party Conference in October 1948. According to this viewpoint, Britain was to continue to play three roles: a European power, the special ally of the United States and the centre of the vast Commonwealth. Thus, the primary aim of British foreign policy was to avoid the choice of having to decide exclusively between these roles.

The essence of British foreign policy over the EDC was, therefore, to offer as little as necessary to the countries involved in the EDC negotiations to allow for the rearmament of Germany, yet not allow British forces to be subject to any form of supranational authority. Thus, if the plan failed, provisions were to be made for the rearmament of Germany to take place within a structure that was more acceptable to the British adherence to the three circles policy.

Within months of the collapse of the EDC and the concomitant plan for a European Political Community (EPC), the British Government took the lead in solving the problem of German rearmament. As Eden had pointed out in 1951, the second stand of British policy should be to offer a less entangling alternative should EDC collapse. The proposal of Eden for the Western European Union allayed the fears of Benelux by involving the British in European military matters and at the same time rearmed Germany and ensured US presence in European defence. For the French Government the disquiet over the incorporation of Germany into NATO was balanced by the revised Brussels Treaty (now WEU), which contained certain safeguards related to the problems of German rearmament. The British commitment to the WEU was to maintain British forces on the Continent and

> 'not to withdraw those forces against the wishes of the majority
> of the Brussels Treaty Powers who should take their decision in
> the knowledge of the Supreme Allied Commander's views.' (52)

The importance of the British commitment to WEU was that the rearmament, and the re-emergence as a sovereign state, of Germany was ensured. The actual offer was little different from that made to the EDC, the difference being the agreement not to withdraw forces without the agreement of the majority of the WEU powers. It was, however, made in one package, in direct contrast to the piecemeal nature of British commitments to the EDC.

CONCLUSION

The dominant theme of Dutch foreign policy in the area of security after the Second World War was one of the movement away from neutrality to a very full commitment to the Atlantic Alliance. As Baehr has noted

> 'a firm policy of anti-communism and of alliance with the Atlantic
> nations on the one hand, a strong commitment to European cooperation
> on the other hand - these have formed the foundations of the
> foreign policy of the Netherlands since the Second World War.' (53)

The move away from neutrality was by no means a straightforward one; neutrality did not disappear as easily as has often been painted. As Van Campen has argued, it is only with the signature of the Brussels

Treaty (17 March 1948) that the period of neutrality ended(54). This
reliance on neutrality had resulted in the Dutch Government basing its
hopes on the collective security of the United Nations. Thus, whilst
the old stance of total neutrality, which had dominated Dutch foreign
policy for decades, was totally discredited by the German invasion on
10 May 1940, the immediate post war period saw the Dutch Government
essentially attempting to adapt that policy to the requirements of the
situation. Thus the moves towards the North Atlantic Treaty were by
no means straightforward and clearcut.

The discredited policy of neutrality had failed primarily because the
conception of politics on which it was based - the balance of power -
had failed. In a post war situation in which such a balance of power
increasingly appeared unlikely to develop this policy clearly required
modification. The initial formulation of this policy was to base aspirations on the United Nations and collective security. However, the
nature of the United Nations was not in line with the interests of the
Dutch. Nevertheless, the Government's position was that it was the
only alternative and they had achieved the most acceptable form of universal organisation that they could.

The German problem illustrates the way in which the reliance of the
Dutch Government on great power agreement gradually diminished. Initially, the Dutch stressed the need for a united Germany in order to
ensure peace and security on the one hand and to allow economic recovery
on the other. However, the large measure of disagreement between the
great powers effectively prevented any concerted action on these demands.
With the failure of the London and Moscow meetings in 1947, a divided
Germany became the most likely development. This overt split between
the Soviet Union, and Britain and the United States resulted in a settlement for Germany that effectively ignored Dutch demands for territorial
adjustments and for economic reparations.

The split between the great powers that occurred in 1947 had the
effect of dividing Europe and, in this division, the Dutch Government
moved gradually towards the Western bloc, gradually - not because there
was ever any thought of agreement with the Soviet Union - but because
there was still considerable opposition within the Netherlands to any
policy which represented a move away from neutrality or at least from
reliance on collective security. The Dutch signature of the Brussels
Treaty and the North Atlantic Treaty were by no means fully supported
in the States-General but, ever since then, the Dutch have manifested
a policy of total support for the Atlantic Alliance. By 1949, therefore, the transformation of Dutch foreign policy from its pre war neutrality stance to one of strong allegiance to the Atlantic Alliance had
occurred.

The debate over the European Defence Community and the Dutch policy
towards NATO since 1950, illustrate the continuity in Dutch foreign
policy. With regard to the EDC, the Dutch Government adopted a position of scepticism - attending initially as an observer. In essence,
the Dutch never saw the EDC as the best way of strengthening what was
the main plank of their foreign policy - NATO. The eventual agreement
over Western European Union represented just that form of strengthening
NATO.

Russell's excellent study of the Netherlands and the Atlantic Alliance
shows that the wholesale support of the Dutch for NATO is based on their
willingness to leave the nuclear defence of Europe to the United States
and on their desire, as a small state, to ensure access to and some
influence over the United States (55). The high level of Dutch activity within NATO reflects this desire.

With regard to security, therefore, the general nature of Dutch foreign
policy from 1945 to 1963 was one of a tentative and temporary reliance
on collective security within the United Nations and a desire for a
peace treaty to create a united and economically strong Germany; this
was transformed, as the international situation developed, into a policy
of membership of the Western bloc with the cornerstone of that policy
being reliance on NATO and the American commitment.

British foreign policy in the area of security was based on the wartime conception of the four power plan - whereby the Big Three (the
USA, the USSR and Britain) and France would cooperate in keeping the
peace in the post war world and in preventing the emergence of Japan
and Germany. This conception coloured the policy of the British
Government towards the negotiations over the United Nations - it was to
be based on great power cooperation. In the immediate post war period,
British policy was severely restrained by economic difficulties and it
was these which determined British policy towards Germany. On the one
hand the British were unwilling to continue with massive financial aid
to Germany in the face of such vast economic difficulties at home, and,
on the other, Britain was determined to see an economically viable
Germany emerge to aid the progress of European economic recovery.

In realisation that the world could split into two blocs, Bevin stated
that the aim of British foreign policy would be to aid agreement between
the United States and the Soviet Union. In reality, this desire for
agreement was most seriously shattered in 1947; this was the decisive
year for British foreign policy. It was the year in which the severe
economic circumstances forced the British Government to cut back on
their overseas commitments - resulting in the speech by Truman pledging
United States' support for the free peoples of the world. It was the
year in which Marshall aid was proposed, and was gratefully accepted by
the British Government. These two features indicate the firm location
of British foreign policy within the American orbit by 1947. At
another level, 1947 represented the final breakdown of the great power
control over Germany and the creation of Bizonia indicated that the
'parting of the ways' was in full swing.

This policy stance by Britain was deepened by the signing of the
Brussels and the North Atlantic Treaties, so that by 1949 Britain was
committed to the defence of West Europe and the Atlantic. This commitment was, however, not total: by that it is meant that neither Labour
nor Conservative Governments were willing to step outside the centre of
the 'three circles'. The policy of the Labour and Conservative Governments over the EDC illustrates this reluctance.

The basic stand of British foreign policy over the area of security
is that, unlike the Dutch, the British Government had no conception of
their role in the post war world as being that of a neutral power. For
the British Government, the initial aim was for great power cooperation

and, as ·this became increasingly unlikely, the aim was for Britain to
act as a mediator.   As, in turn, this policy became impossible to
realise, attention turned to the formation of a Western pact.   This
policy stance was buttressed by the severe economic difficulties facing
the British Government.   From the signing of the Brussels and North
Atlantic Treaties, the major tenet of British policy was that of close
alignment with the United States, although as the problem of Suez and
the British independent nuclear deterrent show, this was only one -
even if the major - strand of policy.   As the British position on the
EDC indicates, Britain was conceived as being in such as international
position as to rule out any total commitment to Europe in security terms.

NOTES

(1) L. G. M. Jacquet, 'The Netherlands', in A. Schou and A. Brundtland
(eds), Small States in International Relations, Almqvist and Wiksell,
Stockholm 1971, p.60.
(2) S. I. P. Van Campen, The Quest for Security, Martinus Nijhoff,
The Hague 1958, p.10.
(3) D. Stikker, Men of Responsibility, Harper and Row, New York 1966,
p.205.
(4) 'Suggestions presented by the Netherlands Government concerning the
proposals for the maintenance of peace and security agreed on at the
four powers conference of Dumbarton Oaks' - as published on 9 October
1944, in Van Campen, op.cit., Appendix One, pp.163-179.
(5) 'Declaration regarding the defeat of Germany and the assumption of
supreme authority with respect to Germany by the Governments of the
United Kingdom, the United States, the USSR and the Provisional Government of the French Republic', in Van Campen, op.cit., Appendix Two,
pp.180-186.
(6) See footnote 4, Appendix One of Van Campen, op.cit., p.168. For
the principles referred to, see pp.178-79.
(7) Ibid., p.172.
(8) Ibid., p.170.
(9) Ibid.
(10) Van Campen, op.cit., Appendix One, p.165.
(11) Ibid.
(12) 'Statement issued by the Netherlands Government, 28 October 1944',
ibid., Appendix Four, pp.203-204.
(13) 'Memorandum of the Netherlands Government containing the claims
of the Netherlands to reparations from Germany', ibid., Appendix Five,
pp.205-218.
(14) Ibid., p.41.
(15) Quoted, ibid., p.57.
(16) Ibid., pp.66-78.
(17) Ibid., pp.93-4.
(18) Ibid., pp.110-1.
(19) Ibid., p.112.
(20) Stikker, op.cit., p.301.
(21) R. McGeehan, The German Rearmament Question, University of Illinois
Press, Urbana, Ill. 1971, p.137.
(22) Ibid., p.157.
(23) R. Russell, 'The Atlantic Alliance in Dutch foreign policy',
Internationale Spectatore, 1969 (2), p.1189.
(24) Ibid., p.1190.

(25) Ibid., p.1191.
(26) Jacquet, op.cit., p.67.
(27) Ibid.
(28) Ibid., p.65.
(29) J. Frankel, British Foreign Policy 1945-73, Oxford University Press, London 1975, p.175.
(30) Ibid., p.177.
(31) Lord Gladwyn, Memoirs 1914-63, Weidenfeld and Nicolson, London 1971, p.113.
(32) J. Wheeler-Bennett and A. Nicholls, The Semblance of Peace, Macmillan, London 1972, p.89.
(33) Ibid., pp.538-9.
(34) M. Gordon, Conflict and Consensus in Labour's Foreign Policy 1914-65, Stanford University Press, Stanford, Ca. 1969, p.105.
(35) W. McNeil, America, Britain and Russia 1941-46, London 1953, p.629.
(36) F. Northedge, Descent from Power, George Allen and Unwin, London 1974, p.38.
(37) Frankel, op.cit., p.182.
(38) 423, H. C. Debs., 4 June 1946, Col. 1835.
(39) M. Fitzsimons, The Foreign Policy of the British Labour Government 1945-51, Notre Dame University Press, Notre Dame, Ind. 1953, ch. 4.
(40) Northedge, op.cit., p.82.
(41) 446, H. C. Debs., 22 January 1948, Col. 390.
(42) Ibid.
(43) Northedge, op.cit., p.95.
(44) Quoted Fitzsimons, op.cit., p.141.
(45) Quoted M. Camps, Britain and the European Communities, Oxford University Press, London 1964, p.13.
(46) Stikker, op.cit., p.302.
(47) A. Eden, Full Circle, Cassell, London 1960, p.33.
(48) Ibid., p.34.
(49) Ibid., p.35.
(50) Ibid., p.36.
(51) Quoted H. Heiser, British Policy With Regard to Unification Effects on the Continent of Europe, Sijthoff, Leyden 1959, p.63.
(52) Northedge, op.cit., pp.168-9.
(53) P. Baehr, 'The Foreign Policy of the Netherlands', in R. Barston, The Other Powers, Allen and Unwin, London 1972, p.76.
(54) van Campen, op.cit., p.145.
(55) See Russell, op.cit.

6 Anglo-Dutch interaction — the Netherlands East Indies

The last two chapters have focussed on case studies of parallel and divergent behaviour; in this chapter, the focus will be on a case study of interaction in order to offer a survey of the foreign policies of the two states that deals with as wide a coverage as space permits.

In order to appreciate fully the importance of the events in Indonesia for Anglo-Dutch relations it is necessary to see both the nature of Anglo-Dutch relations before the conflict and to have some historical background for the conflict itself. It is, therefore, necessary to say something about the nature of Anglo-Dutch relations in 1945 before turning to discuss the historical build-up to the conflict in Indonesia.

What is clear is that Anglo-Dutch relations in the first half of 1945 were very cordial: as Attlee said in the House of Commons on 17 October 1945,

' . . . we are very conscious of the fact that throughout these years the Netherlands Government have stood with us and that the difficulties that face them inevitably arise from the conditions of waging war.' (1)

As Bevin recalled,

'it must be remembered . . . that the Netherlands Government stood by us when we were attacked by Japan. They were, I believe, the first actually to declare war on Japan.' (2)

Thus, the relationship between the two states, before the onset of the differences over Indonesia, was one between wartime allies with little to disagree about, and with both concentrating on the need for postwar recovery. The two states had had considerable economic ties before the Second World War, had allied in the fight against the axis powers, and in 1945 were preparing to build up the new Europe. On the surface, and from the informed press reports at that time, there were no major areas of disagreement. The wartime friendship was, however, to be subjected to strains as the events of the Indonesian conflict unfolded.

The Indonesian conflict centres on the group of islands called, in 1945, the Netherlands East Indies (NEI). The NEI comprises Sumatra, Java, Dutch Borneo, Celebes and fifteen minor islands. The most populous island in 1945 being Java, with a population of 60 million. The islands became Dutch colonies in the 17th century, having been first opened up to Dutch trade in the late 16th century. The main products were rubber, oil, tin and copra - and by 1939 the economic benefit accruing to the Netherlands was considerable. The pressure for independence found its first concrete organisational expression with the formation of the Budo Utomo. When the Dutch declared war on Japan, the NEI was overrun by the Japanese in the first three months of 1942 - most of the Dutch administration fleeing to Australia.

The Dutch administration was destroyed and replaced by Japanese control; more than 60,000 Dutch officials and population were interned. The old social order was overthrown, with the use of the Dutch language being forbidden. The internment of the Dutch and the general treatment of them as inferior to the indigenous population, together with the Japanese use of Indonesian rather than the Dutch language, helped spread ideas of unity. With the Japanese in control, life went on without the Dutch with the Indonesians having a greater say in political life (partly because the Japanese were lacking in knowledge about the NEI). The Japanese consolidated their control over the NEI by obtaining the support of Hatta and Soekarno (later the leaders of the infant Republic of Indonesia), who were willing to cooperate with the Japanese in return for independence. Through Hatta, Soekarno and others, the Japanese spread anti-Western views which further accelerated the nationalist cause. The Japanese carefully controlled this desire for national determination by a series of promises of independence. The result of this process was that, by the time that the Japanese surrendered on 15 August 1945, a strong nationalist movement was ready to seize power; an independent republic was proclaimed on 17 August.

Dutch policy towards the Japanese invasion was outlined in a speech by Queen Wilhelmina on 6 December 1942. She proposed

> ' . . . a Commonwealth in which the Netherlands, Indonesia, Sumatra . . . will participate with complete self reliance and freedom of conduct for each partner regarding its internal affairs, but with the readiness to render mutual assistance.' (3)

In April 1944 the British and the Dutch drew up an agreement over Sumatra (which the British were to reoccupy on behalf of the Joint Chiefs of Staff). However, the Joint Chiefs of Staff transferred the reoccupation of Java from the US Pacific Command under MacArthur to the British South East Asia Command (SEAC) under Mountbatten, a decision taken to enable MacArthur to concentrate on the expected invasion of Japan. The Dutch were opposed to this change, since they had concentrated their limited resources on the US machine in Australia, whereas SEAC was directed from India. The decision was made in late July, with the handover of command to fall to Mountbatten on the surrender of the Japanese. As a consequence of this decision, the civil affairs agreement for Sumatra was now extended to Java - an agreement concluded on 24 August 1945. The main part of the agreement concerned the transfer of power to the Dutch. The agreement said

> '1. In areas affected by military operations it is necessary to contemplate a first or military phase during which the Supreme Allied Commander will, to the extent necessitated by the military situation, <u>de facto</u>, possess full authority . . .
>
> 2. It is agreed that the Netherlands Indies Government will resume as rapidly as practicable full responsibility for the civil administration of liberated Netherlands Indies territory . . .
>
> 3. The Netherlands Indies Government and the Netherlands Indies administrative and judicial services will be re-established as rapidly as possible.' (4)

This agreement clearly envisaged a smooth transfer of power to the
Dutch. Indeed, when the Japanese surrendered, the surrender treaty
ordered the Japanese troops to prevent any political changes and keep
order until the allied troops arrived.

However, despite what might have been expected, the situation in
practice turned out to be much more complex. When the Japanese surrendered, the military responsibility for the NEI fell on SEAC. But SEAC
had had less than one month's notice and, as indeed the Dutch said at
the time, (5) they were, in contrast to the USA, unprepared. The
sudden Japanese surrender found SEAC without any plans for discharging
their responsibility. In the NEI, of course, the Republic had been
proclaimed on 17 August. The Japanese army sat by and did nothing,
despite their treaty obligations noted above. In fact, they allowed
the new administration to start work and actually supplied it with arms
while the Dutch internees were kept in confinement under Indonesian
guard.

Thus, as of August 1945, the situation immediately before the British
became involved in the NEI was that the Dutch stood by the policy
announced in the Queen's speech of 1942. They could not, under this
policy, recognise the Indonesian Republic, a republic that did not intend
to be part of the Commonwealth. They felt it essential to restore the
economy of the NEI before they would even talk of self-government, and
the Dutch felt they could carry this out more effectively than the
Republican leaders. Yet in the NEI, the only government that existed
in September 1945 was that of the Republic, the Japanese having allowed
them to take over full control. The situation was thus that de jure
the NEI was Dutch, but de facto it was Indonesian. SEAC had to abide
by the civil affairs agreement of 24 August 1945, and thus restore the
Dutch to the NEI. But, the primary task of SEAC was to disarm the
Japanese troops and then to release prisoners of war. That was the
setting for the events of the next four years, which strained the friendly wartime relationship between the Dutch and the British.

Although the period of British military involvement was to lead to the
most serious clashes between the British and Dutch Governments, the conflict of opinion over how to undertake the military occupation had earlier origins. As has already been noted, the Dutch opposed the transfer
of the responsibility for the reoccupation of the NEI from the USA to
Britain for the reason that they had concentrated their resources on
the administration of the US. However, the evidence appears to indicate that their true reasons were somewhat more basic. As I. N.
Djajadiningrat writes in his history of the Dutch-Indonesian dispute

> ' . . . Van Mook was of the opinion . . . that the Dutch cause in
> Indonesia would be better served if the archipelago remained
> part of the American command. Moreover, he felt that the existing
> Dutch relations with the Americans were better than those with
> Mountbatten's command.' (6)

This view was strengthened at the Honolulu conference, when MacArthur
accused the British of being interested in gaining economic and political
advantages by reoccupying the NEI. Thus, even before the Japanese
surrendered, there existed an area of friction in British-Dutch relations.

Indeed, even when it was announced publicly on 11 August 1945 that the SEAC would be responsible for the reoccupation of the NEI, a special correspondent of the Manchester Guardian reported that

'. . . The Dutch authorities are quite frank in admitting their
concern over this interregnum. They feel that the business of
handling the islands at the present time is one which requires
tact, patience, and experiences which they only, so far as the
Indies are concerned, possess. They do not feel that either
the British or the Americans have at their disposal the number
of men knowing the languages and minds of the Indonesians
sufficiently well to deal with the situation.' (7)

Despite such feelings, the British Supreme Commander for South East Asia, (Earl Mountbatten), who on 15 August assumed responsibility for the NEI, had to make immediate plans for the reoccupation. However, as he writes in his report to the Combined Chiefs of Staff,

'it was clear that my forces were (not) adequate to secure the
speedy, orderly re-establishment of civil governments . . . I
therefore had no alternative but to instruct the Japanese, through
their Supreme Commander, to maintain order in the areas for which
they had been responsible up to the termination of hostilities . . .
For this purpose I maintained the existing Japanese Chain of
Command.' (8)

Yet, and this is of considerable importance to the events that followed, Mountbatten had no intelligence reports on the NEI. Thus

'. . . I had been given no hint of the political situation which
had arisen in Java. It was known of course that an Indonesian
Independence Movement had been in existence before the war . . .
but no information had been made available to me, as to the fate
of this movement under the Japanese occupation.' (9)

As an indication of the Dutch knowledge of the area Mountbatten recalls

'. . . Dr. van Mook, who had come to Kandy on 1 September 1945,
had given me no reason to suppose that the reoccupation of Java
would present any operational problems, beyond that of rounding
up the Japanese.' (10)

Again, Mountbatten notes a meeting with van Mook and the senior members of the SEAC Netherlands Staff Mission on 3 September, at which preliminary questions concerning the reoccupation had been discussed

'. . . but the Dutch authorities had been unable to give me any
indication of the state of affairs actually prevailing in the NEI.
When I referred to a leaflet which had been prepared for dropping
on Java, instructing the inhabitants to obey neither the Japanese,
nor the self-styled Indonesian Republic, Dr. van Mook informed me
that this appeared to be a mistranslation.' (11)

However, Mountbatten soon became aware that the situation in Java was very different than he had been led to expect. Rather poignantly, the Economist summed up the dilemma facing the British:

' .... If they use their military power to suppress . . . the
Indonesians, they will come under a barrage of criticism from the
Chinese, Russians, Indians and Americans. If they fail to suppress
the local movements they will earn the ill-will of their nearest
neighbours in Europe. The worst of all policies would be to
suppress local movements enough to anger the Americans but not
enough to reassure the Dutch.' (12)

On 28 September, Mountbatten told van der Plas that Britain would not
be involved in internal politics in the NEI. But he replied that this
was contrary to Dutch expectations (13). Britain was expected to keep
law and order pending the arrival of the Dutch troops. This message
of Mountbatten's was repeated by Mr. J. Lawson, British Secretary of
State for War, who stated that ' . . . Britain's obligations to her
allies will not involve fighting for the Dutch against nationalism in
Java.' (14) The Economist felt that this policy was misguided,

' . . . the conclusion is that the Secretary of State for War
(Lawson) is taking it upon himself to dictate policy to the Dutch,
. . . and generally to suggest that the British think this time of
disturbance and uncertainty is a proper time to introduce basic
changes into somebody else's colony for which by the accident of
war and geography they are, for the time being, responsible . . .
The only possible attitude for the British in these delicate
circumstances, is complete solidarity with the Dutch. The
troubles in the Far East must not be detracted from the context
of Britain's foreign relations as a whole, and it becomes daily
more obvious that the best hope for progressive and successful
action in any part of the globe lies in Britain's close association
with France and the Low Countries.' (15)

The problem for the British was complex. The objectives were to
occupy eight key bridgeheads, to disarm the Japanese, then allow the
Dutch to enter through the bridgeheads and take control of the rest of
the islands. However, as the Survey of International Affairs in the
Far East (16) shows, the task of disarming the Japanese required the
help of the de facto authority in Java - the Republic of Indonesia.
Accordingly, Christison (Allied Commander of the NEI) asked for their
assistance. The Dutch saw this as conferring de facto recognition on
the Republic. Furthermore, the Dutch military commanders argued that
the Indonesian forces were not organised, that the populace of Java was
peaceable and that all resistance would collapse as soon as the Allied
forces appeared in strength and showed a determination to put an end to
unrest (17). The British knew a Republic had been proclaimed, but they
did not know the strength of it, believing the Japanese were maintaining
law and order, whereas in fact they were not. Thus Mountbatten had no
instructions on how to deal with the Republic, and only the information
of the Dutch to base his plans on, information which turned out to be
inaccurate. A more immediate problem to Mountbatten was that twenty-
six of his thirty divisions in the NEI were Indian, and India, as Nehru's
protest of 1 October 1945 shows (18), would not permit their use to
return the Dutch to the NEI.

In this difficult situation, the Foreign Office announced on 1 October
1945 that the Dutch Government was the only one in the NEI that the
British Government recognised (19). Furthermore, the British Govern-

ment attempted, unsuccessfully, to persuade the Dutch to allow van Mook to talk with Soekarno and other leaders of the Republic.   The Dutch, according to a report from the British Ambassador in The Hague (Bland), felt that the situation in the NEI was being exaggerated by the British (20).

The problems in Anglo-Dutch relations that arose from the above diffi-culties and differences of opinion were noted in the Press as early as 5 October, when the Chicago Daily News commented that

> 'the British are doing a housekeeping job in Java.   The view is
> that Britain is merely keeping the peace and wants to get out as
> soon as possible.' (21)

The British Prime Minister, in a reply to a letter from the Labour MP, Fenner Brockway, however, discounted allegations that British forces were being used to restore the French and Dutch administrations with a warning ' . . . to be careful about accepting at their face value reports of this kind'. (22)   The Times, in an editorial on 11 October noted that

> ' . . . it may be weeks before the Dutch troops in any strength
> arrive.   In the meantime the Dutch are dependent on the British.
> The British . . . do not wish to become involved in a political
> issue between the Dutch and Indonesians . . . They regard their
> three main tasks in the East Indies as being: to disarm the
> Japanese; to rescue and succour prisoners of war and internees;
> and to maintain order until they are relieved or the political
> issue can be decided.'

The Times concluded that

> 'It is becoming increasingly doubtful whether the British can
> avoid taking sides, or at least appearing to do so to one of
> the parties.   The coming weeks will place a strain on the close
> bonds forged during the war, between the British and Dutch.' (23)

In an attempt to reconcile the difficulties in the NEI, Mr. van Kleffens (the Dutch Foreign Minister) came to London to meet Mr. Bevin.   The Times dramatically noted that ' . . . the British and Netherlands Governments remain in close consultation in face of the swiftly mounting dangers in the East Indies.' (24)   The Manchester Guardian pointed out that

> 'there has been much scope for sore feeling between the two
> Governments here; but it is hoped that as a result of last
> week's conversations (Kleffens and Bevin), misunderstanding may
> have given place to understanding, for whatever faults have been
> committed the emergency cannot be relieved without the understanding
> between our two countries.   For the next two or three weeks res-
> ponsibility for whatever comes about rests almost entirely with
> the British.   After that a Dutch problem will have to be solved
> by the Dutch.' (25)

In the NEI, during this period, the Nationalists were accusing the British of giving protection to the return of the Dutch administration, whilst many British observers felt that the British handling of the situation ' . . . is not being particularly distinguished and is not calculated to raise Britain's prestige in the eyes of the Dutch, of the Indonesians, or of anyone else.' (26)   The British dilemma was succinctly summed up by the London correspondent of the <u>Christian Science Monitor</u> when he wrote that

> ' . . . the British are not a little embarrassed by the turn of events in Java.   They find themselves faced with the distasteful choice of helping the Dutch get back into power in the NEI or encouraging a nationalism that could spread to India and British colonies.' (27)

The Dutch view on the events in the NEI was expressed by the Minister for Overseas Territories, Professor Logeman, who said in the Dutch Parliament that strong representations concerning food supplies and the safety of Dutch nationals had been made repeatedly to Britain.   He added,

> 'I cannot say that the Government of our British ally has remained insensible to these representations, but nevertheless we follow with anxiety the very slow course of events.' (28)

He then openly criticised Britain

> ' . . . It is a serious thing that we, who in this war gave all we could, to our sorrow, must say that we did not find our allies ready and only hesitantly prepared for this common duty (. . . of disarming and evacuating the Japanese occupation forces and restoring the lawful authority) . . . Even demobilisation appeared to have priority over liberation measures for our territory.' (29)

The Dutch felt that if British territory had been at stake, the priorities would have been different.   Van Kleffens, the Dutch Foreign Minister, said in the Hague on 21 October,

> ' . . . the Government and people of the Netherlands, let it be said frankly, have been disappointed, unprepared as they were for it, by a degree of unreadiness on the part of Britain to deal with a situation with which we have been prevented from dealing with ourselves, but there is no point in recrimination, least of all if things improve.   The Netherlands and British Governments are in close touch and must work together on this and other matters as they worked together during hostilities.   The fact that there is no disagreement with regard to fundamentals should facilitate this.'(30)

The British response to both the early problems in the NEI and the Dutch statements can be discerned from Attlee's statement in the House of Commons on 17 October

> ' . . . I need hardly say that His Majesty's Government do not desire to be unnecessarily involved in the administration or the political affairs of non British territories and their object is to withdraw British troops as soon as possible.   Meanwhile not only have we a strong moral obligation towards our Dutch allies as the sovereign power until they are in a position to resume

105

control, . . . but also the maintenance of law and order is
essential to the fulfilment of the military tasks . . . ' (31)

As the end of October approached, Soekarno warned the British that
there would be a blood bath if they continued their ' . . . calculated
policy to reimpose Dutch rule.' (32)   The immediate response to which
was a statement by sixty Labour MP's that demanded that 'our troops
must not be used to restore Dutch and French imperialism.' (33)   The
Dutch response was to press for large scale reinforcements, accusing
the British, according to one report, (34) of taking a lighthearted
view of the situation.   In the NEI, the situation deteriorated rapidly
towards the end of October, with riots in the town of Sourabaya which
culminated in the murder of Brigadier Mallaby.   This led to the outbreak of fighting in the town which resulted in three weeks' bitter
fighting before the town was cleared of insurgents.

The British reaction to the murder of Mallaby and the subsequent
fighting was summed up by the Times:

'What makes many British observers unhappy . . . is their feeling
that much more might have been done on the political front if the
Dutch had earlier shown a genuine desire to get together with
Indonesian leaders and had put forward a generous liberal policy.
It would . . . have put the Dutch more in the right with their
allies.' (35)

The Dutch, in the midst of these disturbances, announced their policy
on the NEI, which was to be one of its independence within a commonwealth.   The Times summed up much British feeling on this by noting
that

'. . . their delay in publishing their statement of policy until
this late hour . . . has merely confirmed suspicions that the
Dutch were thinking in terms of force and force alone in dealing
with this "trouble with the natives"' (36)

The situation was so complex and contradictory, vis-a-vis the statements coming from London, the Hague and Batavia, that Bevin attempted
to clarify the British Government's position with a statement in the
House of Commons.   He stressed that the Government had no intention
of being involved in any constitutional dispute between the Dutch and the
people of the NEI.   He re-emphasised that the Dutch stood with Britain.
when Japan attacked.   He continued
'. . . It was not their fault or the fault of the NEI that they
were unable to assume control.   It is therefore quite clear
that His Majesty's Government have a definite agreement with
them to provide for the Dutch . . . to resume as rapidly as
practicable full responsibility for the administration of the NEI
territories.' (37)

He then pointed out that the British had been given no indication that
their forces would be opposed.   Turning to the situation as it then
was he remarked,

' . . . we are now faced with a very difficult and intricate
situation.   It is impossible for us to avoid becoming involved

in the political affairs of the island in view of the developments that have subsequently taken place.' (38)

Thus, by the end of November, the situation with regard to the NEI was that Britain was admitting that it was involved in its political affairs. Yet the essential problem for Britain, that of what forces to send in and with what orders, still remained. Whilst the Dutch argued that the delay in sending in sufficient troops had caused the situation of insurgence, and thus severely condemned the British, the Indonesians (and the Australians, Russians, and Indians) criticised the British for sending in forces to carry out the task allotted to them. Little wonder that Mountbatten on 21 November still wanted clarification as to whether or not he was to restore Dutch sovereignty, adding that there would be a problem of morale if the troops were to reimpose Dutch rule. (39)

November 1945 thus witnessed the overt recognition by the British Government that they were involved in the political affairs of the NEI. December 1945 was the month when the Dutch and British finally began to consult and attempt to reconcile their differences over the NEI; on 20 December, it was announced that the Dutch Cabinet would meet the British Cabinet at Chequers on 27-28 December. This meeting, although obviously of considerable importance, was, however, only very scantily covered in the British Press and the only detailed comment on it appeared in two articles in the New York Times. These articles pointed out that there was British dissatisfaction with the reactionary policy makers at the Hague and argued that any solution could only come after negotiations between the Dutch and Javanese nationalists. In order to do this it would be necessary to correlate British and Dutch views:

' . . . The official British view is that while fully recognising
Dutch sovereignty in Indonesia, Britain has had to shoulder the
task of disarming the Japanese and restoring order in Java and
therefore has the right to insist that the Dutch go as far and
as fast as they can toward an agreed solution of the problem.
Britain accepts the Queen's speech as the basis for discussion
and . . . backs Dr. van Mook . . . and wants the Hague to send
him back . . . fortified to negotiate with the Indonesian
nationalists.' (40)

However, it was felt that the Dutch would not negotiate with any except the most moderate Indonesian leaders. But the British could not go too far in meeting the demands of the Republic without risking a repe- tition of these events in some of Britain's colonial possessions. Thus, the British felt that because of this and also because they wished for more friendly relations with the Dutch in the post war organisation of Western Europe, then the degree to which they could press the Dutch to make concessions was limited.

Material on the outcome of the Chequers talks is limited to the press reports and the Official Statement. The Times (41) noted that in both British and Dutch circles the talks were held to be 'highly satisfactory'. The Official Statement recorded

' . . . the British Government were acquainted fully with the
consistent and liberal policy which the Netherlands Government

are pursuing and intend to pursue, towards the Indonesian problem.'

The British Government, for their part, reaffirmed

'. . . their obligation to their Dutch allies to establish without delay conditions of security in which it would be possible for the Government of the NEI to continue negotiations with representative Indonesians.' (42)

The reality of the inability of the British to press the Dutch to talk to the Republicans is shown by the phrase 'representative Indonesians'.

Nevertheless, on 10 February 1946, van Mook met Sjahrir, with the background of a hostile UN Security Council debate on the Indonesian question that had criticised the British and Dutch. Van Mook brought a new offer, that of a movement towards independence after a Dutch-Indonesian joint control period; but with no mention of the Republic. Sjahrir returned with a demand for the recognition of the Republic as the sovereign authority of Indonesia; only when this demand was satisfied would cooperation be welcomed. Van Mook proposed the recognition de facto of the Republic, but this was opposed by the Dutch Government. However, by May the Dutch offered de facto recognition to the Republic in areas not under British control.

Meanwhile, in the face of further protests by the British troops, (43) and another demand for the immediate recall of Indian troops, (44) the British and Dutch agreed to introduce Dutch troops into the NEI as from 1 March, to take over from the British. Nearly 6,000 of these arrived in the middle of March with the Dutch news agency, Aneta, reporting that all British troops would be withdrawn from Java 'in the next few months' (45). As a further indication of the speedy nature of the impending transfer of power to the Dutch, the British and Dutch Prime Ministers met, along with other Ministers, at Downing Street on 12 April. It was decided that British troops would not mop up extremists - this task being left to the Dutch when they finally took over. On 25 April, Mountbatten recommended that all British forces should be withdrawn by 1 July 1946, although the transfer was not that quick in practice; Mountbatten was withdrawn as Commander-in-Chief on 8 June 1946, as an indication that the British were committed to withdrawing completely (Stopford took over as Acting Supreme Allied Commander, SE Asia). By 14 July 1946, the Dutch controlled all the NEI except Java, Sumatra and the Riouw Archipelago. Nevertheless, criticism of the actions of the British continued with the NEI Dutch paper commenting that

'General MacArthur would have restored law and order here long ago. He does not travel around in splendid uniforms glittering with decorations, bragging about victories.' (46)

The Dutch-Indonesian negotiations were held up during the Dutch general election of May and then by the kidnapping of Sjahrir in June. Finally, the Dutch called a conference at Malino in July 1946, but the Republicans were not invited. The ensuing confusion over what exactly was happening in the NEI led the British to send Lord Killearn to Batavia to 'lend his good offices in any way calculated to bring about a settlement'. This was combined with a strong request from the

British Government to 'regard Dr. Sjahrir as the real plenipotentiary
of the Indonesian republic'(47).   The Dutch sent out three Commissio-
ners-General to negotiate a settlement in Java, and Killearn was instru-
mental in getting them to meet Indonesian representatives, which included
Republicans.   This led to the Linggadjati Agreement being initialled on
15 November 1946.

By 30 November, the last British troops left Java.   The military
involvement was at an end;   it had been an involvement that had cost
the British 563 troops killed, 1,441 wounded, and 315 missing, out of
the 92,000 men involved (48).   The British thus withdrew, leaving the
Dutch and Indonesians face to face with an agreement accepted in
principle.   They now had to implement it in practice.

November 1946 therefore saw the end of direct British military involvement in the NEI, and it also saw the initialling of the Linggadjati
agreement.   This agreement, which was very general in nature, recognised
that the Republic had de facto authority in the areas of Java, Sumatra
and Madura.   Dutch troops were to be withdrawn from these areas.   The
Dutch and the Republic were to cooperate to establish a sovereign democratic state, to be set up on a federal basis - a United States of
Indonesia (USI) - to be established by 1 January 1949.   This agreement,
however, was attacked both in Indonesia and in the Netherlands.   Despite
these attacks, the Treaty was finally signed by both parties on 25 March
1947.

However, the treaty was not all-embracing with regard to the problems
facing the two states.   There was no agreement on foreign representation;   no agreement on Dutch property in Indonesia;   no agreement about
policing.   Negotiations on these and other matters continued, but
became bogged down.   By the end of June, the US offered the Indonesians
aid if they signed an agreement on outstanding matters.   Britain offered its good offices to help in the worsening situation (49).   But although the Indonesians conceded to all but one of the Dutch demands
(that of a joint police force) the Dutch would not compromise and
pressed for an immediate settlement - partly because the cost of the
Indonesian operation was running at three million guilders a day.   On
13 July Britain offered to set up a neutral commission to establish
internal security in Indonesia - this was refused by the Dutch.   On
18 July, Britain, Australia, China and France urged the Republic to
accept all the Dutch proposals.   But then the Dutch broke off negotiations (19 July) and despite Indonesian proposals of arbitration the
Dutch refused and called in the troops in the '1st police action' on
21 July 1947 (50).

The immediate British reaction to this was expressed in a statement
issued by the Foreign Office on the morning of 21 July.   It stated
that

' . . . it is with the keenest disappointment that His Majesty's
Government have witnessed the breakdown of the ceaseless efforts
during the last eighteen months to promote a peaceful settlement
of the exceptionally difficult situation which has persisted in
Java and Sumatra.' (51)

British fears were centred on the fact that the whole Far and Middle
East would be stirred by the Dutch action, and thus the economic situa-

tion would deteriorate still further.   The British Government clearly
felt that a little more patience on the part of the Dutch would have
been judicious.   Aside from the offer of mediation made in the 21 July
statement by the Foreign Office, Britain was a bystander - but one acute-
ly interested because of its interests in the area.

The Dutch refused this offer of good offices by the British on 22
July - merely 'noting'that it had been made (52).   Other attempts to
mediate by Australia, India and the USA also failed.   The next step
for these mediating powers - especially Australia and India - was to
refer the Indonesian situation to the UN Security Council as a threat
to world peace.   On the day before the issue was debated in the Security Council, Bevin made a statement on the British position; he announced that war materials for Indonesia from Singapore and British Far East
territories had been banned.   Further, the Dutch were to get no training facilities in that area and no supplies of war materials intended
for the NEI would be permitted from Britain.   But the training of
Dutch troops in Britain would not be stopped.   ' . . . After all,'
he said, 'Holland was overrun by the Germans and we entered into very
solemn undertakings to re-equip and to train the Dutch army . . . but we
are not doing this for the purposes of the war in Indonesia.' (53)
Later that evening, Mr. van Kleffens, Dutch Ambassador to the US, rejected British and US offers to mediate.   He said they would serve no useful purpose (54).

The debate over Indonesia then moved to the Security Council of the UN.
Australia took the Indonesian issue to the Security Council under article
39 of the Charter.   The British view on this was that

    'article 39 . . . dealt with the action of one sovereign state
    against another and that the invocation of it showed that
    Australia "inaccurately" believed Indonesia to be a sovereign
    state.' (55)

From then on the British attempted to keep Indonesia out of the UN, first
by asking India to withhold formal representation to the UN until infor-
mal British-Dutch negotiations were finished.   Then, when the Dutch
accepted US mediation (on 1 August) Britain proposed suspending consideration of the Indonesian question until US mediation was completed.   In
the actual UN debate, a truce was proposed - with Britain (as well as
France and Belgium and the USA) abstaining, because it claimed that the
UN had no right to intervene in internal politics.

Bevin explained this vote in the House of Commons on 6 August.

    'When matters are referred to the Security Council, I am anxious
    that the council will adopt a judicial view on what comes within
    their charter and what does not . . . in view of our responsibilities
    for so many territories in the world I feel I must take precautions
    to see that in a slipshod manner the Security Council does not go
    outside their proper jurisdiction.' (56)

After the failure of US mediation on 22 August, the Security Council
discussed the issue again, and resolved, on 6 September, to create a
three member consular commission to attempt to conciliate.   Each participant could choose one representative, then these could choose one more.

The Dutch chose Belgium; the Indonesians chose Australia; Belgium and Australia chose the USA. This commission was formally turned into a Committee of Good Offices on 1 November following a US resolution.

Negotiations continued through the rest of 1947 and through 1948 with the situation still remaining very tense. On 17 January 1948, a truce was signed on the US ship Renville, with the provisions being: a truce; plebiscites leading to the creation of a United States of Indonesia; the Dutch to retain areas seized in the police action. In March an interim Government (not Republican) was set up. The talks between the Republic and the Dutch continued in April under the auspices of the UN Committee of Good Offices, only to be broken off in June by the Dutch - and after being resumed - being broken off by the Indonesians in July. The result of this was that the UN ordered the resumption of talks in August.

In the Netherlands, the elections in July 1948 stirred up some anti-British feelings - feelings that, the Economist pointed out,

'the subject of Indonesia always raises (since Indonesia was the main issue in the election). This takes two forms - memories of the six weeks' delay in reoccupying Java and Sumatra after the Japanese surrender - for which the British were blamed: and resentment at the embargo on arms for the Dutch forces in Indonesia imposed by London last year.' (57)

One complicating factor was the British action in Malaya, where it was vigorously suppressing an insurrection; this led many Dutch to ask what was the difference between the Dutch police action in the NEI and the actions of the British in Malaya. By September 1948, the link between Malaya and Indonesia became more salient to the British with the outbreak in Java of a communist uprising aimed against the Republic, with Bevin announcing on 18 September that he intended to stamp out communist movements (58). The Republic, in fact, was soon able to defeat the communist uprising, after first telling the Dutch to keep out. During this period, negotiations continued, but to no avail, with the result that on 11 December the Dutch announced that the three years of negotiations had finally broken down. The Indonesians became disillusioned, the Dutch impatient. The final effect was that the Dutch opened a second 'police action', capturing all major republican leaders, imprisoning them, and overrunning all major towns.

The immediate reaction to this was that the Australian Government and the US Government felt that the Dutch had bypassed the UN good offices in starting the police action. British official quarters received the news of the Netherlands' military action with 'expressions of regret and dismay' (59). The British sympathised at this time with the Dutch exasperation - especially as the British themselves had been obliged to take similar action in Malaya; but they wished that the Dutch had not forced the issue, and had tried to settle the problem in the same way that Britain settled the Indian issue.

Again, the British were in a quandary as to what to do since the Dutch might present a fait accompli to the UN and the British were not too eager to engage in a public dispute with another European power over an Asiatic territory, especially when any such disputation might be too late to be effective. According to the London correspondent of the New York Times,

the most serious worry of the British soon became that Dutch action
might turn India, Pakistan, Burma and Siam away from any voluntary
association with the European powers to create an anti-communist front
throughout Asia.   His view was that Britain would wait to take a lead
from the United States (60).

    The US did not wait long before taking that lead.   On 21 December they
threatened to cut off aid to the Netherlands - and on 23 December they
suspended Marshall Aid to the NEI.   From then the UN became the centre
of debate on the issue.   Leading the attack on the Dutch were the
Australians who compared them to Hitler and urged their expulsion from
the UN.   In the UN a ceasefire was ordered on 26 December, but the
Dutch ignored it.   The US and Britain attacked the Dutch mildly, but
never enough to put too much strain on the Western states' front against
communism.

    By January, Britain became increasingly concerned about reports that
Asian states might form a 'Monroe Doctrine' against European powers
following the Dutch action.   Thus the emphasis was, for the British,
to end the dispute as soon as possible.   Hence, on 28 January, they
supported a four power resolution in the Security Council.   This called
for: a ceasefire; the release of all political prisoners; a United
States of Indonesia by 1 July 1950; the Good Offices Committee of the
UN to become the UN Commission for Indonesia, with the mandate of carrying out UN resolutions on Indonesia.   This was in effect the end of the
real debate in the UN, although Australia and India took the question to
the General Assembly - with France and Britain abstaining on this vote.

    The Dutch and Indonesians signed the ceasefire order on 7 May when
van Royen (Dutch) and Dr. Mohamed Rum (Republic) agreed under the auspices of the UN Commission.   This Royen-Rum agreement laid the basis
for a round table conference in the Hague.   The final agreement came
on 23 September 1949, with the conference discussing the debt agreement
until 24 October.   This agreement was ratified in Holland on 6 December
1949, and in Indonesia on 14 December.   On 27 December, Indonesia
became a separate state with an independent United States of Indonesia
being formed on 17 August 1950.

CONCLUSION

The policy of the Dutch Government with respect to events in the Dutch
East Indies between 1945 and 1949 is relatively easy to summarise on
account of its consistency: the initial aim of the Dutch Government was
to reoccupy the territory and thereby restore the colonial relationship
that had existed until the Japanese overran the islands in 1942.   Such
a foreign policy objective required the British to enter the islands
immediately and, by a show of force, defeat the Republican movement and
thus allow the Dutch to return to an environment that would permit them
to reassert their rule.   The failure of the British Government to
follow this line of action resulted in severe criticism of them by the
Dutch.

    In such a situation, the Dutch Government's policy became one of
desiring to take over their former colony as soon as was possible.   In
carrying out that policy of reoccupation, especially after the withdrawal

of the British troops in November 1946, the Dutch Government faced
serious difficulties as witnessed by the necessity for the first and
second police actions of July 1947 and December 1948 respectively.
From the initialling of the Linggadjati agreement in November 1946, the
Dutch Government's policy was one of balancing the strong internal
desires to retain control over the NEI, the increasingly costly and
difficult task of controlling events in the NEI, and the nature of world
opinion as expressed in both the United Nations and, more importantly,
through direct contacts with the British and United States Governments.

The fundamental factor in shaping Dutch policy over the NEI was not,
therefore, the insurrection that their troops faced there, but the
nature of the linkage between policy in that issue area and policy in
those of security and economic recovery. With regards to economic
matters, the Netherlands was in a dire situation. For recovery to
occur, aid, primarily from the United States, was necessary. In terms
of security, the Dutch Government, as noted in chapter five, moved from
a policy of neutrality in 1945 to one of wholesale commitment to the
North Atlantic Treaty in 1949. The parallel between this increasing
enmeshment in the Western alliance and the gradual acceptance that the
NEI could not be returned to its pre war status is not coincidental.

Dutch relations with the British over this issue area were a mixture
of both gratitude and criticism. Initially, the Dutch reaction to the
British refusal immediately to reoccupy the NEI with massive forces and
thereby restore Dutch control, was one of hostility and severe criticism
from both the leadership and the media. This initial hostility to
British policy was transferred into one of gratitude for the action
Britain had taken in the light of severe problems that country was facing. Nevertheless, it is clear that the events in the NEI during the
period of British occupation did represent a serious strain on the
relationship between the British and Dutch Governments. When the issue
was transferred to the United Nations, the British policy of refusing to
accept United Nations involvement in the internal affairs of a country
was more to the liking of the Dutch. From then on, however, the British policy became more and more enmeshed in the general Western stance,
led by the United States, which resulted in the linkage between events
in the NEI and in the areas of security and economic recovery. As
noted above, it was this linkage that became the dominant consideration
of the Dutch Government as the Western bloc took shape on the one hand,
and as the difficulties of retaining control over the NEI increased on
the other.

With regard to British policy over the NEI, the immediate contrast to
be drawn with that of the Dutch is that the issue area of the NEI was
never nearly as important an issue to the British Government. Britain,
still one of the big three in 1945, could never see the issue as being
as salient as it was to the Dutch. In a situation in which the British
Government was involved in planning independence for vast areas of its
Commonwealth (including India), it was incongruous, at the same time,
to occupy another power's colonies and proceed to return control of that
country to the colonial power. More simply, the demands on British
resources were severe and wideranging - demands which made the speedy
and low cost settlement of the NEI issue extremely desirable, if not
inevitable given the involvement of Indian troops.

Given these factors, the desires of the Dutch Government with regard to British policy were clearly incompatible with British resources and resolve. The nature of British policy resulted from attempting to balance these conflicting demands - thus the establishment of the eight key bases was at variance with the preferences of the Dutch, and clearly also with the de facto authority in the islands - the Republican Government. Given the British acceptance of claims by nationalist movements in its own colonies and the necessity of cooperating with the de facto authority, their policy with regard to the NEI was essentially a compromise between the demands of the nationalists and the Dutch. As a compromise, it was not acceptable to either side: the Dutch Government felt that it gave too much recognition to the illegal Republican authority; for the Republicans it was seen as the first step on the road to restoring Dutch rule.

The essence of British policy over the NEI during the occupation by British forces was that the occupation was an obligation that could not be reneged on; yet it was primarily intended to allow the Dutch to negotiate with the Nationalist leaders. This policy was manifested in the tactic of obtaining footholds and in the continual offering of good offices.

With the removal of British troops from the NEI, and the consequent raising of the question within the United Nations, the policy of the British Government, although becoming more complex, continued, essentially, to balance demands. Therefore, in the debate on the first police action in the United Nations, Britain's main concern was to prevent the intrusion of the United Nations into the domestic affairs of member states and their colonies - a policy clearly linked to the demands for independence in Britain's own colonies. At the same time, however, Britain had been involved in attempting to persuade the Dutch Government to recognise the demands of the Nationalist leaders and continued to offer its good offices.

The debate over the second police action, which took place in the United Nations in January 1949, saw the policy of the British Government shift to that of openly criticising the Dutch and voting for a motion that demanded the release of Republican leaders and called for a cease-fire. The linkage between these two stances held by the British during the two police actions was the relatively straightforward one that the political situation in South East Asia had changed dramatically; primarily this was due to the virtual defeat of the Nationalist forces in China, and the commencement of the insurrection in Malaysia. Continued hostilities in the NEI would, in the view of the British, result in nationalism being aroused throughout the area and would also make any attempt to develop an anti-communist front much more difficult. But again, as during the occupation of the NEI by British forces, the attitude of the British Government was ambivalent. By 1949, the Dutch were committed to the Western Union and were involved in discussions for the North Atlantic treaty. A rapid solution to the NEI problem without forcing the Dutch to choose between the efforts at creating a Western bloc and its former colony, was the preferred policy stance.

NOTES

(1) The Times, 18 October 1945.
(2) Bevin, in the House of Commons - see The Times, 24 November 1945.
(3) Quoted in The Survey of International Affairs 1939-46. The Far East 1942-46, The Royal Institute of International Affairs, London, p.244.
(4) See H. J. van Mook, The Stakes of Democracy in South East Asia, George Allen and Unwin, London 1950, pp.186-189.
(5) See The Survey on International Affairs 1939-46, op.cit., p.240.
(6) I. N. Djajadiningrat, The Beginnings of the Indonesian-Dutch Negotiations and the Hoge Veluwe Talks, Monograph series - Modern Indonesian Project, Cornell University Press, Ithaca, N.Y. 1958, p.9.
(7) Manchester Guardian, 16 August 1945.
(8) Earl Mountbatten, Report to Combined Chiefs of Staff by Supreme Allied Commander - South East Asia 1943-45, Section II, HMSO, London 1969, p.282.
(9) Ibid., p.289.
(10) Ibid., paragraph 37.
(11) Ibid., paragraph 38.
(12) The Economist, 29 September 1945, p.447.
(13) The Foreign Relations of the United States - Diplomatic Papers 1945. Volume XI - The British Commonwealth - The Far East, Department of State, Washington 1969, pp.1158-92.
(14) Quoted in The Daily Worker, 29 September 1945.
(15) The Economist, 6 October 1945, p.475.
(16) Survey of International Affairs 1939-46, op.cit., pp.240-258.
(17) Mountbatten, op.cit., p.290, paragraph 42.
(18) See News Chronicle, 1 October 1945 - which reports Nehru's protest at the use of Indian troops to suppress a nationalist uprising in Indonesia.
(19) New York Herald Tribune, 2 October 1945.
(20) Foreign Office Records 1945, F7787.
(21) Chicago Daily News,5 October 1945.
(22) The Times, 5 October 1945.
(23) Ibid., 11 October 1945.
(24) Ibid., 13 October 1945.
(25) Manchester Guardian, 15 October 1945.
(26) Ibid.
(27) Christian Science Monitor, 16 October 1945.
(28) See The Times, 17 October 1945.
(29) Daily Express, 17 October 1945.
(30) The Times, 22 October 1945.
(31) Quoted ibid., 18 October 1945.
(32) See Manchester Guardian, 23 October 1945.
(33) The Times, 25 October 1945.
(34) The Daily Worker, 27 October 1945.
(35) See The Times, 10 November 1945.
(36) Ibid.
(37) Quoted ibid., 24 November 1945.
(38) Ibid.
(39) Major-General S. Woodburn Kirby, History of the Second World War - The War Against Japan. Volume V, HMSO, London 1969, p.317.
(40) New York Times, 27 December 1945.
(41) The Times, 29 December 1945.
(42) The statement is printed ibid.

(43) See The Daily Worker, 13 February 1946, for a letter complaining about the role of the British, written by six staff sergeants serving in the NEI and ibid., 20 February 1946, for a report stating that soldiers intend to take direct action against Dutch troops because of the atrocities committed by them.
(44) New York Times, 22 January 1946.
(45) Ibid., 10 March 1946.
(46) Daily Express, 25 April 1946.
(47) The Times, 27 August 1946.
(48) Survey of International Affairs 1939-46, op.cit., p.258.
(49) The Sunday Times, 29 June 1947.
(50) See P. Calvocoressi, Survey of International Affairs 1947-8, Oxford University Press, London 1952, p.396.
(51) Quotations in The Times, 21 July 1947.
(52) Daily Herald, 23 July 1947.
(53) Ibid., 31 July 1947.
(54) Daily Express, 31 July 1947.
(55) News Chronicle, 31 July 1947.
(56) Quoted in The Times, 7 August 1947.
(57) The Economist, 17 July 1948.
(58) The Times, 18 September 1948.
(59) New York Times, 20 December 1948.
(60) Ibid., 21 December 1948.

7 A comparison of the empirical and predicted findings

In this chapter, the three case studies summarised in the last three chapters will be restated in terms of the four strategies of adaptation. These empirically derived strategies will then be compared with the strategies predicted for the two states as derived in chapter three.

The four adaptive strategies that states may follow have already been discussed in chapter three; in summary, they are:

Promotive   where decision-makers choose to promote changes at
                     home and abroad, thereby ignoring the demands of
                     both the essential structures and the external
                     environment.

Preservative   where decision-makers attempt to maintain an equili-
                     brium between changes in both the external environ-
                     ment and the essential structures.

Acquiescent   where decision-makers adjust external policies and
                     essential structures to the demands of the external
                     environment.

Intransigent   where decision-makers attempt to alter the external
                     environment to the demands of the essential structures.

These strategies will now be utilised to assess the broad nature of British and Dutch foreign policies in the issue areas chosen.

A EUROPEAN INTEGRATION

Dutch policy towards the issue of European integration is closely related to the other areas under examination. One clear relationship is that between European integration and the problems caused by the loss of the NEI. Another is the close relationship between Dutch concerns for security and the desire for integration amongst the European countries. Yet another is the interrelationship between moves for European integration and Dutch reliance on NATO as the cornerstone of their foreign policy.

In essence, Dutch policy towards moves for European integration has resulted from the impact of domestic factors and external pressures - and must thus be considered <u>preservative</u>. Dutch policy over the Council of Europe was determined both by the impetus generated by external factors and by the domestic desire to avoid Dutch political and economic policies being excessively influenced by a supranational body. There were clear elements of intransigence in the initial Dutch posture towards the Council of Europe, witnessed, for example, by the Dutch refusal to make proposals to the commission charged with designing the structure. However, partly as a result of domestic pressure, as voiced in the

States-General, and partly due to the clarification of the attitude of the United States towards European integration, Dutch policy towards the Council of Europe became more positive. Indeed, the Government, in the debate over the ratification of the statute, promised to attempt to strengthen the powers of the Assembly.

The proposals for functional European organisations saw Dutch policy again as essentially preservative. Thus, because the Dutch Government realised that economic integration was necessary if the loss of the NEI was to be in any way counterbalanced, and also, in order that economic recovery could occur in the Netherlands, functional economic integration was the preferred form of integration. With the example of Benelux, the Dutch desired, for domestic reasons, the creation of a customs union and the Schuman plan was seen as the first step on the road to such a goal. Nevertheless, the strong internal desire for functional economic integration could be contrasted with the domestic concern to avoid the encroachment of any supranational body on other areas of Dutch domestic policy. Hence the Dutch only participated in the discussions on the Schuman plan on the condition that they were not bound to any preconditions. Dutch concern for a similar move in the field of agriculture was illustrated by the Green Plan of Sicco Mansholt. Yet, acting as a powerful external influence on Dutch policy was the position of Britain, and the Mansholt Plan, along with the Stikker Plan, were both designed to involve British participation in European integration. Dutch policy over the ECSC and the EDC was, therefore, primarily preservative in the sense that it attempted to balance an internal goal - the creation of a customs union in Europe - with an external goal - the participation of Britain in European integration. With regard to the former, the Beyen proposal for a customs union (February 1953) was based both on the desire for such a union and on the desirability of economic preceding military integration. With regard to the latter, the Dutch position over the EDC was fundamentally concerned with balancing internal and external requirements (primarily the participation of Britain in Europe and the continuation of the American guarantee). Dutch policy toward the EPC (European Political Community) is a further illustration of this basic nature of preservation: internally there were strong demands for political integration and yet there were concerns over the degree of French domination within any enclosed European political community. Externally, there was the obvious desire of other states to proceed with some form of political integration and these other states were the partners of the Netherlands in other functional plans.

Dutch policy over the discussions concerning the creation of the EEC and Euratom appear again to be fundamentally preservative. The desire for a customs union was a very powerful internal factor, and the proposal for the EEC represented a policy that would enhance the essential structure of the economic system of the Netherlands. The Dutch were, therefore, seen as the most powerful supporters of integration - primarily because the policy of a customs union yielded, potentially, such vast benefits for Dutch industry and agriculture. In a situation where the old colonial markets had been severely depleted, and in a country where trade was of fundamental importance, the prospect of a customs union was a very worthwhile goal, especially since it might prevent the return, in any economic depression, of the old beggar-my-neighbour policies. Free trade was, henceforth, the basic requirement, for the Dutch, of any economic integration.

118

Despite this very powerful internal factor influencing Dutch policy, a major external factor was of considerable importance - that was the position of Britain. The Dutch, throughout the negotiations, were the strongest supporters of British participation, attempting, in the Benelux memorandum, to open the way for British involvement, and mediating, as the emissary of the Six, between the negotiations at Messina and the British position. A further external factor that affected Dutch policy was the fear that France might accept Euratom and reject the EEC - thus the Dutch Government attempted in the negotiations to tie the two proposals together.

During the negotiations, further internal factors - primarily the concern of the Dutch Government for a free market in agricultural goods and the demand by the Government for a lower common external tariff - affected Dutch policy. In this situation, the coincidence of adverse internal relations and the concern of the Dutch Government over the dominant external consideration - the question of British membership - coalesced in the discussion within the Netherlands as to whether the Dutch Government should withdraw from the EEC/Euratom negotiations and join in with the British. However, this was not a viable policy alternative primarily because of the influence of the external factor that the other European powers - notably the other Benelux powers - were set to go ahead with the EEC/Euratom plans.

Once the treaties had been signed and ratified, Dutch policy again concentrated on obtaining some form of reconciliation with Britain. Yet again the preservative nature of Dutch policy is clear, in that the advantages of the EEC/Euratom proposals related to powerful internal and external factors. The internal economic advantages were obvious, but there was also the important political consideration that the treaties represented the increasing stabilisation of the Dutch regional environment. Given that what the British were proposing with the Free Trade Area was not a customs union, Dutch policy, whilst still welcoming British participation in the Communities, was essentially aimed at developing the EEC. Despite attempts, such as the Luns Plan, to balance the advantages of British participation within a wider framework with the existing and potential benefits accruing from the EEC, Dutch policy concentrated on liberalising the trade policy of the EEC. Thus policy towards the EEC/Euratom was basically preservative since it was based on the attempt to balance internal - mainly economic - requirements with external political considerations.

The debate over the European Political Union (EPU) is the best example of Dutch attempts to pursue a preservative policy. Dutch policy during the Fouchet negotiations was primarily aimed at obtaining an invitation for British participation; indeed it became a condition for continued Dutch involvement in the project. The Dutch Government attempted to divert attention from political union discussions by proposing more regular heads-of-state meetings, and by calling for parallel discussions in WEU. The Dutch policy of delaying any agreement until Britain was invited received a boost with the decision by the British Government to seek membership of the EEC; indeed, after that announcement the Dutch did not send any proposals to the Fouchet Committee. Furthermore, the Dutch Government attempted to ensure that two further limitations were placed on any EPU. First, it should not be allowed to interfere in the other European Communities - for fear that it would result in Franco-German domination. Second, it should not impinge on matters which had been discussed within NATO. With the announcement of the second French plan, the Dutch refused to sign any agreement until Britain was admitted to the Communities.

The Dutch position was not based on the desire for supranationalism, since British membership was strongly proposed despite clear indications that any British stance would be fundamentally Gaullist. Dutch policy over the EPU was, therefore, the result of two major sets of forces: there were internal ones stemming from the Dutch reluctance to accept any supranational control that might interfere with other areas of policy, since the Dutch felt strongly that even in any supranational body, political power was not equal; there were also external ones, resulting from the concern that the political constellation of the proposed EPU would be in contradiction with the more salient policy goal of the strengthening of the Atlantic Alliance. British membership of the EPU was the common denominator in any conception of how to overcome these difficulties. It would counteract both the protectionist nature of French conceptions of the European enterprise and the French attempt to extend political control over the economic communities. Externally, British membership would provide a much more Atlanticist base to European integration. Given that this Atlanticist posture was the cornerstone of Dutch foreign policy, then their stance towards the EPU discussions was essentially one of ensuring the continued predominance of this Atlantic connection; hence the stress by the Dutch on the fact that the EPU should not be concerned with defence, rather that it should be, in reality, a contribution to the strengthening of the Atlantic Alliance within the framework of that Alliance.

In summary, the Dutch attitude over the EPU represented a straightforward attempt to balance external and internal pressures. The fundamental aim was to avoid, on the one hand, the setting up of any organisation which could bring French political power into economic affairs; on the other, there was an equally strong desire to prevent the establishment of a European third force, as envisaged by De Gaulle, within, or even possibly outside, the framework of NATO. Championing British membership represented the outward manifestations of this preservative policy stance. The Dutch reaction to the veto of British membership can be cited as a further instance of this policy stance, in that both the reasons for wanting British membership, and the reaction of the Dutch Government to the veto, were based on an attempt to balance external and internal demands.

British policy towards European integration from 1945-61 has been described as the long haul to Europe; certainly, there is a danger of examining the data in a teleological way. Nevertheless, there can be no doubt that British policy underwent a fundamental transition in the period. In the immediate post war period the traditional British policy of non involvement in European affairs was heightened by the contrast between the situations of the European powers and that of Britain. Furthermore, the dominance in British elite thinking, of the conception of the three circles - with Europe as the least important of these - meant that British policy towards Europe was one of 'with but not of'. In terms of the adaptive behaviour approach it would seem appropriate to term such a policy intransigent. The primacy of the Commonwealth link, and the British conception of its role in world politics, resulted in policy being essentially determined by domestic factors. There were,

120

of course, external elements influencing British policy, but the dominant set of factors was domestic. Thus, Churchill's famous 1946 Zurich speech can be seen primarily as one based on the translation of domestic values and requirements into international politics: Britain required, for economic and political reasons, the creation of a strong Europe, but not one that would involve British participation.

The Labour Government's conception of Europe was very similar to that of the Conservative leadership, although for slightly different reasons. The main factor in Labour's policy towards European integration was again domestic: it was the desire to prevent any, especially a non socialist, control over the British economy. Given the nature of the transformation of British society envisaged, and, in part, already in progress, the Labour Government was concerned not to become involved in any European venture that was based on principles of supranationalism. In addition, the continued desire for American aid meant that European integration, because it might result in American withdrawal from Europe, was undesirable.

This policy of intransigence underlined the British Government's reaction to the series of proposals made on European integration during the first years of the post war period. In the negotiations over the formation of the Council of Europe, British policy was determined by domestic factors and took the form of attempting to prevent any non governmental control of the organs of the Council. Furthermore, it obtained the agreement that the Consultative Assembly would not discuss defence matters. In line with the conception of the three circles and the primacy of Commonwealth links, British policy was opposed to any proposal for European federation, especially one that was of a different political texture. The return of the Conservative Government in 1951, although the party was associated with a more far-reaching commitment to Europe, produced no real change in this intransigent policy; however, the Eden Plan, to coordinate integration in the various fields, was the first indication of a move to a <u>preservative</u> strategy. Thus, although domestic concerns were still of considerable importance, the Eden Plan, by attempting to coordinate integration in areas in which Britain was not involved(the Schuman and Pleven Plans), represented the clear influence of an external factor. In other words, British policy, by the early 1950s was motivated not only by domestic factors and conceptions but also by the very fact that integration was occurring in Europe and that this integration required some reaction from Britain.

Whereas the Eden Plan represented an indication of a transformation to a <u>preservative</u> strategy, with regard to specific measures, British policy was essentially motivated by domestic concerns. British policy towards the Schuman plan was determined basically by the nature of the enterprise envisaged and the effect that this would have had, not only on the Labour Government's doemstic policy, but also on the entire notion of control of the British economy. Indeed, the preconditions, whether real or whether used as an excuse by the British Government, required a commitment both to the pooling of resources and to supranationalism. Despite the superficial differences, neither party was willing to give up control of such large sectors of the economy. When the Conservatives returned to power in 1951, they refused to join the ECSC. Yet, again, given the existence of this community, British policy attempted to achieve some sort of balance between domestic factors and this external factor. Nevertheless, it is believed that despite these preservative tactics after the creation of the ECSC, British policy was essentially intransigent, in that the dominant factors in the formation of British policy were domestic. Even the attempt to subsume all integration within the Council of Europe and the signing of an Association Agreement with ECSC were reactions on the basis of domestic considerations as to the consequences of not so doing.

The proposal for a Green Pool was dealt with in an intransigent manner; the proposal envisaged supranational control over agriculture and, again, Britain refused to consider such a development, preferring to see the debate moved to the OEEC. Similarly, the case of the EDC involved considerable influence from domestic factors. Yet, as noted in the discussion of the EDC in the security issue area, the nature of British policy was also affected by external factors. On the one hand, the British refusal to join was in line with the general intransigent nature of its European policy, yet on the other the attempts made by Britain to give some form of guarantee to the EDC powers was the result of external factors (primarily, the need to rearm Germany in the face of the Soviet threat). It seems necessary to conclude that, unlike the Schuman Plan, the Green Pool Plan and the Council of Europe, British policy over the EDC was essentially preservative.

British policy towards the EEC/Euratom proposals seems to witness a return to the intransigent posture. The desire of the British Government to remove such considerations to the OEEC, and, when this failed, not to take part in the negotiations, illustrates the predominant role of domestic factors in determining policy. In essence, the EEC was not an attractive proposition to the Government because of its inclusion of agricultural matters, because it involved supranational supervision of the harmonisation of economic and social policies, and because it would, as a customs union, have involved some severance of Commonwealth ties. The British proposal for a Free Trade Area was the positive manifestation of this essentially intransigent policy stance since it proposed the exclusion of agricultural products from the FTA, the continuation of Commonwealth preferences and no supranational control. Following the signing and ratification of the Treaty of Rome, British policy was based on the need to prevent the first round of tariff reductions within the EEC resulting in a deflection of British trade.

Yet the very ratification of the Treaty of Rome and the coming into existence of the EEC and Euratom seems, in the adaptive behaviour terminology, to indicate a change in British strategy towards European integration. From the time that the EEC and Euratom were in existence, British policy was formed both by internal factors and the powerful external factor of the existence of the Communities (and, thereby, the need to come to some arrangement with them). The discussions within the Maudling Committee of the OEEC illustrate this attempt. However, the limited nature of the offer made by Britain to the Six indicates the degree to which British policy was still predominantly determined by internal considerations, and, therefore, was still intransigent. The failure of the attempted reconciliation and the formation of the European Free Trade Association are further examples of the basic intransigence of British policy towards Europe. Although the very existence of the Communities was of significance in the formation of British policy, it was still domestic considerations, primarily the effect of any proposals on British industry and agriculture, that dominated policy discussions.

The turnaround of July 1961, when the British Government announced its intention to seek membership of the European Economic Community, does seem to indicate the fundamental shift in British strategy towards European integration from an intransigent strategy one to one of preservation. The decision to seek entry was the result not only of domestic factors but also of powerful external ones. On the domestic front, the problems of the British economy could be contrasted with the initial success of the Six. Yet, externally, the effects of the continuing process of decolonisation and the realisation that, following the failure of the 1960 summit, Britain could no longer be seen as in the same league as the United States and the Soviet Union, meant that the turn towards Europe acquired significance in terms of external factors. The decline of the special relationship and the problems of continuing with the development of high technology weaponry meant that powerful external forces made the decision to apply for membership of the EEC not just a matter of serving domestic considerations. In that respect, the decision to apply for membership of the EEC represents the transformation to a preservative strategy of foreign policy.

In summary, British policy towards European integration was essentially a policy of intransigence, which was transformed after the ratification of the Treaty of Rome, into one of preservation. It is important to note that British policy was, by no means, simply intransigent; there were preservative features in elements of policy - especially the EDC. Nevertheless, it is clear that the dominant factors in forming British policy towards Europe were domestic - primarily, the desire to avoid supranational control over domestic policy and, especially with the ECSC and the EEC, the desire to avoid any fundamental change in the nature of British agriculture and industry, with Commonwealth ties and economic links acting as an additional factor. It was these factors that dominated considerations of British policy towards Europe, allied to conceptions of Britain's role at the centre of the three circles. With the exception of the EDC, British policy followed a fundamentally intransigent posture until the signature and ratification of the Euratom and EEC treaties. The decision to apply for membership of the EEC represents not only the impact of domestic concerns over the success of the new community, but also a realisation that membership would aid external considerations as well. Thus, by 1961 British policy towards European integration was essentially preservative, seeking to balance both internal and external demands in a way that was not characteristic of previous British policy towards Europe.

B SECURITY

From the mid 19th century to the end of the Second World War Dutch foreign policy was based on the principle of neutrality. The period of World War One and the inter war years was one in which this policy of passive rather than active neutrality dominated Dutch policy. In the adaptive behaviour terminology such a policy was intransigent. Although the stark nature of the failure of that strategy might indicate that it would be changed immediately the country was regained, and although many Dutch writers at the time saw the strategy as dead, its burial took much longer. In the immediate post war period, Dutch policy was based on the conception that Dutch interests would be best served either by great power agreement or by collective security vested in the United Nations. Such a conception was essentially intransigent, relying, as it did, on the re-establishment of some form of balance of power in Europe, whether by the great powers or by the United Nations.

Dutch policy towards the United Nations was based on the desirability and necessity of great power agreement and on the necessity of small countries having some say in decisions. In line with its pre war policy of independence and neutrality, the Dutch Government objected to any automatic sanctions over the use of force. Although Dutch proposals over the United Nations were not accepted, the Dutch Government clearly preferred an international organisation to none. The Dutch attitude towards the structure of the United Nations and the Government's rejection of any regional groupings indicate that in the immediate post war period Dutch policy was essentially intransigent. There were promotive elements in the policies (promotion of international law; attack on any great power veto; demands for standards of correct international behaviour to be included in the charter; distrust of regional groupings) but, fundamentally, Dutch policy was not motivated by these factors. Nor was Dutch policy essentially determined by the external environment. Although the nature of the post war world political arrangements was clearly of importance to the Dutch, the impetus for their policy positions over the United Nations, regional groupings and great power agreement, came not from the external situation, but from internal factors - the need to rebuild and protect their essential structures. Just as neutrality was essentially an intransigent posture, so was the policy of the Dutch in the immediate post war environment. Any confusion that might occur from calling Dutch policy intransigent in the light of balance of power theory on the acquiescent role of small states is the result of missing the central point of the adaptive behaviour approach: that is that it is the sources of foreign policy that determine the strategy. In the case of Dutch foreign policy both before and after the Second World War, the source of the posture of neutrality and the source of the immediate post war posture of independence was internal. Neutrality was seen as a policy that enhanced the essential structures, not as a policy imposed from without. An acquiescent policy in the Rosenau approach is one followed by a state solely as a result of decisions made by other actors - for example, it is the strategy followed by a small state in an alliance system. By opting out of such postures, by basing foreign policy primarily on the requirements of internal essential structures, Dutch foreign policy both between the wars and in the immediate post war period was essentially intransigent.

Similarly, Dutch policy towards Germany in the immediate post war period was essentially intransigent in the sense that Dutch demands for territorial adjustments and economic reparations arose from domestic considerations. On the other hand, the realisation that Germany had to recover in order to allow the Dutch economy to recover was essentially an internally derived stance. It was the interaction between these two domestically determined positions that formulated Dutch policy towards Germany. However, as the question of the settlement over Germany became increasingly bound up with the nature of Soviet-Western relationships, this policy of intransigence met with very little success. After the decisive year of 1947, Dutch policy towards Germany moved,

fundamentally, to one of <u>acquiescence</u>, in the sense that what determined
the policy stance taken by the Dutch Government over Germany was primarily dictated by the nature of Dutch relations with Britain and the
United States in the field of European security. As with the NEI, Dutch
policy, initially solidly based on domestic considerations, became, in
the light of more significant policy areas, determined by what occurred
in those other areas.   Thus, for the Dutch Government, events in
Germany, although of considerable importance, were less important than
events in the wider European theatre.   The importance of the Western
alliance, as represented by the Brussels Treaty and the NAT in the face
of the breakdown of post war, great power cooperation, entailed the total
acquiescence of policy over Germany to the interests of this alliance.

From the formation of NATO, the general trend of Dutch policy has been
one of continued support for the Atlantic Alliance: the Atlantic Alliance
has been the cornerstone of Dutch foreign policy.   From the emergence
of the open split between the Soviet Union and the West in 1947, Dutch
policy swung behind the Western alliance.   Whereas in debates in 1946
and 1947, the Government had cited collective security and international
cooperation as the aims of their foreign policy, by early 1948 the
Netherlands had signed the Brussels Treaty, which was clearly directed
at both Germany and the USSR and involved automatic military sanctions.
Thus, by the end of 1948, the Government placed, as its dominant aim in
its foreign policy, closer association with other western powers in the
light of the Soviet threat.   By 1949, this closer association was
translated into the NAT.   In terms of the adaptive behaviour approach
such a policy stance was basically <u>preservative</u>; it was preservative
because it represented the effects of both internal factors (the desire
for security and economic recovery) and external factors (the breakdown
of the post war, great power agreement and the inability of the United
Nations to ensure collective security).

From 1949, Dutch policy was overwhelmingly of a <u>preservative</u> nature;
the debate over the EDC illustrates this clearly.   In this debate
the primary aim of the Dutch Government was to avoid supranational control over Dutch troops and money, reflecting the strong desire of the
Dutch Government to prevent themselves, as a small country, being dominated, primarily by France.   This was further illustrated by the necessity for guarantees by Britain and the United States to the Dutch.
Thus, whilst, on the one hand, Dutch foreign policy over the EDC was
determined by internal concerns, on the other, powerful factors in that
policy were the nature of American policy, and the position adopted by
the British.   For the Dutch Government, although forced, by the activity of other European powers, into support for the proposal, it was
never seen as the best way of strengthening NATO.   Fundamentally,
because the EDC represented a regional grouping within NATO, the Dutch
attitude was determined by the stance it took on NATO itself.   Yet that
policy towards NATO was not born out of weakness - i.e. it was not an
acquiescent policy.   Dutch policy towards NATO has been based on the
premise that such an alliance offers a small state like the Netherlands
opportunities for influence that it could not otherwise have.   In this
sense, Dutch policy towards NATO has been essentially <u>preservative</u>.

British policy over this issue area is less difficult to fit neatly
into one of the four strategies.   During the interwar years, British
foreign policy was, according to the adaptive strategies, essentially

preservative - in that it was derived from both domestic and external
sources. In the immediate post war period, British policy was based
on the premise that Britain was still one of the big three, had been
victorious in war, and was ready to attempt some form of post war
settlement. Discussions over the nature of the United Nations were
based on the dual assumptions of the desirability of continued great
power cooperation and the preferred non intervention of the United
Nations in sensitive areas such as decolonisation. The change of
government in 1945 did not bring the vast change in policy that might
have been expected on the basis of pre war pronouncements by the
Labour Party. The level of agreement between Labour and Conservative
leaders over foreign policy can be contrasted with the depth of disagreement over domestic matters.

Yet, if the degree of agreement between the leaderships of both main
parties in the immediate post war period was high, this does not mean
that domestic factors were not important. The overwhelming domestic
concern - the essential structure that intruded most significantly into
foreign policy - was that of the economy. The level of domestic economic difficulties was very high. Frankel has commented that this
economic situation ' . . . constituted the major restraint on her free-
dom of manoeuvre both at home and abroad.' (1) Exacerbated by the
ending of lend-lease, this fundamental economic weakenss coloured British
foreign policy in virtually every dimension. Thus, British policy towards Germany was primarily determined by both the problems of the
domestic economy, which entailed the speedy curtailing of aid and relief
of the economic burden, and the necessity of resolving the German problem in the light of the dominant issue in international politics - the
nature of great power relations.

In the same manner, British policy over support to Greece and Turkey
was determined by the desirability of removing a burden on the domestic
economy and by a consideration of the necessity of preventing the spread
of perceived Soviet influence. As Bevin argued in the Commons, British
policy was guided not by ideology but by a prudent empiricism that aimed
at guiding British policy to adapt a hostile and unfavourable international situation to the prosperity of the common people. Indeed, the
attitude of Labour Party activists changed during the year of 1947 from
one of hostility to the United States to one of more empathy and trust,
especially after the Marshall Plan. Nevertheless, the Truman Doctrine
and the Marshall Plan may be seen as the results of the impact of domestic factors on British foreign policy. Thus in Germany, Turkey, Greece
and Palestine, as well as in the issue of decolonisation, domestic,
primarily economic, factors had a considerable impact on British foreign
policy.

Yet it is necessary to point out that external factors were also of
crucial importance in the determination of British foreign policy. The
perceived Soviet threat was of fundamental importance in the creation
of the defence arrangements that culminated in the NAT. Since four
power cooperation had so clearly failed at the United Nations, and since
the spectacle of the creation of a Soviet bloc loomed large, the British
proposal for the creation of what became the Brussels Treaty Organisation,
and the resulting creation of NATO, can be seen as foreign policy behaviour of essentially a preservative character.

126

From the date of the signature of the NAT, British policy followed a relatively straightforward _preservative_ strategy. The British atti- tude to the EDC, although complicated by Churchill's initial association with the idea, was fundamentally of a preservative nature. On one side of the debate, the nature of external demands meant that some form of rearmament of Germany was necessary, yet on the other side of the debate, joining in a European venture such as the EDC would have been in contra- diction to the prevailing domestic view of Britain's place in the world. In other words, the nature of Britain's essential structures - primarily the links with the Commonwealth - were seen as a reason for avoiding participation in the EDC. British policy, therefore, was to offer, reluctantly, virtually anything short of actually joining. The Eden proposal, which led to the creation of WEU, is evidence of the preser- vative nature of British foreign policy - since it effectively balanced British perceptions of the external demands and requirements with the enhancement and maintenance of the essential structure of the Common- wealth relationship.

In summary, then, British foreign policy over the issue of security was primarily one of a _preservative_ nature. Indeed, in a very recent article on the adaptive approach, Petersen argues that 'the foreign policy of post war Britain is a paradigmatic example of this orienta- tion'. (2)

C THE NETHERLANDS EAST INDIES

From the material summarised in chapter six it would appear that Dutch policy over the Indonesian issue area was essentially one of _intransi- gence_. Their unwillingness to negotiate with the Republic, their criticism of British policy for not returning the NEI to them, and their imposition of the first and second police actions, are all factors pointing to the conclusion that the essential strategy being followed by the Dutch over the NEI was one of _intransigence_. The final agree- ment, however, which gave independence to the NEI must be seen as essen- tially _acquiescent_ because it was carried out primarily because of ex- ternal pressure. As the support for the Dutch position weakened in the United Nations, as the United States suspended Marshall Aid to the NEI, the previously intransigent nature of Dutch foreign policy gave way to a policy of acquiescence. This change was fundamentally due to the linkage between Dutch policy in the NEI and the general drift of Dutch security policy towards a NATO based stance - a stance in which the Atlantic link was the dominant, overriding guarantee of Dutch security.

The British policy stance over the NEI was essentially one of an _acquiescent_ nature. From the time that British troops, as a result of an Allied commitment, entered the NEI, until the time they left, British policy was basically one of balancing the demands of the various external pressures - the Dutch, the Republican leaders, the Commonwealth, the United States, etc. - with the desire, arising out of domestic pres- sure, to withdraw. But, unlike the preservative strategy, British pol- icy was essentially concerned with balancing the external pressures. The high level of pressure applied by the Dutch to restore the colony to their control by dismantling the structure of the Republic, had to be balanced against the pressures from the Republican leaders and from world opinion not to act to restore someone else's colony. Fundamentally, the NEI was a peripheral issue in British foreign policy, determined by the nature of the external pressures and constraints. When the issue moved to the United Nations, British policy adopted a very different stance. Because of the precedent involved at a time in which British decolonisation was being planned, the British Government was clearly concerned to prevent the United Nations, under article 39, from interfering in the internal politics of a member state. As Bevin stated in the Commons, the Government was anxious to prevent the Security Council from going outside their proper jurisdiction. With regard to the police actions, British policy was the result of a combination of two factors: the first was a desire to prevent an open dispute with a fellow member of the nascent Western defence system, over an Asiatic territory; the second was a concern that Dutch action might make the process of decolonisation more difficult, as well as making an anti-communist front more difficult to maintain, thereby threatening the British essential structures of territory (in the form of overseas possessions) and economic assets. In sum, therefore, British policy during the period from the withdrawal of the troops from the NEI to the granting of independence was essentially preservative.

A COMPARISON OF THE PREDICTED FORMS OF BEHAVIOUR WITH THE EMPIRICALLY DERIVED FINDINGS

In the final section of chapter three, the adaptive behaviour approach was utilised to yield predictions as to the nature of the foreign policy behaviour of Britain and the Netherlands. This section will compare these deductively obtained theoretical propositions with the inductively derived empirical propositions, as outlined above.

The theoretically derived propositions were obtained by relating the national genotypes of Britain and the Netherlands to the dependent variable of adaptive strategy via the use of the intervening source variables. The propositions obtained were as follows:

Proposition One   Britain will initially pursue an intransigent foreign policy strategy that will be transformed into a preservative strategy.

Proposition Two   The Netherlands will initially pursue an acquiescent foreign policy strategy that will be transformed into a preservative strategy.

On the basis of the three empirical case studies undertaken in chapters four, five and six, foreign policy strategies in the terminology of the adaptive behaviour approach were derived. In summary, the foreign policy behaviour of the two states, in terms of the adaptive behaviour approach, was:-

Britain   European Integration In the immediate post war years, British policy was fundamentally intransigent towards European integration. During the early 1950s there was an indication of a move towards a preservative strategy, although the basic nature of British policy only became preservative with the 1961 decision to apply for membership of the EEC. Thus policy was

initially _intransigent_, being gradually transformed
into a _preservative_ strategy.

Security British foreign policy was basically _pre
servative_.

Netherlands East Indies (NEI) British policy was
essentially _acquiescent_ during the period of occupation but was transformed into a _preservative_ strategy when the issue went to the United Nations.

The Netherlands _European Integration_ Dutch policy has been, in
essence, _preservative_ throughout the period examined.

Security Initially Dutch policy was basically
intransigent - with, as in the NEI, an ultimately
acquiescent strategy in the case of its demands over
Germany. However, Dutch policy became essentially
preservative following the signing of the NAT.

NEI Dutch policy was overwhelmingly _intransigent_
in the dispute, finally being transformed to one
of _acquiescence_ with the final granting of independence.

In comparing this behaviour with that predicted an initial problem -
and one which will be discussed in detail in the next chapter - is that
of aggregation. In other words, it appears to be very difficult to
conclude from the empirical case studies what the general form of
behaviour was, especially when there is a contradiction between the three
issue areas. For example, how, in the case of Britain, are the two
areas of the NEI and European integration to be weighed? In the case
of the NEI, British policy moved from _acquiescent_ to _preservative_; in
the case of European integration it moved from _intransigence_ to _preser-
vative_. Clearly, to state now what the initial stance of British
foreign policy was involves a value judgement as to the nature of
importance of the two areas. Whilst, given the peripheral nature of
the NEI for Britain, this might not appear to be too problematic, it
does offer serious difficulties in the case of the contrast between the
European and the security areas. Similarly, in the Dutch case, whilst
in both the NEI and security, Dutch policy moved from _intransigent_ to
acquiescent and _preservative_, in the area of European integration Dutch
policy was consistently _preservative_. Do two _intransigent_ strategies
outweigh one _preservative_ strategy?

Given this difficulty what can be pointed out is that the predictions
were not very accurate. Rosenau's proposition regarding Britain -
that it would initially pursue an _intransigent_ foreign policy strategy -
was only supported in one of the three issue areas studied - that of
European integration. In the issue area of security the strategy was
preservative; in the NEI issue area it was _acquiescent_. Rosenau's
prediction that the foreign policy strategy of a state such as Britain
would become _preservative_ was largely justified. It needs to be
pointed out, however, that there are problems with this prediction,
which will be outlined in the next chapter, and it is felt that these
problems seriously reduce the apparent utility of such a prediction.

Rosenau predicted that the Netherlands would pursue an <u>acquiescent</u>
foreign policy strategy that would be transformed into a <u>preservative</u>
strategy.   Again, this prediction appears to be largely inaccurate.
In no case was the initial Dutch policy <u>acquiescent</u>, nor did it become
so except in one area.   This is a striking conclusion.   Rosenau
actually cites the Netherlands as <u>the</u> example of the type of society
which he later classifies as most likely to follow an <u>acquiescent</u>
foreign policy strategy.   Again, however, the approach accurately predicted that the Netherlands would follow a <u>preservative</u> strategy yet,
as noted previously, there are problems with this prediction and this
will be commented on in the next chapter.

On the basis of this comparison it would seem justified to state that
the predictions of behaviour outlined in chapter three would appear to
be at variance with the forms of behaviour that emerged from the case
studies.   With the proviso that both states did in general adopt <u>preser-
vative</u> strategies, the predictions as to the nature of behaviour were
almost totally at variance with the empirical findings.

NOTES

(1) See J. Frankel, <u>British Foreign Policy 1945-73,</u> Oxford University
Press, London 1974, p.182.
(2) N. Petersen, 'Adaptation as a framework for the analysis of foreign
policy behaviour', <u>Cooperation and Conflict</u>, Volume XII, 1977, p.224.

8 A review of the adaptive behaviour approach

Having outlined the procedure that was used to test the adaptive behaviour approach, and having compared the predictions as to the foreign policies of the two states with the empirical findings, the approach can now be examined in detail. In this chapter, the approach will be reviewed at three levels:

A The ability of the approach to predict foreign policy behaviour.
B The process of operationalisation.
C Problems of the approach arising out of its use in this study.

Before dealing with these reviews, it is important to point out that the approach has attracted critical attention from other authors. In an article that examines some of the major systems approaches in international politics, Stephens (1) examines Rosenau's adaptive behaviour approach. He criticises Rosenau on several grounds: <u>first</u>, he argues that the essential structures are much too vaguely defined to allow them to serve the purpose that Rosenau requires of them - that is to relate specific behaviour patterns to changes in the essential structures. <u>Secondly</u>, Stephens argues that there is no evidence that societies have essential structures that must be maintained. <u>Thirdly</u>, he points out that Rosenau, although conscious of the need, has failed to specify the criteria that define where one stage in a national system ends and another begins, i.e. the limits within which the essential variables can be fulfilled; the alternative would be to maintain that national societies are always adapting since they tend to persist for long periods of time. Stephens argues that by failing to provide such criteria, Rosenau requires the analyst to make moral judgements about a society's performance of the essential functions. Fundamentally, Stephens stresses that the danger of Rosenau's formulation is that

' . . . since most of the societies that we study are ongoing ones, there is a real risk that we will merely accept continued existence as evidence of the fulfillment of the essential structures within the requisite limits.' (2)

<u>Fourthly</u>, Stephens indicates that Rosenau fails to test those activities that are adaptive and maladaptive for any given structure, thus heightening the tendency to view almost any activity as adaptive if the system continues to exist, especially since Rosenau deems adaptation and transformation to be the same. Finally, Stephens notes three developments that must occur for Rosenau's approach to serve as a jumping-off place for students of international politics. They are: that the proposition that systems require that requisites must be fulfilled be established; that the range within which they can be fulfilled and the system remain the same system be determined; that the activities that can fulfil a given essential structure be listed. He concludes

' . . . until this is done, Rosenau's adaptive systems analysis will remain, at best, a vague program for inquiry that is based

partially on a flimsy analogy between the behaviour of social
and organic systems.' (3)

As was discussed in chapter three, McGowan has critically evaluated
Rosenau's work on adaptive behaviour and has found several problems
with his formulation.   Fundamentally, he believes that although the
approach does allow the generation of falsifiable hypotheses, there are
four main criticisms that can be made of them: <u>first</u>, they are not
deduced from his assumptions about the nature and motivation of actors.
<u>Second</u>, they are only weakly related to each other and in some cases
appear inconsistent.   <u>Third</u>, there is no explicit time variable;   the
approach is basically static.   <u>Finally</u>, certain presumed causes of
behaviour are ignored (change in the international environment, dyadic
relations) (4).   Additionally, McGowan argues that if Rosenau's assumption is that preservation is the strategy each state will ultimately
adopt, then where will the dynamics of international politics come from?
Are not other variables involved in that transformation?   These problems
prevent Rosenau's work from being ' . . . a general positive theory of
foreign policy' (5).   Nevertheless, as has already been noted, McGowan
argues that

> ' . . . in comparison to other attempts to construct positive
> theories of foreign policy at a high level of generality, Rosenau's
> efforts have achieved an unmatched level of rigour and scope.   If
> general positive theories of foreign policy are our common goal,
> then Rosenau's work represents as far as we have as yet (1974)
> progressed.' (6)

Petersen argues that Rosenau's treatment of interdependence as a para-
meter and not as a variable is fundamentally misconceived as it not only
varies between states and in differing issue areas but it is also only
a modern phenomenon (7).   Another fundamental problem of Rosenau's
approach, Petersen points out, is that it is too reliant on the analogy
with biological systems.   Not only are social systems far more complex,
they are also voluntaristic rather than determinist.   By dichotomising
the concept of adaptation, Rosenau limits its utility to only a very
small number of events: it should be widened to deal with the satis-
ficing functioning of the essential structures.   Petersen also argues
that it omits consideration of how adaptation takes place.   Finally,
he finds a set of difficulties concerning the relationship between
independent and dependent variables that together result in serious
problems in the derivation of propositions (8).   Despite these problems,
Petersen then attempts to reformulate the approach, although he does not
then test or operationalise his reformulated approach.

The common denominator in each of these perceptive and cogent critiques
of the approach is, however, that in no case does the critique emerge
as the result of subjecting the approach to testing.   Clearly, if the
approach is to be of utility in comparative foreign policy analysis it
should be capable, <u>inter alia</u>, of successfully predicting the forms of
adaptive behaviour adopted by the states.   Thus, it is believed that
the attempt to test the approach that is reported on in this study will
provide a wider basis for a critique of the approach.   Indeed, on the
basis of this attempt to test the approach a series of problems were
found with it;   in some cases the problems had already been mentioned in
the literature as summarised above, in many other instances the problems

generated by actually attempting to test the approach had not been discussed in the extant literature. This chapter will now consider these
problems:

A THE ABILITY OF THE APPROACH TO PREDICT FOREIGN POLICY BEHAVIOUR

As has been discussed, the method of testing the approach adopted in this
study has been to examine the behaviour of the two states in three issue
areas. However, whilst this appears to be the only way of testing the
approach, there are serious problems involved in combining the results of
the three case studies. To assess the overall strategy would seem to require some - by necessity subjective - value judgement as to the relative
importance of the areas studied (something that Rosenau himself warned
against in his original article on pretheory). To deem British foreign
policy as, say, initially intransigent would reflect the value judgement
that one area of foreign policy - European integration - was more important, was of greater weight, than those of the NEI and security. To restate the problem: if the approach is to serve as the basis for comparative foreign policy research it must be capable of testing empirically;
if it is to be tested against empirical data it must proceed by assessing
the predicted strategies against actual behaviour; to obtain one strategy of behaviour requires either the implicit value judgement of the analyst as to what is the nature of foreign policy behaviour of the state(s)
involved or the analysis of foreign policy via case studies in which the
summation of these sectoral studies into an overall evaluation would seem
to be problematic. This seems to serve as an important limitation on
the approach.

   It is, therefore, seen as a significant limitation of the approach
that it was unable to predict accurately the initial strategies of the
two states: in fact, in the case of the Netherlands, the predicted
strategy (acquiescent) was at the opposite end of the spectrum to that
which it followed (intransigent). From the difference between the
predicted forms of behaviour and the actual behaviour, the utility of
the approach in the examination of British and Dutch foreign policies is
very small; however, there are some further criticisms of the approach
that arise directly out of the attempt to apply it. It needs to be
stated that initially the approach appeared to offer considerable advantages to the comparative study of foreign policy: not only did it have
tremendous heuristic value but it seemed, by utilising the pretheory
approach within a framework that yielded testable propositions (i.e.
clearly identified the independent and the dependent variables - state
characteristics and the four adaptive strategies), to fit the criteria
of the form of analysis which could galvanise comparative foreign policy
research. It was expected that, whilst the empirical material might
reveal inconsistencies between predicted and actual behaviour, the study
could conclude by offering suggestions as to how these might be recon-
ciled within the framework - for example, by developing the categories
or the continua used. The process of operationalisation however, has
turned out to illustrate some more fundamental weaknesses within the
approach that have not been pointed out in the theoretical writings.

B THE PROCESS OF OPERATIONALISATION

McGowan, as has already been noted, argues that the adaptive behaviour
approach suffers from serious internal theoretical weaknesses. These
weaknesses

' . . . relate to the logical character of (Rosenau's) concepts
and definitions, and most particularly, to the absence of a
deductive structure of definitions, axioms and general theorems
that is essential if one is ever going to be able to explain why
the relationships summarized in . . . (Figures 3.1 to 3.4) . . .
hold - if indeed they are correct.' (9)

In a recent survey of the state of the art, McGowan has gone so far as
to argue that

' . . . the one sustained attempt to construct a recognizably scientific (i.e. falsifiable) general theory of foreign policy by Rosenau
suffers from such serious logical faults that it is merely a weakly
related set of typologies.   If Rosenau's work is the closest our
discipline has so far come in its search for general and middle
range theory, we have a long way to go.' (10)

In addition to these problems of the approach noted by McGowan the
attempt to operationalise and test it in this study has thrown up a
further set of difficulties with the internal structure of the approach.
After all, the utility of the approach is determined, more than anything,
by its capacity to be tested; if it is not open to testing against
empirical data, then its utility remains at the heuristic level.   Accepting that the method of testing does not significantly weaken the conclusions, then the following problems of operationalising the approach seem
to be critical.

(I) Rosenau's assumptions about foreign policy, how it is made, and
how it aids adaptation, are not explicit.   The result of this is that the
construction of the theoretical relationships contained in the various
tables is not open to testing or analysis.

(II) Rosenau offers few guidelines for the operationalisation of his
approach.   Whilst in his initial statement of the approach he discussed
the means of operationalising the concept of the essential structures,
(11) he does not extend this to cover the process of testing the hypotheses.   In fact, the tables summarising the theoretical relationships
contained in the approach are difficult to find in Rosenau's work and,
when found, are very complex and awkward to use.   It was left to McGowan
(12) to collate the various tables in one article.

(III) The operational measures used by Rosenau to determine the national
genotypes of societies are arbitrary and controversial.   National genotypes are obtained by the eightfold division of states following from the
dichotomous treatment of three attributes;   size, polity, development.
Each of the three operational measures is open to question, although
again these measures were only made explicit in a 1974 article (13). The
dichotomous operational measure of size is stated as being whether or not
a country has a population of more than 23,376,000 (14).   Thus, Britain
is a large state whilst the Netherlands is a small state.   Yet, if other,
potentially equally acceptable measures of size were used - for example,
square miles of territory - the classification of the two states would
change and thus the predicted foreign policy strategies would alter.

The measure of the polity which determines whether a state is classified as open or closed is the existence of a free press (15).   It does
not appear necessary to list the problems in operationalising this definition.   Clearly what counts as a free press is a significant value
judgement and certainly many would argue that the placing of, for example,
Britain in the open, free press column is hardly a clearcut issue.   Again,

134

as with size, different classifications of Britain and the Netherlands in terms of an open or closed polity (on the basis of e.g. elite rotation, number of parties, governmental control of the legislature), would result in different foreign policy strategies being predicted.

The third dichotomous measure is that of the developed or underdeveloped nature of the economy of the society. This is operationalised by calling all states with a GNP per capita of over $402 rich and those with a lower GNP per capita poor. Whilst this seems the most acceptable measure of the three, it is nevertheless the case that it is only one out of a potentially large series of measures and is one which could hide vast differences in the composition of the economic structures involved.

Given the arbitrary nature of the operational measures and because alternative measures of the national attributes could well result in different foreign policy strategies being predicted, the internal construction of the approach seems to be built on shaky foundations.

(IV) A further problem relating to the internal construction of the approach relates to a specific aspect of the operationalisation procedure and that is that in some cases the allocation of strategy prediction is extremely difficult. As noted in chapter three, the Netherlands was predicted as following an acquiescent strategy only after relating a further set of variables to strategy types. According to figure 3.2, a country with the same ranking of source variables as that possessed by the Netherlands' national genotype could follow either an acquiescent or a preservative strategy. The eventual prediction as to Dutch foreign policy behaviour could only be obtained after utilising figure 3.3, which relates national genotypes to strategies. The point here is that Rosenau's own theoretical figures do not make it clear how to proceed, yet clearly a prediction that a state will follow one of two strategies does not appear to be very useful. In other words, and this builds on a point made previously, the tables that contain the theoretical relationship involved in the approach do not lend themselves to the generation of clearcut hypotheses.

(V) This problem leads to a further difficulty in the theoretical structure of the approach. Although the expressed task of the approach is to relate the independent variable of national genotype to the dependent variable of adaptive strategy, the intervening variables - the source variables - have an ambiguous place in the development of hypotheses. These source variables are not testable, either in composition or in the ranking of them for each national genotype, yet in the case noted in the previous section, they offer a different prediction than that obtained by looking at the national genotype. Again, this appears to indicate a fundamental weakness in the approach in that the precise theoretical link between national genotypes and source variables remains implicit and obscure, whereas it is essentially a crucial part of the theoretical structure of the approach.

(VI) It is also necessary to point out that the approach sees change in foreign policy strategy as occurring within a national genotype i.e. that Britain, a large, rich, open polity would transform its foreign policy strategy from intransigent to preservative. Yet it would seem to be the case that the national genotype of a society can change over time; for example, the GNP per capita could rise from $401 to $403 and the state would change genotype from poor to rich. Similarly the state could undergo a population increase to take it from just under to just over 23,376,000 and thus from small to large. Yet such genotype changes are not dealt with explicitly in the approach. The only such possible interpretation is that Rosenau, by viewing preservation as the long run equilibrial strategy, sees all societies becoming large/small, rich, open polities. Yet this interpretation is both extremely controversial, and implicit rather than explicit. In summary, it is either an implicit assumption of Rosenau, in which case it is both debatable and illustrative of the manner in which his assumptions impinge on the theoretical relationships within the approach, or it is not an assumption he makes, in which case he is guilty of ignoring the very real possibility of genotype transformation. Furthermore, it is important to note that Rosenau's definition of the unit of analysis - the national society - suffers from similar problems of vagueness and imprecision.

(VII) There is also a problem with the approach in that it deals with something called foreign policy. Not only does such a level of analysis concentrate attention on very broad, general sweeps of behaviour, but it also assumes that there is something called policy that is a coherent, straightforward set of behaviour. The former problem - that of the gross level of behaviour dealt with - is discussed in the series of criticisms based on the case studies. The latter problem, however, is more methodologically contentious in that it makes the important assumption that there is something long term, rational and linked together called policy that is something other than a series of individual decisions. By deliberately eschewing the individual decision approach to foreign policy analysis, Rosenau is arguing implicitly that something called policy can be discerned from the series of unrelated, uncoordinated individual decisions. This problem is exacerbated by the fact that Rosenau nowhere defines policy, either in terms of its timespan or its composition, notably the difference between foreign and domestic policy. Yet in the operationalisation of the approach in this study, whilst the emphasis was on the overall nature of foreign policy in the issue areas, this could only be discerned by examining key decisions. Whilst it is believed that it is necessary to examine foreign policy behaviour in order to arrive at hypotheses about states' behaviour, this notion of policy clearly requires much more careful consideration than has been the case hitherto. This problem is made much more complex by Rosenau's use, as a key variable, of the notion of interdependence, a notion which by definition questions the very distinction between foreign and domestic policy.

(VIII) A further problem that arose out of the operationalisation process was simply that of what behaviour to examine. Although the approach is concerned with broad sweeps of policy, to assess the overall strategy would seem to require some value judgement by the analyst as to what constituted the adaptive strategy involved. Yet, given that an examination of case studies was the only alternative to this, there still remain problems of combining the results in differing issue areas. To do so would involve a significant value judgement by the analyst as to which issue area was dominant.

(IX) Finally, the adaptive behaviour approach suffers from several of the major technical problems common in Rosenau's work. Although it was intended to be the theoretical framework for the generation of hypotheses regarding the relationship between foreign policy behaviour and national genotypes, it ends up by creating one more typology; indeed, this present study is the first known attempt to test it. Furthermore, there has been a noticeable tendency in Rosenau's work to create frameworks, leaving the task of filling in the details to others (linkage politics, foreign policy as an issue area, pretheory). The lack of attempts to do just that results

in the charge that Rosenau's frameworks are unworkable, and if the
present lack of attempts to utilise the adaptive behaviour approach continue, that criticism will be made about it as well. As has been noted
previously, the adaptive behaviour approach is based upon Rosenau's
deepseated and firmly held methodological commitment to the possibility
of creating a general theory of foreign policy behaviour. Yet it must
be restated that this is an extremely controversial methodological issue,
and is one which is exacerbated by Rosenau's abstract presentation.
Rosenau's determinism is clearly indicated in the approach by his use of
analogy - the national society is an organism, with essential structures
which must adapt to the environment or perish. However, Rosenau is
guilty of the charge of having his cake and eating it since he includes
within his source variables the individual and role characteristics of
the decision-makers. By so doing he is open to the charge that these
variables are included to account for that part of behaviour that the
environmental variables do not account for.

C THE PROBLEMS OF THE APPROACH THAT ARISE OUT OF ITS USE IN THE CASE
STUDIES

The use of the approach in this study has indicated that there exists a
set of fundamental weaknesses in it, which, when combined with the problems outlined in the above two sections appear to limit very seriously
the utility of the approach. These weaknesses can be conveniently considered under nine headings:

(I) Gross categories of behaviour

One problem of the approach that has been most clearly illustrated by
the case studies is that the approach can only deal with extremely gross
categories of foreign policy behaviour. By terming the foreign policy
behaviour of a country as, say, promotive, this tells us very little
about the nature of that foreign policy. Naturally, this is not sur-
prising, nor is it a criticism of the utility of the approach, if the
analyst wishes to deal in such general terms. Certainly, it appears
to be the express purpose of the approach to deal at very general, broad
levels. Yet even given this aim, there are two problems arising from
the gross level of behaviour dealt with. First, within one issue area,
to say the foreign policy of Britain is preservative may well offer
little in the way of indication as to the nature of that foreign policy
behaviour. Although this point will be discussed in a slightly different context below, it seems to be a limitation on the utility of the
approach to have to call the behaviour of a state preservative or intransigent, even within one issue area. To label behaviour in that
sense says little about the style or the performance of foreign policy -
or even the content!! Thus preservative behaviour could be achieved by
many different means: diplomacy, war, economic blockade - to use only
broad strategies.

Similarly, the mere labelling of British policy as, say, preservative
over the NEI does not help us understand why, in one vote, the British
representative at the United Nations abstained, while in another vote
he voted in favour of United Nations' action. Again, to call British
policy over the EDC preservative does not help us in understanding
the Eden proposals of 1954 - both these proposals and the British refusal to join the EDC were examples of a preservative strategy. To see
Dutch policy over European integration as consistently preservative is
of little utility in explaining the Dutch attitude to, on the one hand,
the Council of Europe, and, on the other, the EEC. The subtleties of

policy, the contradictions amongst individual and specific objectives
are all subsumed under a one word description of policy in one area. As
such, the ascribing of a strategy to behaviour seems to miss out the
nuances and the details of that behaviour, details or nuances that might
well be more important than the strategy itself in the formation of responses by other governments.

The second problem of the gross categories of behaviour dealt with by
the approach concerns the fact that the categories are so loosely defined that anything can be fitted into them. Not only do the points
made above, concerning the difficulties of utilising the approach in one
issue area, apply, but the problem of labelling foreign policy in terms
of one strategy seems almost to miss the wood for the trees. Forgetting
the difficulties of making an overall judgement on the nature of any
state's foreign policy behaviour, any such judgement would appear to be
so gross as to allow actual policy and the way it is performed to be
anything at all. For example, if Britain was said to have pursued a
preservative foreign policy strategy since 1945, then this would have
allowed Britain to have joined the EEC, or not; to have an independent
nuclear deterrent, or not; to give up its colonies, or not. Thus the
very decisions that might appear to the participants to be the crucial
ones could all be subsumed, whatever their nature, into one strategy.
Again, the possession of an acquiescent strategy per se may not be as
important as the way in which external forces are balanced - as for
example, in the case of British policy during the occupation of the NEI.

(II) Measurement

Given these problems of the gross categories of behaviour dealt with in
the approach and the difficulty in testing it, there arises an associated problem which refers to the question of 'what counts as relevant behaviour in a given issue area?'. The example from the research was that
of British policy over the EDC. When looked at in terms of British policy over the security issue area, the policy was, as was the general nature of British policy, preservative. Yet, when looked at in terms of
British policy towards European integration, the policy, although naturally still preservative, was in direct contrast with the general intransigent nature of British policy towards European integration. Such a finding would appear to indicate that some rather specific criteria need to
be developed to utilise the approach for the analysis of different issue
areas. Although this finding seems to show a benefit of the approach,
in that it encourages the examination of the location of a particular
policy decision (i.e. was the EDC an abnormal decision for European policy or was it primarily a matter for security policy?), the approach
would seem to require some method of resolving these inconsistencies. In
other words, the approach would appear to require some criteria to measure the location of a particular policy decision in one issue area or
another. Thus, the approach suffers from the problem of an inability, in
its present form, to assign specific policy decisions to behavioural issue
areas. Furthermore, this difficulty is exacerbated by the absence of criteria to determine how to aggregate policy stances that cross issue area
boundaries. The example of British policy towards the EDC illustrates
these problems of measurement and indicates that to resolve them some
specific criteria for measurement would need to be developed.

(III) Time

The approach also omits the variable of time and this appears to be a
most significant omission. At one level, the results of this study,
i.e. the disparities between the empirically and theoretically derived

strategies, could be dismissed on the lines that the approach is a recent one and is thus concerned with the contemporary time period and is unable to deal with earlier periods. Thus, it could be argued that the approach is related to an interdependent world - a view that is supported by some of Rosenau's statements. A case study such as this one would, therefore, be seen as outside of the approach's time scale since the world studied was not an interdependent one. Yet, it would be necessary to reply that the approach is either an attempt at a general framework for the comparative study of foreign policy, or not. If it is not, and the variable of interdependence is the independent variable, then the whole basis of Rosenau's approach, of analysing foreign policy behaviour in terms of source variables, is mistaken and misdirected. If this is the case, and if the approach is indeed applicable for all forms of international society - as any general foreign policy approach would, by definition, have to be - then the inconsistency between the form of behaviour predicted by the approach and that derived from the case studies would appear to be both a valid and a serious objection to the approach. By being rather obscure about the variable of interdependence and thus the time period that the approach refers to, Rosenau is open either to the charge that the general theory is, in fact, a partial approach or to the criticism that it is inaccurate.

At another level, the problem of the lack of a time dimension in the approach represents a most important limitation on its utility. The theoretical predictions as to the foreign policy behaviour of the two states indicated that both would adopt a preservative strategy - a prediction substantiated by the empirically derived strategies. However, it is believed that this prediction is of very little utility since no time dimension is involved. Not only does the omission of a time dimension mean that the prediction is very difficult to test, but, when combined with the criticism of the gross categories of behaviour noted above, the prediction is virtually meaningless. It will be recalled that a preservative strategy means only that a national society's foreign policy will be characterised by an attempt to balance internal and external forces. As noted previously, the categories are very broad indeed, and thus to argue that states will balance internal and external forces tells us very little about actual foreign policy behaviour. Although the charge by many analysts that all states balance both forces, indeed that that is the very essence of foreign policy, would seem to be countered by the specific definition of the strategy offered by Rosenau, the preservative strategy does appear to be an extremely wide one. Such a catch all strategy would seem to apply to most states in an interdependent world and, as such, would seem to be of very little use as a specific category. Thus, since in the contemporary world it would appear to be the case intuitively that, like Britain and the Netherlands, most states follow a preservative strategy, the vast differences in the way that strategy is performed, the variations in the manner in which external and internal forces are balanced, would seem to reduce considerably the theoretical utility of such a category and predictions associated with it.

(IV) Adaptive-maladaptive behaviour

A further problem of the approach illustrated by the case studies was the difficulty in distinguishing between adaptive and maladaptive behaviour. Rosenau notes that in actual foreign policy behaviour, some actions may be adaptive, other maladaptive, in relation to the preservation of the essential structure. Yet this seems to be almost tautological.   As Thorson has pointed out

> ' . . . a foreign policy which results in any of the essential
> structures not being present is termed maladaptive.   This, of
> course, is equivalent to saying that any foreign policy which
> results in the destruction of a nation-state is maladaptive.' (16)

The problem is that the term adaptation is used in two distinct ways
by Rosenau: on the one hand, it is utilised to differentiate that
behaviour which is in line with the strategy adopted from that which
is not, i.e. maladaptive behaviour;   on the other, it is the general
term for the change of foreign policy.   Thus under the second usage
of the term, a state may adapt by behaving maladaptively.

The effect of this distinction between the two uses of the term is
that not only may a state be seen as adapting by following a maladaptive
strategy, but also the only way a state can transform its strategy is
via maladaptive behaviour, i.e. is by behaviour that is maladaptive in
terms of the prevailing strategy.   To illustrate the first point:
the invasion of the Netherlands in May 1940 is as clear an example of
maladaptive behaviour as can be imagined.   Yet this maladaptive
behaviour which, in the short run, resulted in the destruction of the
Dutch state (or at least of certain of the essential structures), was
just as clearly a major catalyst in allowing Dutch foreign policy to
adapt to the post war world.   Thus, in virtually the most extreme case
of maladaptive behaviour imaginable, the eventual effect of that behaviour was adaptive.   In other words, no behaviour can be outlined that
would make the distinction between adaptive and maladaptive behaviour
a meaningful one.   Even if a state is at present under occupation, it
cannot be argued that the state will always be so controlled, i.e. the
state may eventually be able to adapt to the new circumstances.   This
is exacerbated by the absence of a time dimension in the approach.
Thus, at one level, the distinction between adaptive and maladaptive
behaviour is virtually meaningless.   As Thorson noted

> ' . . . a cat (a mechanism usually thought to be adaptive)
> may put his paw in the flame (a maladaptive behaviour) in
> learning that getting too close to the fire is not good for
> cat paws.' (17)

At another level, the distinction between adaptive and maladaptive
behaviour is difficult to apply and that is in the case of strategy
transformation.   In other words, it is clear that behaviour that will
mark the transformation of foreign policy strategy will be maladaptive
according to the strategy being discarded.   Hence the decision of the
British Government to apply for membership of the EEC might well mark
the transformation of strategy to one of preservation, but it might also be seen as an example of maladaptive behaviour within an intransigent
strategy.   Clearly, to distinguish between adaptive/maladaptive behaviour in terms of strategy transformation requires either considerable
value judgements or the type of precise measure of policy location that
was previously noted as being absent.

(V) Strategic-tactical behaviour

A problem with the approach which follows on from several of the criticisms noted above is that it fails to offer any criteria to distinguish

140

between strategic and tactical behaviour. Because of the gross level
of behaviour that the approach is concerned with, and following on from
the problems of distinguishing between adaptive and maladaptive behaviour and the lack of a time dimension, the approach cannot deal with the
fact that one strategy might be served by tactics of another strategy.
How does the analyst distinguish between strategy and tactics? For
example, British policy towards European integration was basically
intransigent, yet in the case of the Eden Plan, this policy proceeded
by utilising the tactics of a preservative policy. Similarly, Dutch
policy towards Europe - essentially preservative - utilised, for specific policy matters, the tactics of an intransigent strategy. The
point of this criticism is not to hint at inconsistency in policy, but
to point out that any strategy may well be composed of various tactical
measures that would usually be associated with other strategies. The
approach fails to offer any means of coping with this situation, and
again the analyst is forced to rely on value judgement in distinguishing what is strategic from what is tactical. Furthermore, as Lawrence
Freedman has pointed out with reference to the work of Allison, what
may appear to be a certain form of behaviour at the present may reflect
previous decisions on the basis of alternative forms of behaviour (18).
In such a situation, calling a strategy preservative or intransigent
is again an oversimplification and reflects a particular view of the
dynamics of the situation.

(VI) Exclusive nature of categories

Another reservation about the usefulness of the approach that arises
from the case study is that the categories are too rigid. Behaviour
is framed in terms of either being X or Y. If behaviour is acquiescent then it is wholly so. This, on the basis of the case study, is
an oversimplification, and it would appear to be a basic problem of
the approach. However tempting it is to do so, the universe of foreign policy behaviour does not fit into a two-by-two matrix. Rather
than be concerned with either/or type statements about foreign policy
behaviour it would be more useful to discuss the more or less dimension
of that behaviour. For example, what accounted for the various mixes
of strategies? How different issue areas had different mixes and how
mixes of strategies changed? Again, the approach is unable to cope
with the dynamics of category change, since it does not specify when
and how, say, a preservative strategy emerges from an acquiescent one.

(VII) Determinism

Possibly the most serious problem with the approach, and one which
appears to limit the utility of it, is that it omits the area of
decision-making. Given the relationship within the approach between
independent and dependent variables (national genotype and adaptive
strategy) the whole question of the process of decision-making is treated not as an intervening variable, but as an exogenous one. By
implicitly deeming as irrelevant the whole area of debate surrounding
the nature of the relationship between perceptions and reality, the
approach turns its back on what is to many analysts a crucial level of
analysis in the study of foreign policy behaviour. In so doing, by
treating the relationship between decision-making and behaviour as, in
essence, irrelevant to strategy adoption and performance, the approach
is essentially determinist. This would seem to be a most significant

141

error in the approach.   On the basis of the case studies it is justified to argue that in many cases the crucial variables in determining
foreign policy behaviour were the perceptions of the decision-makers
and the time lag between changes in the environments and the clear
perception of these changes.   In other words, the whole theme of British foreign policy since 1945 can be seen more profitably in the light
of perceptions and time lags than as a determinist response to a changing national genotype.   This problem of determinism appears to be a
fundamental one; decision-making is primarily a social, voluntary act
or set of actions.   The adaptive behaviour approach does not include
this process as either an independent or dependent variable in its
analysis.   Not only does this mean that the actions of the participants
in foreign policy decision-making are exogenous, but it also means that
their perceptions and the relationship between these and the operational
environment are of little consequence.   If anything, the approach
appears to be closest to Allison's rational process model of decision-
making - but it is so unconsciously and without any consideration of
the alternatives.

Furthermore, the approach is teleological in the sense that it sees
preservative strategies as the long run requirement for national societies.   As noted previously, this prediction is of little utility for
the study of foreign policy behaviour, but it does imply a certain view
of international politics, which is never made open to analysis.   Why
preservation and not intransigence should be the long run equilibrium
for national societies is not made explicit except in vague references
to interdependence.   As such, the approach reflects considerable
implicit value judgements of its author on the dynamics of international
politics, judgements which are not empirically verifiable.

(VIII) Definition of foreign policy

Although stressing interdependence as an important factor in the adaptation of foreign policy strategies, the approach fails to appreciate
that interdependence has the effect of questioning the whole nature of
what is foreign policy behaviour.   Although this was a problem identified by Rosenau in his work on foreign policy as an issue area, the
adaptive behaviour approach ignores the point that as interdependence
increases the whole conception of what is foreign policy becomes essentially contestable.   Thus, as much of the recent work on interdependence
stresses, the overlap between domestic and foreign policy results in the
boundaries being difficult to distinguish.   In this situation, and
given the degree of interaction between the four essential structures
and external factors, the analysis of foreign policy behaviour may only
cover part of the relevant behavioural field.   In addition, the very
problem of actual survival in such an interdependent world would appear
to miss the point that it is the enhancement of essential structures
not their survival that becomes crucial.

(IX) Dyadic relationships

Given that an initial aim of this study was to examine the interaction
of Britain and the Netherlands, it must be deemed to be a noticeable
limitation on the approach that it is of very little utility in the
examination of a dyadic relationship.   It was hoped that the approach
would shed light on, or offer interesting insights into, Anglo-Dutch

relations. Indeed, if it is the general theory that it purports to be, then it would be expected that, _inter alia_, it would offer some perspectives on interaction within a given dyad. However, on the basis of the case study of Anglo-Dutch interaction over the Netherlands East Indies 1945-50, the approach has very little utility in such a study. To say that over the NEI, whilst the British pursued an acquiescent strategy the Dutch followed an intransigent policy, is to offer precious little in the way of insight into actual behaviour. This is compounded in the case of interaction within a dyad by the problems of the approach noted in the previous eight sections. Whilst such problems reduce the utility of the approach for a general comparative analysis of foreign policy, they are much more limiting in the case of dyadic interaction.

In summary, on the evidence of the case studies undertaken in this present work, the adaptive behaviour approach has serious problems that reduce its utility in the comparative analysis of foreign policy behaviour. Not only have the case studies indicated serious drawbacks in the approach, but the results of the comparison of the theoretically and empirically derived strategies indicate that, when subject to testing, the approach does not predict foreign policy strategies accurately. Although the degree to which the methods of testing weaken these conclusions will be examined below, there appear to be serious problems in the approach on the evidence of this study.

Having listed the various problems with the approach it is necessary to point out that even if there are serious problems with the approach under consideration in this study, this does not mean that the whole comparative foreign policy analysis approach started by Rosenau is doomed to failure. It is believed that the adaptive behaviour approach, like so much of Rosenau's work, is a significant improvement on the single country case study approach in the task of creating general theory. That task may prove impossible to achieve, but certainly the deficiencies of the approach considered in this study should not be seen as ruling out the endeavour totally. There are important strengths of the approach: it is extremely heuristic; it does lead, albeit with some difficulty, to the generation of falsifiable hypotheses, thereby representing a significant and worthwhile improvement over previous approaches; it has acted as an island of theory, serving as the focal point of the Inter-University Comparative Foreign Policy Project (ICFP) (19) and, thereby, aiding the production of a series of papers aimed at producing falsifiable hypotheses concerning the relationship between actor types and foreign policy behaviour (20).

In summary, the adaptive behaviour approach does have serious drawbacks, yet it is as far as the comparative study of foreign policy behaviour has progressed. It is the belief of this writer that there is no reason why such a goal is unobtainable; there is nothing inherent in the material to prevent the generation of falsifiable hypotheses.

It is now necessary to discuss the degree to which the methods of testing weaken the conclusions arrived at in this chapter. As was discussed in some detail in chapter three, there were serious problems in the operationalisation of the approach and clearly, given the disparity between the theoretically and the empirically derived strategies on which the conclusions of this study were based, it is important to examine these difficulties. The conclusions are very critical of the approach, and since this is the first known attempt to test it, it is important that these conclusions are not the result of the methods of testing.

The first factor that does weaken the conclusions of this study is simply that this study is only one out of a vast possible universe of such studies. As such, the conclusions arrived at must be tentative since this study could well be the exception to the norm. Thus, the severe problems found in the approach's ability to predict the foreign policy strategies of Britain and the Netherlands might be outweighed by the overwhelming ability of the approach to predict successfully the behaviour of many other states in similar case studies. Such a limitation is inevitable in a single case study. Furthermore, it is important to point out that although this study examined two countries' foreign policies, it did so only in three issue areas and over a short period of time. Again, this would seem to be an inevitable and significant limitation on the findings of this study. However, it is important to point out that there is no alternative to such a procedure. Given that the approach deals in macro foreign policy behaviour and given that the methods of testing it required a two country study, then the limited nature of the case studies was axiomatic. Moreover, it is believed that the method of testing was necessarily selective in order to offer as extensive and fair a test of the approach as was possible. Furthermore, whilst the present study is only one out of a large potential sample, the inductive method of testing the approach means that such tests have to commence somewhere. Whilst it is accepted that the results of this study cannot be conclusive by themselves, the method of testing has been made as explicit as possible in order to allow replication of the study. It must also be pointed out that the problems found with the approach are so extensive, and many relate to the theoretical structure of it, that it appears unlikely that they are unique to this particular case study.

A second potential limitation on the conclusions of this study is related to the precedure adopted in this study to operationalise the approach. There are three areas in the operationalisation process that potentially could weaken the conclusions arrived at in this study: the generation of the theoretical propositions; the generation of the empirical propositions; the methodological relationship between the two. With regard to the generation of the theoretical propositions a potential limitation on the results of this study is simply that since Rosenau does not give much in the way of advice on how to operationalise the approach, then the method adopted in this study might well be incorrect. If this were so, then the assigning of theoretical strategies to the two states would be erroneous and thus the conclusions derived from the case studies would be unwarranted. Yet, it is believed that the process of operationalisation has been carried out as explicitly as possible and has been based on a reading of all the relevant material. Having used Rosenau and Hoggard's national genotype classification as a check on the classification arrived at by this writer, and then having followed these genotypes through the relevant figures in chapter three, to obtain the adaptive strategies, it is argued that the generation of the theoretical hypotheses was carried out as carefully as possible. Again, the possibility of replication has been catered for.

The generation of the empirical adaptive strategies is also a potential limiting factor on the conclusions of this study, since this was the area in which most judgement was required from this writer. Again, if the assigning of the empirical strategies was incorrect, then the conclusions as to the ability of the approach to predict behaviour are illfounded. Whilst it is accepted that the actual generation of these strategies involved the assigning by this writer of one of the four available strategies to a welter of empirical material, it is believed that the process adopted to carry out this task was as explicit and fair as possible. By summing up the foreign policies of the two countries in the three issue areas in the language of the adaptive strategies, it is argued that any errors in the procedure are observable. There appears to be no way round the fact that at some point an analyst has to carry out such a task, but it is believed that in this study the process has been carried out fairly and in accordance with the structure of the approach.

The final problem of operationalising the approach is that the two sets of strategies are obtained by procedures that involve different methodological assumptions. The distinction here is between historical-inductive strategies and scientific-deductive strategies. It could be·argued that these two sets of strategies are not strictly comparable and that any conclusions derived from such a comparison must be treated with considerable caution. Whilst accepting the point that the strategies have been generated according to different methodological criteria, it is argued that this does not detract from the findings of this study. Clearly there can be no other way of testing the approach but to compare its predictions with actual behaviour. To argue that such a test is inconclusive is to consign not just this approach, but all attempts at theoretical analysis, to the position of being merely heuristic or more or less illuminating. In this study it is believed that the method of testing was the only one available and that the findings of the study have not been coloured to any significant extent by this problem of the two sets of methodological assumptions involved.

A final area of the study that is potentially a limiting factor on the conclusions arrived at is that of the material examined in the empirical sections of the analysis. One important caveat concerns the use of mainly secondary sources. As noted in chapter three, it is a limitation on this study that the source material is of a secondary nature, but it is believed that this limitation does not detract significantly from the conclusions arrived at. Although it must be admitted that the picture of reality painted in the empirical sections of the study is based on incomplete evidence, it is argued that the explicit presentation of the material combined with the wide choice of sources reduces the gaps in the coverage. Again, it must be stressed that, had the aim of this study been to examine specific decisions per se, then the type of evidence used in the empirical case studies would have been more critical. Certainly, in terms of behaviour, it is strongly argued that the level of generality dealt with in this study is adequately catered for by the sources utilised.

A final problem arising from the methods of testing refers to the analysis of foreign policy as interpreted in this study. Because of the nature of the examination of foreign policy followed in this study, it would appear to be necessary to point out that, as has been noticed previously, as the degree of interdependence increases the definition of what is foreign policy changes. In other words, perhaps by concentrating on overt foreign policy issues, this study has not fully examined the relevant adaptive behaviour of the two states. Nevertheless, such a focus of analysis is determined by Rosenau's theoretical framework.

In summary it is clear that some distortion may have been introduced into the conclusions of this study by the method of testing the theoretical approach. It is the firm belief of this writer, however, that this distortion is of a very small order, that the method of testing is the only possible one, and that the conclusions arrived at are fundamentally accurate.

Finally, this study will conclude by offering suggestions as to possible areas of modification in the adaptive behaviour approach, although it must be stressed that this study has indicated serious weaknesses with the approach that may be so serious as to prevent the development of the approach. There appear to be two technical, and two more fundamental, areas where modification would be possible and desirable.

An initial technical modification, which would seem to be essential for further testing of the approach, would be the tightening up of the theoretical structure. As was noted in the previous section, there is a whole series of difficulties with the theoretical structure as it is at present. Most notably, the relationship between the independent, intervening and dependent variables requires attention so that it becomes possible to deduce from national genotype characteristics the dependent variable of the adaptive strategy. At present these are merely intuitively related. Such a modification would require the dichotomous measure of national genotype characteristics to be re-examined, possibly developing a set of measures for each of the three measures.

A second technical area that would benefit from modification is that of the nature of the strategies, notably the distinction between adaptive and maladaptive behaviour; it would seem possible but, at present very difficult, to introduce some quantitative measure of the degree of optimality of the essential structures. Similarly, some improvement is necessary in the nature of the categorisation of strategies. As noted in this chapter, some method of cumulating the various strategies in the issue areas is necessary. Furthermore, some means of making the categories more meaningful is necessary, since at present they offer little indication as to the nature of policy.

However, from the problems of the approach noted in this chapter, it must be concluded that such technical modifications alone would appear to be unlikely to increase substantially the utility of the approach. Such an increase would seem to require much more fundamental revisions of the approach and even these may be unable to overcome some of the many difficulties it suffers from in its present form. Although, as recently as Autumn 1977, Petersen has argued that the approach is a viable one. He points out that

' . . . the much needed corrections of the model . . . are possible, and that a theoretically and empirically viable reconstruction of

146

the model is, therefore, feasible.' (21)

Yet, as he points out later on in the article

'. . . just as the proof of the pudding lies in the eating,
so the "proof" of . . . adaptive behaviour lies in its
applicability to empirical research.' (22)

If such a reconstruction of the approach is to occur it would seem
to require, in addition to the technical changes noted previously,
modification in two main areas.   One area would be further development
on the lines of Hansen's and Petersen's modifications of the approach in
the light of the recent literature on the concept of interdependence.
Thus, the nature of foreign policy behaviour might be made dependent
on the degree of interdependence, but this would again require considerable elaboration of the concepts and variables involved, and thereby
possibly becoming over-complex for a general model.

A second area where fundamental modification is required is in the
approach's treatment of decision-making, since the present determinist
approach fits uneasily into a subject area in which choice and perception play so important a role, certainly as far as the literature is
concerned.   If changes, such as those noted above, could be combined
with developments in the use of interdependence and decision-making as
independent and intervening variables, then some reconstruction of the
approach would appear to be possible.   Yet such an approach would still
be unable to offer any help to a study of interaction;   any attempt to
relate the adaptive behaviour approach to dyadic relations would seem
to be of little utility.   Any progress in accounting for dyadic interaction requires primarily a significant reformulation of the information
available on the concept of image.

In conclusion, this study must end by pointing out that the utility
of the adaptive behaviour approach, on the evidence of its use in examining the foreign policies of Britain and the Netherlands in three issue
areas, is small.   The empirical investigation yielded foreign policy
strategies that did not fit well with those predicted by the theory and
thus, given that the strategies were generated correctly, this is one
area of weakness in the approach - its predictive capacity.   Secondly,
the process of operationalising resulted in other serious weaknesses
in the approach being discovered.   Finally, the examination of the
approach in this study revealed a set of difficulties with it.   Thus,
whilst the approach has considerable heuristic value and whilst it is
an appealing research strategy, the problems of it noted in this case
study would appear to limit seriously the claim that it might serve as
the basis for comparative foreign policy analysis.

It has been noted that there are necessary modifications to be made
to the Rosenau formulation if it is to be of utility, and it has also
been noted that there are more wideranging developments that might be
utilised to reconstruct the approach.   Yet it is argued that even if
these modifications were made, the approach would be unable to aid any
study of dyadic relations.   Whilst it is hoped that further work, and
certainly further testing, is carried out, possibly on the lines of
development opened up by Hansen and Petersen or on the lines suggested
above, the overwhelming conclusion of this study is that the approach

147

suffers from such serious problems that these attempts would seem to be unlikely to make the approach a viable paradigm for comparative foreign policy analysis. On the basis of this study, one thing is certain: Rosenau's claim in 1976 that foreign policy analysis was a normal science is clearly undermined substantially by the problems found in the theory that he saw as providing the paradigmatic base for that normal science.

NOTES

(1) J. Stephens, 'An appraisal of some system approaches in the study of international systems', International Studies Quarterly, Vol. 16, 1972, pp.321-49.
(2) Ibid., p.343.
(3) Ibid., p.347.
(4) P. McGowan, 'Problems in the Construction of Positive Foreign Policy Theory', in J. N. Rosenau (ed), Comparing Foreign Policies, John Wiley, New York 1974, p.38.
(5) Ibid.
(6) Ibid.
(7) N. Petersen, 'Adaptation as a framework for the analysis of foreign policy behaviour', Cooperation and Conflict, Vol. 12, 1977, p.225.
(8) Ibid., pp.227-234.
(9) P. McGowan, 'Problems in the Construction of Positive Foreign Policy Theory', op.cit., p.41.
(10) P. McGowan, 'The Future of Comparative Studies', in J. N. Rosenau (ed), In Search of Global Patterns, Free Press, New York 1976, p.227.
(11) J. N. Rosenau, The Adaptation of National Societies, McCaleb-Seiler, New York 1970, pp.21-28.
(12) P. McGowan, 'Problems in the Construction of Positive Foreign Policy Theory', op.cit., pp.25-44.
(13) J. N. Rosenau and G. Hoggard, 'Foreign Policy Behavior in Dyadic Relationships: Testing a Pre-theoretical Extension', in J. N. Rosenau (ed), Comparing Foreign Policies, op.cit., pp.121-3.
(14) Ibid., p.121.
(15) Ibid., p.122.
(16) S. Thorson, 'National Political Adaptation', in J. N. Rosenau (ed), Comparing Foreign Policies, op.cit., pp.73-4.
(17) S. Thorson, 'Adaptation and Foreign Policy Theory', in P. McGowan (ed) Sage International Yearbook of Foreign Policy Studies, Vol. II, Sage, Beverly Hills, Ca. 1974, pp.123-4.
(18) L. Freedman, 'Logic, politics and bureaucratic politics processes', International Affairs, Vol. 52 (3), 1976, pp.434-449.
(19) For a history of the project see: J. N. Rosenau, P. Burgess and C. Hermann, 'The adaptation of foreign policy research', International Studies Quarterly, Vol. 17 (1), 1973, pp.119-44.
(20) For a list of these papers see ibid., pp.142-44. Many have been published in J. N. Rosenau, Comparing Foreign Policies, op.cit.
(21) Petersen, op.cit., p.222.
(22) Ibid., p.248.

Index

France 57, 58, 59, 60, 61, 62, 63,
64, 65, 66, 68, 72, 75, 81, 82,
83, 85, 87, 88, 89, 91, 92, 96,
103, 104, 106, 109, 110, 119,
120, 125
Frankel, J. 6, 7, 10, 26, 37, 38,
65, 66, 68, 77, 78, 89, 90, 98,
126, 130; on National Interest
10-11, 15.
Freedman, L. 141, 148
French-Italian Customs Union 58
Fritalux 58

Gaitskell, H. 72
Gambia 42
Germany 57, 59, 61, 62, 64, 66, 73,
79, 81, 82, 83, 85, 86, 87, 88,
89, 91, 92, 95, 96, 119, 125,
126, 127, 129
Ghana 19
Gladwyn, Lord 89, 98
Gordon, M. 90, 91, 98
Greece 42, 91, 126
Green Pool 58, 61, 69, 70, 118, 122
Greenstein, F. 5

Halperin, M. 7, 37, 46
Handelman, J. 8, 37
Hanrieder, W. 7, 31-32, 39; on
Compatibility and Consensus
32-36
Hansen, P. 46, 55, 147
Harlech, Lord 73
Hatta 100
Heiser, H. 77, 78, 98
Hermann, C. 54, 148
Hilsman, R. 7, 37
Hoggard, G. 52, 53, 55, 144, 148
Holsti, K. 7, 12-16, 38

India 19, 42, 103, 105, 107, 108,
110, 112, 113
Indonesian Republic 100, 101, 102,
103, 107, 108, 109, 111, 112, 114,
127
Inter-University Comparative Foreign
Policy Project (ICFP) 143
Israel, 7
Italy, 65, 87, 88

Jacquet, L. 79, 88, 97, 98
Japan, 99, 100, 101, 102, 103, 104,
105, 112
Jenkins, J. 52, 53, 55
Jervis, R. 7, 37

Kegley, C. 4
Kennedy, J. 73, 76
Kenya 19
Killearn, Lord 108, 109
Knorr, K. 37
Korean War 6, 16, 86
Kuhn, T. 2, 5, 8

Lakatos, I. 5
Lawson, J. 103
League of Nations 80, 89
Lieber, R. 67, 68, 70, 72, 73, 77,
78
Lindblom, C. 7, 37
Linggadjati Agreement 109, 113
Linkage Politics 7, 20, 25-32,
34-35
London Conference (1947) 92, 95
Logeman, Professor 105
Luns, J. 64, 119

MacArthur, General D. 100, 101,
108
Macmillan, H. 70, 72, 73, 76
Malaya 111, 114
Mallaby, Brigadier 106
Mansholt, S. 58, 118
Marshall Plan 56, 73, 82, 84, 91,
92, 96, 112, 126, 127
McGeehan, R. 97
McGowan, P. 41-43, 44, 45, 54,
55, 132, 133, 148
McNeil, W. 90, 98
Mendes-France 88
Merritt, R. 55
Messina Talks 60, 61, 70-71, 76,
119
Molotov, V. 82
Monnet, J. 60, 61
Morgenthau, H. 8, 37
Moscow Conference (1947) 92, 95
Mountbatten, Earl L. 100, 101,
102, 103, 107, 108, 115
Musgrave, A. 5

National Genotypes 18-19, 22-25,
42-44, 47, 52-54
National Interest 7-11, 15, 16
National Role 7, 11-16
Nehru 103

Netherlands 1, 3, 19, 23, 31, 36,
42, 46, 47, 49, 50, 52, 53,
54, 96, 128, 129, 130, 134,
135, 139, 140, 144, 147; and
Brussels Treaty 83-85, 94-95,
125; and Council of Europe

Three Circles Conception 66, 67, 75, 93-94, 96, 120-121
Treaty of Rome 60, 62, 70, 71, 74, 122, 123
Truman Doctrine 83, 91-92, 96, 126
Truman, H. 84, 96
Turkey 91, 126

Ullman, R. 37
United Kingdom 1, 3, 23, 31, 36, 46, 47, 49, 50, 52, 53, 54, 81, 82, 83, 84, 86, 87, 88, 97, 119, 120, 125, 128, 129, 130, 134, 135, 137, 139, 140, 142, 144, 147; and Brussels Treaty 92, 94, 96-97; and Commonwealth 63, 66, 67-68, 71, 73, 76, 93-94, 113, 120-121, 127; and Congress of Europe 66, 67; and Council of Europe 57, 67, 68, 70, 75, 121, 122, 137; and Euratom 71, 122, 123; and European Coal and Steel Community 58, 61, 68-69, 70, 75, 121-122, 123; and European Defence Community 69-70, 75-76, 93-94, 96, 122, 123, 127, 138; and European Economic Community 60, 61-62, 63, 64, 70-73, 76-77, 119, 122-123, 128, 133, 137, 138, 140; and European Free Trade Association 62, 63, 71-73, 76, 122; and European Integration 57, 65-73, 75-77, 120-123, 128-129, 133, 137, 141; and European Political Community 70, 94; and the German Problem 91-92; and Green Pool 58, 69, 70, 122; National Genotype of 52-54; and Netherlands East Indies 99-114, 127-128, 129, 133, 137, 142-143; and North Atlantic Treaty Organisation 92-93, 96-97, 126; and United Nations 89-90, 96, 126; and West European security 89-94, 96-97, 125-127, 129, 133; and Western European Union, 59, 94, 127
United Nations 80, 81, 83, 89, 90, 92, 95, 110, 111, 112, 113, 114, 124, 126, 127, 128, 129, 137
United Soviet Socialist Republic 19, 42, 56, 66, 76, 81, 82, 83, 85, 86, 89, 91, 92, 95, 96, 103, 107, 123, 124, 126

United States 19, 23, 42, 63, 66, 73, 75, 76, 81, 82, 83, 84, 86, 87, 88, 89, 90, 91, 92, 93, 94, 95, 96, 97, 100, 101, 102, 103, 109, 110, 111, 112, 113, 117, 118, 121, 123, 125, 127
United States of Indonesia 109, 112

Van Campen, S. 77, 79, 82, 83, 84, 85, 86, 94, 97, 98
Van der Plas 103
Van Kleffens 80, 104, 105, 110
Van Mook, H. 101, 102, 107, 108, 115
Vasquez, J. 37
Verba, S. 7, 37

Waltz, K. 2, 5
Western European Union (WEU) 59, 70, 71, 76, 88, 89, 94, 95, 127
Wheeler-Bennett, J. 91, 98
Wilhelmina, Queen 100
Wilkenfeld, J. 39
Willis, F. 77
Woodburn Kirby, S. 115
Wright Mills, C. 21

Zinnes, D. 29-30, 38